AVIATION PSYCHOLOGY:
A SCIENCE AND A PROFESSION

Aviation Psychology:
A Science and a Profession

Edited by
KLAUS-MARTIN GOETERS

Ashgate

Aldershot • Brookfield USA • Singapore • Sydney

Published by
Ashgate Publishing Limited
Gower House
Croft Road
Aldershot
Hants GU11 3HR
England

Ashgate Publishing Company
Old Post Road
Brookfield
Vermont 05036
USA

British Library Cataloguing in Publication Data
Aviation psychology : a science and a profession
    1. Aeronautics - Psychology - Congresses
    I. Goeters, Klaus-Martin
    155 . 9 ' 65

Library of Congress Cataloging-in-Publication Data
Aviation psychology : a science and a profession / edited by Klaus
    -Martin Goeters
           p.   cm.
    Includes bibliographical references (p.).
    ISBN 1-84014-325-8 (hardcover)
    1. Aviation psychology. I. Goeters, Klaus-Martin.
    TL555.A94 1998
    629.132'52'019--dc21   97-46524
                                                CIP

ISBN 1 84014 325 8

Printed and bound in Great Britain by
Biddles Ltd, Guildford and King's Lynn

Contents

Glossary of abbreviations

(A)AF	(Army) Air Force
AASD	After Action Stress Debriefing
AATP	Anti-Airsickness Training Program
AC	Assessment Center
ACSWG	Air Crew Selection Working Group
AFQ	Acronym for Follow-up Questioning
AFSG	Air Force Sub-Group
AMC	Acceptable Means of Compliance
AMS	Aeromedical Section
AQP	Advanced Qualification Program
ATC	Air Traffic Control
ATP(L)	Airline Transport Pilot (Licence)
ATS	Air Traffic Services
BASI	(Australian) Bureau of Air Safety Investigation
CAA	Civil Aviation Authority
CAIR	Confidential Aviation Incident Reporting
CAO	Civil Aviation Orders
CASA	Civil Aviation Safety Authority
CBA	Computer Based Assessment
CBT	Computer Based Training
CCT	Complex Coordination Test
CI(T)	Critical Incidents (Technique)
CMAQ	Cockpit Management Attitudes Questionnaire
CPL	Commercial Pilot Licence
CRM	Crew Resource Management
DAC	Dynamic Airtraffic Control Test
DFS	Deutsche Flugsicherung
DLR	Deutsches Zentrum für Luft- und Raumfahrt e. V.
DMT	Defense Mechanism Test
DTG	Determinationsgerät
EAAP	European Association for Aviation Psychology
ENJJPT	Euro NATO Joint Jet Pilot Training
F/E, FE	Flight Engineer
F/O,FO	First Officer
FAA	Federal Aviation Administration
FAR	Federal Aviation Regulation
FCL	Flight Crew Licensing

FIS	Flight Information Service
F-JAS	Fleishman - Job Analysis Survey
FMAQ	Flight Management Attitudes Questionnaire
FMS	Flight Management System
FOI	Flight Operations Inspector
FOF	Fear of Flying
GAF	German Air Force
GEMS	Generic Error Modelling System
GFT	General Failure Types
GM	General Manager
GND	Ground
HF	Human Factors
HF StG	Human Factors Steering Group
HPL	Human Performance & Limitations
IATA	International Air Transport Association
ICA	Instrument Coordination Analyzer
ICAIO	International Civil Aviation Organisation
IEM	Instructional & Explanatory Material
IFALPA	International Federation of Air Line Pilots Associations
IFR	Instrument Flight Rules
ILS	Instrument Landing System
IMASSA	Institut Médicine Aérospatiale - Service de Sant des Armées
IMC	Instrument Meteorological Conditions
IP	Instructor Pilot
IR	Instrument Rating
JAR	Joint Aviation Requirements
KLM	Royal Dutch Airlines
LAME	Licensed Aircraft Maintenance Engineer
LOFT	Line Oriented Flight Training
MCC	Multi Crew Cooperation
MDA	Minimum Descent Altitude
MEL	Minimum Equipment List
MMPI	Minnesota Multiphasic Personality Inventory
MORT	Management Oversight and Risk Tree
NASA	National Aeronautics and Space Administration
NATO	North Atlantic Treaty Organization

NDB	Non-Directional (Radio) Beacon
NEO	Neuroticism - Extraversion - Openness to experiences
NPA	Notice of Proposed Amendment
NT(S)	Non-Technical Skills
OASIS	Occurrence Analysis and Safety Information System
OHP	Overhead Projector
OPQ	Occupational Personality Questionnaire
OPS	Operations
PCI	Personality Characteristics Inventory
PF	Pilot Flying
16 PF(T)	16-Personality Factors (Test)
PIC	Pilot In Command
PNF	Pilot Not Flying
PPL	Private Pilot Licence
PTSD	Post Traumatic Stress
PUS	Permissible Unserviceability Schedule
RAAF	Royal Australian Air Force
RCT	Rudder Control Test
RG(T)	Repertory Grid (Technique)
RPT	Regular Public Transport
SDS	Spatial Disorientation Simulator
SIAM	Systemic Incident Analysis Model
SOF	Student Orientation Flight
SOP	Standard Operating Procedure
STANINE	Standard Nine (Scale)
TCAS	Target Collision Avoidance System
THC(T)	Two-Hand Coordination (Test)
TOM	Test Of Multiple task performance
TQM	Total Quality Management
TSB	Transportation Safety Board
TSS	Temperament Structure Scales
UN	United Nations
UT	University of Texas
VHF	Very High Frequency

Introduction

General Course Manager:

Klaus-Martin Goeters

1 General introduction

Klaus-Martin Goeters
DLR - German Aerospace Research Establishment, Department of Aviation and Space Psychology, Germany

The European Association for Aviation Psychology EAAP held its 22nd conference in Sabaudia (Italy), 22-27 September 1996. The conference was opened by Capt. Mike Stonehower (EAAP President 1994 - 1996) followed by Silvano Silenzi (Head of Alitalia Flight Safety) and Klaus-Martin Goeters (General Course Manager of the Conference).

The concept for the conference was that of a basic course in aviation psychology. Therefore, the conference was divided into five main sessions representing the basic areas of aviation psychology. Each course was scheduled for one full day and consisted of lectures and practical exercises. Table 1 shows the order of the courses and lists the course managers and the participating co-lecturers.

Capt. Marcello Ralli was responsible for the local organisation of the conference: choice of hotel, bus transfer, spouse program, grants, and, and, and....This huge amount of work was performed with excellence and helped the attendees of the conference (approximately 140) feeling well.

The course program of the conference is to be seen in relation to the ongoing development of the European aviation regulatory of the Joint Aviation Authorities (JAA). JAA uses for instance the term 'Approved Psychologist' in some of its requirements (see JAR-FCL 3.240). In reaction to such requirements EAAP is going to set professional standards in the main areas of aviation psychology. In this context a registration procedure is established by which members of EAAP either can qualify as
• Aviation Psychologist or
• Aviation Human Factors Specialist.

The 22nd EAAP conference was the start to a series of lectures. The reader will find more information about the registration and the EAAP course program in the next chapter presented by Kristina Pollack, president of EAAP elected at the 22nd conference.

Table 1   Course program of the 22nd EAAP Conference, Sabaudia (Italy), 22-27 September 1996

Course	Course Manager	Co-Lecturers
1. Human engineering	René **Amalberti**	Jean **Paries**, Claude **Valot**, Florence **Wibaux**
2. Selection	Hans-Jürgen **Hörmann**	Per **Byrdorf**, Hinnerk **Eißfeldt**, Klaus-Martin **Goeters**, Pieter **Hermans**, Hemmo **Mulder**
3. Training	André **Droog**	Patricia **Antersijn**, Oscar **Elizalde**, Werner **Naef**, Karsten **Severin**, Marieke **Verhoef**
4. Psychological counselling & intervention	Reiner **Kemmler**	Wolfgang **Roth**, Antonio **Tundo**
5. Human Factors accident investigation and prevention	Robert **Lee**	Brent **Hayward**, Alan **Hobbs**, Kristina **Pollack**

Most of the contributions to this book are written by the lecturers of the conference. Since the title of the book is *Aviation Psychology: A science and a profession*, the papers presented in this book not only contain scientific results, but also give recommendations how to implement psychological knowhow in the world of aviation, which is a field still dominated strongly by technology. The contribution of psychology to aviation is to make this complex man-machine-system more efficient and more reliable. In this book the reader will find many approaches how this can be reached.

Although the concept of the conference induced a clear structure of content, the lectures varied very much in a number of aspects: level of abstraction, scientific standard, practical relevance, style, redundancy with other courses, etc..This variety is also reflected by the papers of this book. The course structure of the conference gives the order for sections of the proceedings: Each course has its respective section in this book and is presented by the original course manager and his co-lecturers. Usually a section consists of different chapters. The sections are independent units: tables and figures are numbered chapterwise only, while references are listed section-wise. An harmonization and integration of the different papers are applied mainly to the basic aspects of layout. One particular means of integration is the glossary of abbreviations used in the book. This may be helpful for newcomers to the field. The reader finds the glossary adjacent to the table of contents.

The use of feedback for training purposes is one of the basic principles of learning. The general course manager applied this principle by asking the attendees to give systematic ratings on different aspects of the conference. The results of this feedback procedure are described in the last chapter of this introduction. This feedback gives an excellent input to the planned EAAP course program in aviation psychology and human factors issues, thus helping to increase the standards of aviation psychology.

Since the 22nd EAAP Conference was organized as a course in aviation psychology these proceedings can be seen as a basic text book for this subject. Many have contributed to the completion of this book. The editor likes to acknowledge the help and work of all the course managers and lecturers, who mostly did this work besides their regular occupational commitments. Two names must explicitly be mentioned: Brent Hayward did excellent work in preparing Section 5, so only little work was left for the final version. Karen Thomas prepared the camera-ready copy of this book. This was a huge amount of work since the original papers differed very much in their format, text program, graphics etc. The excellent layout of this book is primarily her merit.

2 EAAP professional standards in aviation psychology

Kristina Pollack
Swedish Armed Forces, Flight Safety Department, Aviation Psychology, Sweden

The European Association for Aviation Psychology (EAAP) is an independent, non-profit professional association. Its main goal is to promote scientific aviation psychology knowledge in the applied field of aviation.

In the context of safety and in relation to the technical development, the balance between technology and the human, has become more and more critical. With regard to incident and accident reports the focus of human factors in aviation has to be expanded. Therefore the need for aviation psychology knowledge in the aviation community has grown significantly during the years.

The psychological requirements of the operator were early recognised in the aviation history. In the late seventies the accident investigation boards opened up the possibilities to investigate the human factor area through the competence of aviation psychology. The training program for Crew Resource Management (CRM) built on aviation psychology knowledge and operational experience, was introduced in the aviation community in the late seventies and early eighties. The human factor concept consequently expanded from more or less being related to ergonomics to a more system / organisational context. The awareness of the importance of the human factor issues to reach safety has increased dramatically.

In this context EAAP, as a professional aviation psychology association, is concerned about the recent need for application of human factors in aviation, civilian as well as military. Present and future Joint Aviation Requirements in Europe (JAR) are following this general tendency. More and more human factors regulations are introduced and they are asking for suitable qualified personnel to implement such human factors requirements (JAR-OPS, JAR-FCL).

The recognition of the importance of human factors in aviation, principally based on findings in accident and incident investigations, is a great window of opportunity for human factors competent people, but at the same time calls for a guarantee for quality and proficiency of practitioners in order to ensure the required professionalism. For this reason EAAP has as a professional association for aviation psychology initiated a *Register of Aviation Psychologists and Human Factors Specialists in Aviation.*

Registration of aviation psychologists and human factors specialists

Through registration, EAAP wants to provide a professional standard on which civil and military authorities as well as aviation organisations and industry (ACAS, accident investigation boards, airlines, aviation schools, ATC, aviation industry, etc.) can rely on.

The minimum requirements to be registered as Aviation Psychologist by EAAP are:

- full member of EAAP
- university degree in psychology to be able to work independently as psychologist.
- three years experience by working in one or more of the applied aviation psychology fields in the aviation community.
- demonstrated and approved familiarity with the aviation environment
- well achieved EAAP training courses of two domains and fulfilling documented minimum recurrent aviation psychology training every third year (publication of papers and/or reports, attendance of conferences and / or training courses set by
- EAAP /JRC (Joint Research Centre, Ispra).

The label "Aviation Psychologist" is reconsidered every third year. In case of non completed achievement of the criteria a temporary standard can be delivered on request with appropriate restrictions.

The minimum requirements to be registered by EAAP as Human Factors Specialist in aviation are:

- associate membership of EAAP
- relevant professional education in the area of human factors in aviation
- three years experience by working in one or more of the applied aviation psychology fields in the aviation community.
- demonstrated and approved familiarity with the aviation environment
- well achieved EAAP training courses of two domains and fulfilled documented minimum recurrent aviation psychology training every third year (publication of papers and/or reports, attendance of conferences and / or aviation psychology training courses set by EAAP/JRC (Joint Research Centre, Ispra)

The label Human Factors Specialist in Aviation is reconsidered every third year. In case of non completed achievement of the criteria, a temporary standard can be delivered on request with appropriate restrictions.

Training

In co-operation with the Joint Research Centre (JRC) of the European Commission, EAAP started a training cycle in September 1997 in Ispra, Italy for Aviation Psychologists as well as for Human Factors Specialists in Aviation. The courses will cover the five major areas identified by EAAP and found relevant to train Aviation Psychologists and Human Factors Specialists.

These areas are:
- Human Engineering
- Selection (Assessment)
- Training
- Psychological Examination, Counselling and Intervention (individual / organisational)
- Accident Investigation and Prevention — ϽT&M .

The goal of this modulated course system is to be professionally updated in the aviation psychology areas. It is to provide opportunities for professionals to discuss, design, develop and evaluate common standards. It is as well to provide common proper goals, methods, contents and systems in the field of human factors in aviation according to prevailing regulations under JARs as well as to the regulations and needs for military aviation, ATC and other partners in this context.

The 22nd Conference of EAAP in Sabaudia was the starting point of the described course system. The only interest of EAAP in this crucial phase of today's development is to be a professional partner in the work for safety and efficiency in aviation. Our intention is to offer a support to an appropriate setting of a professional standard in the field of Aviation Psychology and Human Factors in Aviation.

3 Evaluation of conference feedback

Klaus-Martin Goeters
DLR - German Aerospace Center,
Aviation and Space Psychology, Germany

The European Association for Aviation Psychology held its 22nd conference in Sabaudia (Italy), 22 - 27 September 1996 as a basic course in aviation psychology. The conference was divided into five main sessions representing the basic areas of aviation psychology:

1. Human Engineering,
2. Selection,
3. Training,
4. Counselling and Intervention,
5. Accident Investigation and Prevention.

In the second half of the morning session of the last course 'Accident Investigation and Prevention' a survey was given to the conference attendees which asked them to rate the five courses.

Each course was rated with regard to its practical relevance, scientific quality, form of presentation, hand-outs / materials and time management. The ratings were given on a five point scale from 1 (= poor) to 5 (= excelent); 3 was labeled 'medium'. On this scale also the general conference organisation (a) and information (b) should be assessed. Beside the ratings also written comments could be given.

A total of 81 rating sheets were collected after the conference; 80 could be used for a quantitative evaluation, 1 had to be excluded due to undefinite answers. The 80 attendees whose rating sheets were taken into consideration could be grouped into 54 psychologists, 9 pilots, 11 pilots & psychologists. 6 others (AT - Controller, Engineer etc.) cannot be taken as a clearly identifiable group and therefore are also excluded from further discussions.

Quantitative evaluation

The grand mean for all ratings is 3.63. This shows that the response to the conference is mostly positive, but not always with the highest scores.

Group means and standard deviations for the five courses and the five criteria are presented in Table 1 and 2 respectively. The overall assessment of the courses ranges from an average of 3.20 for the course 'Training' to an average of 4.43 for the course 'Accident Investigation' (see Table 1). While here clear differences are to be observed the group averages for the five criteria vary in a narrow range (see Table 2).

A more differentiated picture is given by Table 3 where means and standard deviations for the three major groups of attendees are shown with respect to the factors 'Course' and 'Criterium'. Also means and standard deviations are presented for general conference organisation and information. The reader can deduct from this set of data his own impression. One should have in mind that the difference between the three groups of attendees are only in few cases statistically significant due to the small sample sizes and the relatively large standard deviations. Therefore, one can use the information of Table 3 primarily to identify trends and relative positions. In order to help in this respect in every attendees group for each criterion the minimum mean is marked by one star and the maximum mean by two stars.

The 'shooting star' of all five courses is the course of 'Accident Investigation'. This course received maximum averages by all three groups in scientific quality, hand-outs and time management. In practical relevance and form of presentation it received maximum averages by at least two groups. It is interesting that in practical relevance this course also received a minimum average. This obviously reflects different attitudes of psychologists and pilots with regard to this aspect. The high quality rating of the course 'Accident Investigation' is without any doubt justified, but being fair with the other courses it should be mentioned that the ratings might be influenced by recency effects since all ratings were given during this (last) course.

In contrast to the course 'Accident Investigation' the course 'Training' received minimum ratings by all three attendees groups in the criteria 'scientific quality' and 'time management' but the other three criteria showed neither any minimum nor maximum averages.

The courses 'Human Engineering', 'Selection' and 'Counselling' showed not that clear and unanimous results. In two cases 'Counselling' showed maximum average ratings and received no minimum average. Thus its general assessment is more positive. In the courses 'Human Engineering' and 'Selection' the minimum indications are unsystematically scattered (four minimum averages in each course). The rest falls between minimum and maximum averages with one exception 'Human Engineering' shares a maximum average in scientific quality with 'Accident Investigation' in the 'Pilot and Psychologist' combination group.

The ratings for the general conference management are presented in the last two rows of Table 3. The conference organisation was rated fairly high by all three groups. For the information ratings we find a difference between psychologists and pilots, but at least the psychologists and psychologists & pilots groups indicated a positive assessment.

Table 1   Means (M) and Standard Deviations (SD) of all ratings with regard to the five conference courses

Course	M	SD
Course 1: Human Engineering	3.45	0.70
Course 2: Selection	3.36	0.68
Course 3: Human Factors Training	3.20	0.70
Course 4: Counselling and Intervention	3.74	0.76
Course 5: Accident Investigation	4.43	0.45

Table 2   Means (M) and Standard Deviation (SD) of all ratings with regard to the five criteria

Criteria	M	SD
Practical Relevance	3.84	0.68
Scientific Quality	3.59	0.67
Form of Presentation	3.71	0.53
Handouts/Materials	3.58	0.48
Time Management	3.44	0.61

Table 3   **Means (M) and Standard Deviations (SD) of groups of attendees who rated 5 courses in 5 criteria**

Course	Criterium	Psychologists (N = 54)		Pilots (N = 9)		Psych.&Pilots (N = 11)	
		M	SD	M	SD	M	SD
Course 1: Human Engineering	prac. rel.	3.45	0.99	3.75	0.89	4.09	1.04
	sc.quality	3.63	0.94	4.14	0.90	4.18**	0.98
	form of pr.	3.15*	1.03	3.44*	1.24	3.55	1.21
	handouts	3.50	0.85	3.11*	0.60	2.91*	0.94
	time man.	3.19	1.10	3.44	1.33	3.09	1.14
Course 2: Selection	prac. rel.	3.77	1.06	3.44*	0.88	3.64*	1.03
	sc. quality	3.54	1.09	3.88	0.35	3.55	1.04
	form of pr.	3.27	0.66	3.78	0.83	3.20*	0.82
	handouts	3.08*	0.93	3.13	0.35	3.00	0.42
	time man.	3.08	1.06	3.33	1.12	2.80	1.03
Course 3: Training	prac. rel.	3.64	0.90	4.22	0.44	3.82	1.08
	sc. quality	3.09*	0.97	3.43*	0.53	3.00*	1.30
	form of pr.	3.23	0.89	3.89	0.93	3.55	1.37
	handouts	3.15	0.70	3.44	0.88	3.00	1.00
	time man.	2.62*	1.13	2.75*	0.71	2.64*	0.92
Course 4: Counselling	prac. rel.	3.87**	0.97	4.13	0.64	3.73	1.27
	sc. quality	3.25	1.07	3.86	1.07	3.27	1.42
	form of pr.	4.06	0.90	4.56**	0.73	4.09	1.14
	handouts	3.50	0.94	3.33	0.87	3.27	1.27
	time man.	3.81	1.06	3.67	0.87	4.09	1.22
Course 5: Accident Investigation	prac. rel.	3.24*	0.84	4.78**	0.44	4.55**	0.98
	sc. quality	4.04**	0.75	4.55**	0.53	4.18**	0.75
	form of pr.	4.42**	0.67	4.50	0.53	4.45**	0.69
	handouts	4.84**	0.42	4.56**	0.53	4.80**	0.42
	time man.	4.40**	0.61	4.11**	0.78	4.55**	0.52
General	organisation	4.23	0.73	3.89	0.93	4.00	0.77
	information	4.13	0.73	3.00	0.93	3.73	1.10

Qualitative evaluation

Written comments on the conference showed a large variety. The positive comments were like these:
- good first attempt for teaching basic knowledge;
- good conference management.

The negative comments were like these:
- nothing new learned; waste of time;
- program too dense, better time management;
- impossible to teach psychologists and pilots in the same session;
- English of native speakers too fast.

The extremes reflect the large heterogenity of the attendees and their demands. Besides the extremes the majority of comments expressed proposals for improving the courses:
- distribute written material before the conference;
- working groups should be smaller and should get more time;
- concentration on specific (advanced) topics to motivate the professionals;
- improve the team management of the lecturing group;
- EAAP policy regarding certification must be clearer.

As feedback is always a precondition for stimulating a learning process the collected information gives EAAP a guideline for improving its future course program.

Section 1

Human Engineering

Course Manager & Section Editor:

René Amalberti

4 Human Factors in aviation: An introductory course

René Amalberti */**
Jean Pariès ***
Claude Valot *
Florence Wibaux **
*   IMASSA, Departement Sciences Cognitives et Ergonomie, France
**   DGAC-SFACT Human Factors, France
***   Dedale Company, France

This section gives a broad overview of Human Factors in crew training, aircraft design and certification, and aviation safety policies. It is not intended to be exhaustive but only to outline the main trends and landmarks in the growing field of Aviation Human Factors. The paper is divided into four sections: the first section gives an overview of the history of Human Factors in aviation, the second section focuses on Human Factors for crew training, the third section focuses on design and certification, and the fourth and last section focuses on the evolution of safety models and data-bases. Human Factors for maintenance as well as for air traffic controllers are not adressed in this chapter.

A tentative picture of Aviation Human Factors

A single discipline versus a mosaïc of disciplines?

There are several ways to tell a story, depending on what role you played in it. This is exactly what happens with Human Factors. Depending on who you are in the Academy or in the Aviation Industry, Human Factors will not refer to the same concept, nor bear the same emotional charge.

In the Academy, Human Factors have long been assimilated into ergonomics, aiming at describing human capabilities and limitations: anthropometry, sight, hearing, memory and numerous other human 'hard' limitations. Several Human Factors and Ergonomic handbooks have been published with the objective to tell the designers the best way of shaping controls and designing displays, of using colors, of arranging the workplace, and so on and so forth. The Aviation Industry has been keen on integrating this kind of know-how into cockpit design since the 40's. The domination of the US industry was outstanding, and the US Academy was talking to the US manufacturers. No significant competition came from outside the USA and very few original Human Factors activities existed in Europe, with the exception of a few Medical Research

Centers often specializing in personnel selection. Therefore, until the end of the seventies, no real divorce existed between the Industry and the Academy about Human Factors.

Then, in the mid-eighties, came Charles Billings's NASA team with names like Clay Foushee, John Lauber, David Nagel and some other well known associated fellows, like Bob Helmreich and Earl Wiener. The impact of this group of people on Aviation Human Factors has been absolutely tremendous. With the introduction of the CRM concept (Crew Resource Management), they shifted the focus of Human Factors towards pilot behaviour and training issues. Human Factors issues then expanded from a bunch of designers with the manufacturers to thousands of people with the airlines around the world. ICAO's Dan Maurino was instrumental in promoting the CRM concept worldwide. But the success has been so great that during more than a decade many people in the Aviation Industry watched CRM as the ultimate form of Human Factors in aviation. Some manufacturers hired Human Factors people to incorporate CRM courses into their transition training programs rather than investing in Human Factors studies for design (the first Airbus CRM dates back to 1990). Finally, the success was such that it has overshadowed other aspects of the Billings's team work, and especially their extremely important work on automation and Human Centered Design.

In the late eighties came Jim Reason's ideas on human error, with a considerable impact on the understanding of aviation safety. A second shift of the Human Factors focus took place. Reason and some other contributors (Westrum, Perrow), again with the intrumental support of ICAO's Dan Maurino, introduced the central paradigm of a systemic approach to safety, enlightening the role of accident precursors through latent organizational failures, corporate and national cultures and beliefs. This new approach was a continuation of the previous shift: from individual pilot performance to team (crew) performance, then from team performance to organizational performance; the individual was fading behind these collective dimensions.

It is only recently, in the early nineties, that cognitive ergonomics has made its way into the Aviation Industry. Cognitive ergonomics was not new in other industries. In the Nuclear, Chemical and Offshore Industry, the design of automated or semi-automated control rooms, triggered in the late seventies, the emergence of a new discipline termed 'Cognitive Ergonomics'. Its main developers were primarily European (Rasmussen, Bainbridge, Reason, Hollnagel, de Keyser, Leplat, Hoc, Cacciabue, etc.). Its central goal was twofold: keeping the human 'in the loop' of understanding and controlling the situation (human-centered design), and improving human reliability (reconciling safety with human error). A characteristic of cognitive ergonomics has been the preference for field studies; task analysis and an 'ecological' approach to human performance, instead of the lab studies and traditional methods of experimental psychology. Ironically, cognitive ergonomics took a long time to be transfered to the Aviation Industry. Aircraft manufacturers, especially those designing automated aircraft, may have been reluctant to cooperate with people obviously featuring negative attitudes towards automation.

To sum up, a first generation of Human Factors know-how (often termed Human Factors) addressed the pilot-cockpit physical and perceptive interaction. It has been incorporated into aircraft design without apparent difficulty. Human limitations and capacities were identified in laboratories, translated into design norms, and those norms were implemented by design engineers, often without any Human Factors specialist in the design staff. A second generation of Human Factors can be identified as the CRM generation. It focused on the crew (team) and their internal and external interactions with the environment. It has been the starting point for pilot education in Human Factors. It has now reached the status of a worldwide requirement, and is currently being extended to all the other frontline operators: cabin crew, maintenance, dispatch, handling, etc. A third generation of Human Factors broadened its scope to address aviation safety as a systemic process, including organizational and sociological aspects. It has been the starting point for a real safety paradigm shift which is still developing. This has led to the re-engineering of accident investigations, and beyond that, to the re-engineering of aviation safety reporting systems and to re-thinking the airlines safety policies. A fourth and last generation of Human Factors is represented by cognitive ergonomics; addressing the cognitive dimensions of human / machine interaction, as well as the cognitive dimensions of other interactions (e. g. communication between humans). This can therefore be the starting point for an important shift in aircraft or aviation systems design; reviving the ideas found in the first Human Factors generation.

Aviation Human Factors today

According to the above description, 'Human Factors' are an artificial construct of various disciplines and concepts. They refer to academic domains which range from experimental psychology to sociology, and through the cognitive sciences. The Aviation Human Factors practitioners also have varied backgrounds. They include about as many people originating from Engineering Sciences as from the Life or Social Sciences. Moreover, most practitioners are researchers, who are still involved in the research environment, and most of whom are poorly aware of industrial realities, practical needs and constraints.

However, Human Factors can also be seen as a more global and logical construct, with a set of hierarchical paradigms and a set of goals forming a step-wise layered model:

- At the bottom layer is the first goal: to design physical interfaces compatible with basic physiological and psychological human characteristics and limitations (perception thresholds, time on duty, fatigue, etc). Achieving this goal also calls for a reduction of the dispersion of individual characteristics by the mean of personnel selection. At this level, the 'good design' not only has to respect the average thresholds but to accommodate the worst potential features of the selected people (e.g. cope with the minimum visual acuity in the population, not the average one). This is the area of 'classic' Human Factors and this is obviously still required in the design process.

- With the second layer, the goal is to design the interfaces, to organize the systems and to train the end-users to reduce the number of control errors, or to reduce the number of unacceptable consequences of these errors. This domain requires a mix of competences from engineering sciences, safety science (human reliability analysis), experimental and cognitive psychology, and social sciences (the systemic approach to safety).

- The next layer is more challenging. Here the goal is to design cognitive interfaces (information transfer media) to provide the end-user with the best situational awareness. The challenge is that situational awareness by definition is something evolutive and fragile. Cognitive ergonomics are at the core of this approach. The key words are the *cognitive control* of a dynamic situation (being able to filter and comprehend those aspects of the situation which allow you to act in a proper and safe manner). A critical condition for such a control is the proper management of the *cognitive compromise* between several contradictory dimensions: in-depth understanding of details versus large scale monitoring of the big picture, strategic anticipation of the future versus tactical reaction to real time information flow, maximum (economic) performance versus optimal safety, short term cognitive resource investment versus long term fatigue management, and so on and so forth.

- The ultimate layer refers to more philosophical issues: such questions as 'what role should be allocated to Humans in future flight decks'? This is probably the primal question, and the one to be answered before any consistent answer can be offered to the problems at the lower layers. At this level, there is no 'hard' scientific models, no 'hard' data, just convictions. Therefore at this level, Human Factors specialists are neither systematically right nor wrong. However, they are often simply in the best position to trigger or stimulate the debate, and to refocus the thoughts of the Industry on individual and collective needs.

Unfortunately, as we have seen above, Human Factors have developed from the bottom layer, while a more logical approach would have been to agree on the top philosophy first (the role of humans within the technical system). That philosophy could then support and direct the lower layers. This irony has often confined Human Factors to the subsidiary role of a narrow technique for subsystems specification, instead of a core discipline for global design. As a consequence Human Factors aspects have often been considered too late in the design process, at a time when the system philosophy was already established and closed to modifications. Not surprisingly, Human Factors were then bound to play an essentially cosmetic role, far from being a mentor of the design process.

A need for modesty, but a real opportunity for Human Factors people in aviation

For years and years, aircraft have been designed with indisputable success, although very little 'Human Factors' stuff was integrated into the design process. As a matter of fact, manufacturers have not hired many Human Factors specialists, at least in Europe, but they have designed most systems with a great deal of innovative engineering, and a great deal of Human Factors 'good sense'. Like it or not: this methodology, often based on technocratic creeds and naive models of human behaviour, and still criticized as such by dozens of current Human Factors papers, has led to the highest safety level of the transport industry (less than 2.10^{-6} fatal accident per million departures). For example, a recent NTSB study reported that when fatalities per million miles are compared, USA air transportation is eleven times safer than that of big trucks.

It would be somewhat arrogant - and naive - for the Human Factors community to assume that, had they been associated in a more systematic manner in the design process, they would have made a better result. Being able to pinpoint the drawbacks of a given system does not make you a better designer of that system. Unfortunately, the Aviation Industry will not hire Human Factors people on their capacity to criticize, but merely on their capacity to create practical design solutions. However, the situation is promising. The Aviation Industry is facing a spiralling challenge; the traffic will double within a few years, more performance will be required, more pressure will be put on the system, more and more competition will arise, while the safety level must be enhanced to meet public expectations.

From local sub-systems to the whole aviation system, the complexity is growing. The Aviation Industry has clearly understood that the human capability to keep control (for front line operators as well as for decision makers) will be central to future safety challenges. This is a unique opportunity for Human Factors. But will Human Factors specialists meet the challenge? It is not that clear cut. Human Factors specialists first need to understand aviation culture, they need to grow aware of technical realities and limitations, to develop more practical methods for interface design and evaluation. To sum up, they need to learn how to act as team players within a very demanding world.

Unfortunately, there are currently very few people in the Human Factors community who fit these requirements. Therefore, the first and most urgent challenge to the Human Factors community is probably to teach and train the life & social sciences' students properly before aircraft manufacturers lose hope to find the right people and turn to their 'in house' resources or to alternative methodologies.

A touch of politics

It is impossible to sketch a picture of Human Factors in the aviation industry without mentioning the importance of political issues. It has not been very difficult to introduce Human Factors and CRM into the airline industry and the pilot training process. But aircraft design and safety policies have been a totally different story. Three aspects, at least, are worth mentioning.

Firstly, the United States has been leading this competition and has been the most influential nation in aviation regulation since World War II. Europe is slowly challenging this US hegemony with the successfull growth of Airbus. But the situation remains a fierce US domination, even for Human Factors issues. The recent FAA task force report[1], which succeeded in moving the industry when so many other actions were unsuccessfull, is a good example of this influence. In the context of historical domination, the growth of Airbus inevitably resulted in extremely tense competition with the largest US American manufacturer, the Boeing Company. Such competition reaches far beyond pure technical aspects. On both sides, political support was involved at the highest level. Airlines are not necessarily always free to decide when purchasing aircraft. It would then be naive to believe that Human Factors issues can just soar in the neutral serenity of cloudless skies slap in the middle of the economic war missiles. Human Factors issues are and will be called upon to rationalize the philosophy on both sides and to overshadow more prosaïc reasons: the challenger is bound to promote new solutions, while the titleholder is keen on status quo.

Secondly, and almost independantly from the previous point, the (same) politicians are more and more inclined to require an absolute safety level, a 'zero accident' situation. This puts tremendous pressure on the aviation industry. In a situation of fierce competition, any accident can be used by ill-intentioned people. This leads everybody to a defensive position instead of a collaborative one.

Thirdly, there is no way to develop future Human Factors regulations outside a solid and permanent harmonization between the European Joint Aviation Authorities (JAA) and the American Federal Aviation Authority (FAA). The JAA set up a Human Factors Steering Group (HFSG) in 1995. However, the synergy from both sides of the Atlantic is still fragile and the obstacles are numerous. But the situation is improving, mainly thanks to the willingness of a small group of people. An FAA/JAA Human Factors Harmonisation Working Group is expected to be formed soon and a set of consistent HF regulations and recommendations can be expected by the end of the year 2000.

Conclusion

To conclude this long introductory section, Human Factors in Aviation has many and varied approaches. On the one hand, the variety of approaches, the value of fundamental Human Factors research and the new challenges in aviation are good opportunities to promote Human Factors within the industry. Regulations will only follow real needs and realistic solutions. On the other hand, this is a critical time for Human Factors specialists because Human Factors specialists now have to

---

[1] FAA Human Factors Team report the Interfaces Between Flightcrews and Modern Flight Deck Systems, June 1996.

meet industrial challenges. They are welcome by the industry, they will have the budgets, they will (soon) have the support of regulatory requirements. They must do the job, now.

Outline of Human Factors in aviation training

The needs

Many aspects of Human Factors pilot training are often identified with CRM because of its success. The value of CRM is recognized throughout the world. The goal within this training is to provide crews with a standardized approach for both human-human and human-machine cooperation. Examples of cooperation failures are numerous in recent accidents. The concept is now extended to maintenance people, apron staff, dispatchers, Air Traffic Controllers and all front line operators. For an expanded discussion of CRM, see the dedicated chapter in this book.

However, despite the value of CRM training, it does not cover all the needs of Human Factors training. Other efforts are required to address the growing complexity of the aviation system and its sub-systems. For example, at the organizational level, the increasing number of mergers, and the internationalization of airline structures calls for specific training to address the cultural and cross cultural issues as well as the emotional dimensions of an unstable work environment. Another area of concern is the adaptation of the aviation training system to the glass-cockpit generation of aircraft. We will focus on this issue in the rest of the section.

Training for the glass cockpit

The Human Factors problems of pilots flying within the glass-cockpit environment can be divided into two categories[2]. Firstly, the transition course from non-glass to glass-cockpit is very demanding (see Pelegrin & Amalberti, 1993 for a complete discussion of the problem). Most of these problems however tend to disappear with experience in the glass-cockpit and with appropriate specific training, namely dedicated glass-cockpit Crew Resource Management training (see for example Wiener, Kanki and Helmreich, 1993).

Nevertheless, some problems come from the new (cognitive) style of glass-cockpit instrument panel display which delivers more and more textual (written or spoken) information in English (one could call them 'class-cockpits', although a significant number of pilots around the world are poor English speakers). A study conducted within Airbus Training showed that the failure rate of pilots

---

[2] See for an extended vision of automation problems some reference chapters and books: Wiener, 1988; Amalberti, 1992; Gras & al, 1994; Woods & al, 1994; Parasuraman R. Mouloua M., 1996; Amalberti, 1997; Billings, 1997; Sarter & Amalberti (in Press).

transitioning to the A310 or A320 was correlated to their age. A closer look showed that the age itself was a good indicator of the level of English (figure 1).

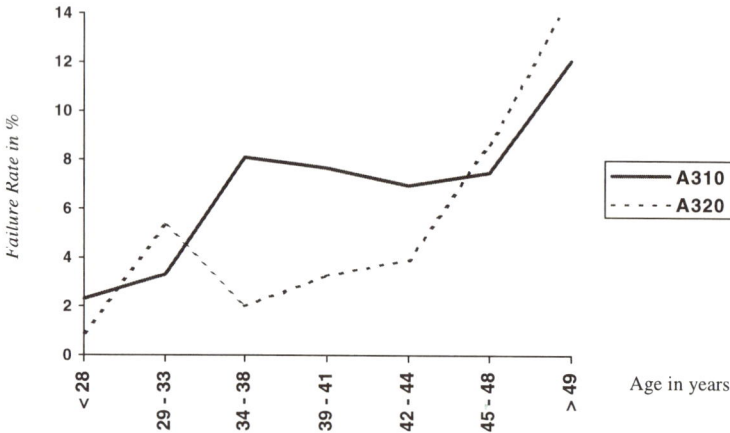

Figure 1   Pilot age and failure rate when transitionning on glass-cockpit
Note: Most of these pilots failing at the first check have a final success after one or several remedial sessions.

This is basically a cultural problem, and it is probably one of the highest priorities. Providing the pilots with a proficient level of English or customizing both the interfaces and the documentation, are two main solutions which will help to address the existing situation. But it seems a bit unrealistic to expect either a proper translation of all the information into all the existing languages, or to expect that all pilots reach a level of English enabling them to handle stressful situations as easily as if they used their mother tongue. Limiting the amount of textual information delivered in the cockpit, to the benefit of intuitive and cross-cultural symbology, may be a solution to prevent the recurrence of the same problem.

Some difficulties also tend to persist after the initial adaptation phase. Flight management programming is both attractive and time consuming. Moreover, most pilots lack a fundamental grasp of the internal logic of automation and evaluate the gap between their expectations (governed by what they would do if they had the controls) and what the computer does. Woods and al (1994) and Sarter & Woods (1991-92-95) coined the words 'automation surprises' to name these sudden and unpredicted system behaviours which are often but not exclusively due to autopilot mode reversions.

Furthermore, pilots flying automated aircrafts have a problem to maintain their manual flight expertise. They may also progressively lose confidence, and tend to hesitate to revert to manual flight in complex and demanding abnormal situations; these are precisely the conditions when manual flight is requested (because of automation failure) (see Amalberti, 1993, for a specific discussion of that issue). Some accident scenarios (like the Airbus A300-600 crash at Nagoya Airport in 1994) indicate that automation can even be felt as a refuge solution when the aircraft behaviour is no longer understood or controlled.

As a matter of fact, beyond the question of confidence, a major issue for research is raised, and that is 'how to understand the organization of pilot knowledge and the dynamic control of cognition?'. The acquisition and organization of pilot's knowledge can be summarized by a three stage model (Amalberti, 1993) (see figure 2).

Trust and expertise
Glass-cockpit   a/c

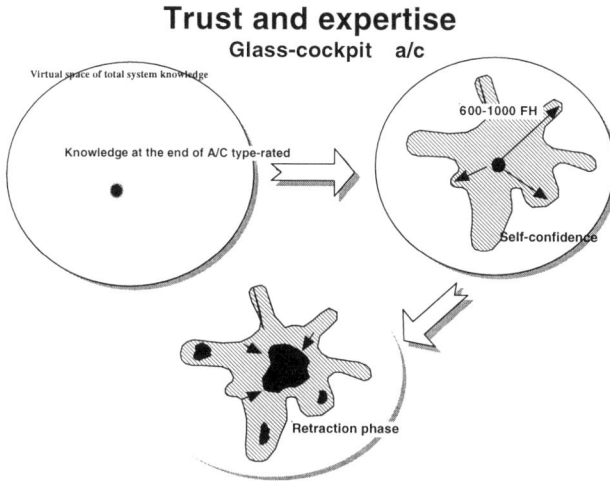

Virtual space of total system knowledge

Knowledge at the end of A/C type-rated

600-1000 FH

Self-confidence

Retraction phase

Figure 2   Trust and expertise in the glass-cockpit aircraft

The data supporting this model comes from:
(i) literature about experimental psychology and the influence of a three stage model for describing the acquisition of expertise introduced by Anderson, (1985)
(ii) incident / accident investivations and
(iii) from a systematic investigation of pilots' knowledge about the Flight Management System at different stages of experience.

This last investigation was made in two phases. Firstly, Amalberti and Valot spent six years investigating the structure of knowledge of fighter pilots (Amalberti & Deblon, 1992; Amalberti & Valot, 1993; see a complete summary of these studies in Amalberti, 1996). In parallel with this study, a similar approach was made (based on the in-house Airbus data base - Cosynus - see Pelegrin and Amalberti, 1993) with 1000 Airline transport pilots during their transition course into the glass cokpit at Airbus Training, and with many airline transport pilots one or several years after their transition course (by the mean of interviews).

Secondly, a thorough study on pilot's knowledge relative to the structure of the Flight Management System (FMS) was conducted jointly in 1995 by IMASSA, Sextant Avionique and Dedale to develop the next generation of FMS (Valot, Grau & Gervais, 1995, IMASSA-Dedale-Sextant in house confidential report). The result of this in-house study is convergent with the results found by Wiener in 1988, by Sarter & Woods in 1992, 1993 and 1995 and by Billings in 1997 on the fundamental heterogeneity of professionnal pilots' system knowledge, due to the complexity of the system and the difficulty to grasp at the same level all the details of system architecture.

The first stage of the model is the knowledge available at the end of the transition course. At this stage, pilots are aware that they still have to discover most of the system. They use the system without routines. Anderson terms this stage the cognitive stage.

Then, pilots fly the system and enter into the second stage. They expand their knowledge until 700 to 800 flight hours (roughly 1 to 2 years). They learn multiple solutions to carry out the job with the system and they gain confidence in themselves. And finally, they stop to expand the knowledge, when they consider that they know enough to carry out their job (positive confidence level based on metaknowledge). However, because of the complexity of the system, the exploration and the knowledge acquisition are not homogeneous for all sub-systems. Pilots can become good specialists of certain sub-functions of the FMS, and may almost ignore the neighbouring functions. Training practices tend to contribute to such results. For example, the FAA Human Factors task force was somewhat amazed at hearing from a major US airline that FMS vertical profiles were not taught to pilots. It was left to each individual crew to decide to explore them and use them in flight. Moreover, the same task force was briefed by the experienced chief pilot of another large airline about the details of system architecture of an advanced glass cockpit, and then was told the following day (by the same chief pilot) that his briefing was incorrect. This shows the extreme difficulty for pilots to synthesize and aggregate in a proper way the disseminated knowledge they have on the system.

The third stage of the model is a retraction of the expertise to an operative sub-set of knowledge and skills suitable for daily operations. The margins generated by this retraction provide pilots with an estimation of the level of risk associated with their own know-how (metaknowledge). It is easy to understand that little practice in manual flight does not generate self confidence, even when the procedures are formally well known. As far as (psychomotor) skills are concerned, the natural process of self confidence building is highly sensitive and rather well tuned. The less the practice, the greater the retraction phase, and the lower self confidence will be. On the other hand, concerning automation management skills, a residual formal knowledge may more easily hide the amplitude of the retraction. A confidence bias often results from this asymmetrical metaknowledge. Pilots become increasingly hesitant to switch to a manual procedure, and tend to develop active avoidance of these situations whenever they feel uneasy. They demonstrate a growing tendancy to recover the automated system by any means when something is wrong. They improvise, reset circuit breakers, without a clear view of the procedure, and sometimes without any procedure (see Plat & Amalberti, in press). However, crews may have enough flexibility to accommodate unknown situations provided they have enough time to set up a new mental plan of action, and provided the cooperation between the two crew members is effective. Consequently, another lesson of experience is the extreme sensitivity of glass cockpits to inter-human relationship (conflicts), especially when intuitive and non-educated cooperation is required.

Solutions

This model of crew expertise has a number of consequences for training. The final heterogeneity of expertise is obviously not the will of pilots. This is not specific to Airbus, nor to Boeing but merely an effect of system complexity which exists throughout the industry. Since the fundamental mechanism of ecological safety (capacities of humans to warrant a certain level of safety) relies upon the accuracy of metaknowledge (see Amalberti, 1996), the main training goal should not be to teach pilots all the details of the system architecture during months, but merely to teach them how to be more accurate in estimating what they know and do not know, and also to teach them generic, safe and simple solutions to recover the control of the situation, when necessary.

There are five main directions towards these goals. Firstly, careful attention should be paid to pilots transitioning for the first time to the glass cockpit and to crew pairing with inexperienced pilots in glass cockpits. Secondly, an easy-to-follow simplified and operative model of system architecture should be taught during the transition course (even though it is formally - technically - a wrong model). It should provide crews with a more global grasp of the systems architecture and functional interconnections. Thirdly, the stability of this basic functional architecture should be kept as far as possible through different aircraft types. The 'family' concept developed by Airbus (thanks to fly by wire) can obviously facilitate the acquisition by regular Airbus crews of a robust model of the aircraft, provided the transition time is not shortened too much. On the other hand, the family concept will make the transition between different aircraft manufacturers more difficult if there is no standardization. Fourthly, crews should be trained in order to avoid losing manual flying expertise, especially when the handling is very demanding (rare manoeuvers). Lastly, CRM is more important than ever in glass cockpit aircraft because of the need for more co-ordination, clear cut task sharing and conflict avoidance.

Most of these points have already led to recommendations to the Authorities (FAA Human Factors Task Force report, June 1996 and JAA draft regulations, JAA Human Factors Steering Group- Subgroup Design and Certification, February 1997).

The (future) regulations

The future JAR-FCL (Flight Crew Licencing) is now expected to be implemented by mid 1999. The JAR-OPS (Operations) is expected a little sooner (mid 1998).

This section briefly describes the work principles of the Joint Aviation Authorities (JAA). The JAA form a 'club' of 16 Western European member States, plus 8 candidates from Eastern Europe. The JAA aim at developing a common set of regulations for Aviation (exclusive of Air Traffic Control which is dealt with within a broader club of nations: the ECAC -European Civil Aviation Conference). The JAA permanent staff is reduced to a few people located in Hoofddorp (near Amsterdam airport). The JAA works with Committees forming the knowledgeable representatives of member states. There are four main Committees (Operations, Flight Crew Licensing, Maintenance, and Certification) and two additional Committees (Research, and Human Factors), which all report to the Secretary General. Each of these Committees have dedicated Subcommittees and Subgroups, e.g. the Medical Subcommittee is part of the Flight Crew Licensing Committee. Any time a new regulation or a change is proposed by a Committee and accepted by the JAA Headquarters (Secretary General and Executive Board - including the Directors General of Aviation of the member states), an NPA (Notice of Proposed Amendment) is issued to initiate the process of searching feedback from the member states' aviation industry. Depending on the feedback, the amendment would be accepted or returned to the Committee for modification.

For the purpose of harmonization between the FAA and the JAA, Harmonization Working Groups are formed at regular intervals. The harmonization process is extremely important for Design and Certification, but less important for Operations and Flight Crew Licensing. This is why that regulations about CRM and Human Factors education (ATPL certificate) are not similar on the two sides of the Atlantic. CRM will also become mandatory in the FARs (Federal Aviation Regulations) for pilots, cabin crew and dispatchers by the end of 1998, but the suggested syllabi will remain simpler than in the JARs and there will be no requirement for CRM in Command Course, Transition Course and Recurrent Training. Conversely, CRM is already mandatory in the US for all airlines choosing the AQP (Advanced Qualification Program) for their Transition Course.

Table 1 summarizes the main regulations related to Human Factors training. The regulations for CRM are not part of the JAR-FCL, but are included into the JAR-OPS.

Table 1   Main HF regulations related to training in JAR-FCL (expected 1999) and JAR-OPS (expected late 1998)

Paragraph	Status	Content
JAR-FCL 1.470 & related AMC	Already in JAR-FCL	Human Factors syllabus for the HF certificate for ATPL. A JAA task force is planned to be formed in 1997 for one year to develop a JAA training handbook relevant to Human Factors and limitations.
JAR-FCL 1.240 & related Appendix	Already in JAR-FCL	Skill & proficiency check for aeroplane type/class ratings and ATPL. Specific requirements for the evaluation of crews' non technical skills (applied research launched 1997, detailed modalities expected in 1998)
JAR-OPS 1.940	Already in JAR-OPS	Requirements for crew pairing depending on the minimum experience of each crew member.
JAR-OPS 1.945 & 1.965 and related AMC & IEM	Already in JAR-OPS	CRM for transition courses, recurrent and command course
	HF steering group's proposal	CRM syllabi and modalities (duration, instructors qualifications, etc.). Clarification for ab-initio CRM (for who, when, what content)
	HF steering group subgroup formed, results expected 1998	HF harmonization effort betweeen JAR-OPS & JAR-FCL

Human Factors in design and certification

Human Factors and airworthiness regulations objectives

Human Factors are not totally absent from the regulations for certification. But they currently are a general reminder that systems should respect human limitations and capacities. They include statements like '...the landing may not require exceptional piloting skill or alertness' (excerpt from JAR 25.125).

The airworthiness requirements concerning the cockpit, as for any other subsystem of the aircraft, are *not* aiming at any 'best possible' design, but they intend to specify the minimum objectives to be matched by an applicable design. This is a very basic principle of any certification. As far as Human Factors in cockpit design and equipment are concerned, the minimum objectives currently set by the airworthiness code are more or less limited to the following:

- to guarantee that the minimum crew (i.e. after one crew members incapacitation) is still able to do the job without excessive workload or fatigue (ref: FAR/JAR 25-1523)
- to provide the crewmembers with acceptable comfort and protection against outside conditions, so that they can do their job without excessive effort, concentration or fatigue (ref: FAR/JAR 25-771)

- to provide the crew with sufficient visibility to the outside (ref: FAR/JAR 25-773)
- to minimize the risks of mistake in the controls use, particularly through a standardization of the shape and movement of the primary flight controls (ref: FAR/JAR 25-777; 781)
- to minimize ambiguities in the information displayed by the instruments (ref: FAR/JAR 25-1303; 1321; 1322)
- to provide the crew with relevant alerting information about unsafe functioning states of any equipment or system, and to allow appropriate crew action (ref: FAR/JAR 25-1309).

However, these generic requirements are accompanied by a set of 'special conditions' adapted to the specificities of each particular aircraft. These special conditions may well include extensive and detailed requirements for systems like CRT display flight instruments.

The methodology used to check the compliance of a proposed design with a relevant airworthiness requirement heavily depends on the explicit versus implicit nature of the requirement. Explicit requirements are directly expressed in terms of design characteristics. For example, FAR/JAR 25-781 quotes: 'cockpit control knobs must conform to the general shape ... in the following figures'. In this case, the compliance of a proposed design is rather easy to check, and direct examination of descriptive material (drawings, scale models, mock-ups) can be used. However, most of the Human Factors related issues are covered by implicit requirements, expressed in terms of general outcomes to be achieved. For example, FAR/JAR 25-777 (a) quotes: 'each cockpit control must be located to provide convenient operation and to prevent confusion and inadvertant operation'.

In this second case, the *methodology* used to evaluate the ability of a proposed design to reach the objective obviously *is a critical part* of the certification process. A first possible source of difficulty is the interpretation of the regulatory objective itself. A second possible source of difficulty is in the evaluation of an acceptable means of compliance. To guide all these interpretations, some requirements are complemented with advisory material, including *interpretation guidelines* and / or indications on *acceptable means of compliance (AMC)*.

The needs

The aviation industry has to manage the conflicting goals of increased performance (more traffic at lower cost) and improved safety in a worldwide environment of extreme competition for survival. Since human errors are recognized to be involved as a major factor in about 70% of the accidents, it is more and more accepted within the industry that better consideration should be given to human error management in the design features of a flight deck.

However, design engineers and flight test professionals have growing difficulty to evaluate a proposed design as appropriate and acceptable. As a matter of fact, almost the only tool currently in use to evaluate the acceptability of a new design in terms of Human Factors in a certification process is a *test pilot judgment*. This judgment is based on the authority and manufacturer test pilots' comparative experience: on the one hand their experience from actual or simulated flight exposure in the test cockpit (several thousands of flight hours for major test programes), and on the other hand their previous experience with existing or past designs.

This test pilot assessment methodology is naturally affected by some biases. Firstly, it is based on the assumption that the experience of test pilots on previous aircraft is transferable on the new one. This may not be true for large evolutions in human-machine interface design. Secondly test pilots are not a representative sample of the airline pilot population. They have a very specific knowledge of the aircraft, which leads to different mental models of the aircraft. They do not share the same routine operations and the same constraints, and therefore the cognitive processes involved at the crew / aircraft interface are probably not the same for these two groups of pilots. Furthermore, typical figures for the number of individuals involved in test pilot flying is about ten, and the exposure time about two thousand hours. This is to be compared to the frequency of critical events or combinations of events in airline operation, which is more likely to be of the order of one per hundred thousand hours.

Furthermore, the certification process *cannot wait* until the first aircraft prototype is built to get started. No manufacturer would take the risk of becoming involved in such highly expensive development programs without reasonable guarantee that the projected designs were certifiable. Consequently new designs are submitted to regulatory authorities to get some 'certification' agreement well before a prototype aircraft is built. In this situation, pilot judgement cannot be exercised in a real cockpit, a real flight context, but has to be exercised in a mock-up or other form of simulated environment.

Finally, test pilots and designers should ideally refer to the behaviour of the 'average pilot' and test the system and evaluate the potential risk of mismatch. But what is 'average pilot' behaviour? Is there such a thing? Helmreich et al (1996) for example have shown that attitudes towards automation show major differences when compared between Europe, America and Asia. Some pilots turn on automation when they are in trouble, although others turn it off. The rapid global appreciation of the aviation industry reveals the extent of these cultural differences. In the seventies, 80% of the world market and all major manufacturers were in the USA. In the eighties, 80% of the world market as well as all major manufacturers were located in the USA or Europe. The next millenium could see 60% of the market and major manufacturers in Asia. Needless to say, there is an urgent need to know more about the range of expected reactions from pilots originating from non western countries. Indeed such models are at the core of the design of system logics and system protections.

Solutions

Solutions to the previous difficulties will not be trivial. The search for solutions should first be directed towards the optimization of existing know how, instead of revolution. Human Factors specialists can play a positive role in this optimization process.

However, the challenges will be hard to meet, for several reasons:

- 'Turf' protection behaviour from all categories of people, including the Human Factors community, slows down the transfer of knowledge from academy to industry.
- Cognitive ergonomics, which are at the core of the required efforts, are not intuitive, even less intuitive than any other of the Human Factors branches. This requires a minimum education in cognitive psychology and cannot be summarized into recipies and hard calculations.
- The time schedule of any aircraft design process has been shortened by drastic proportions as an effect of the competition. Most of the existing Human Factors methods for design evaluation are long, probably too long; the industry needs new methods compatible with its constraints.
- Human Factors methods must respect the current design and certification process, which has proven effective, even though it could be amended.
- Human error management is an extremely difficult subject to address when it comes to design and certification (there is more about this in the last section).
- No significant progress will be achieved without real feedback about previous decisions. This implies that design choices should be documented, that all tests should be conducted with a clearly explicited methodology and that all the results should be made available. This is not the case today. Although the industry acknowledges the theoretical value of such 'traceability' it hesitates to implement it because it could result in freezing creativity and increasing liability problems.

Human Factors education of many designers and certification specialists is a key condition for success. However, the standard university curriculum is not the right formula for people already involved in these demanding jobs. Nevertheless, several attempts to educate design engineers are on the spot either through in-house programs (Airbus, Aerospatiale) or through specific institutions or associations (e. g. the EAAP training program).

There is no magic Human Factors recipe to overcome the limitations of existing methods to address human error in design. These existing methods are based on Human Reliability Assessment (see JAR 25.1309). We do not know how to consider the potential for propagation of basic human errors which remain undetected. We do not know how to address the situation where the crew's mental representation is inaccurate or inappropriate. We do not know how to use the frequency of errors in an evaluation test: should we reject a design just because of one severe error, committed on one day, by one pilot? Or because the majority of pilots would make the same minor error?

The systematic introduction of documented tests at specific milestones of the design process would certainly help to support and keep trace of the main design decisions. The participation of airline pilots to such tests has often been presented as a basic condition for efficiency, which is probably true. However, experience indicates that poor design can result from airline pilot judgement as well as from test pilot judgement. How to organize the participation of airline pilots is still difficult to judge. What pilot population should be involved? How should the individuals be selected? What should be expected from them: passive performance measurement or active opinion? When should they be involved in the design process? At the end of major certification programs? Certification authorities are nowadays calling for operational 'route proving' experimental flights. These flights enable the opportunity to evaluate the aircraft in airline-type environments, including 'natural' and artificially induced failures, with crews being composed of airline and test pilots. Such programs have included more than one hundred flights on some occasions. But what is the benefit of including airline pilots at a stage when the design is frozen?

It is expected in the future to add Human Factors regulations at both the design process level (philosophies, policies, traceability, methodologies) and at the product level (re-visitation of regulation on automation design). However developing these regulations will necessarily take a long time. A working group between the FAA and JAA, with the active participation of the manufacturers, could be the right answer to develop, within five years, some feasible (easy methods) and reasonable (low cost) Human Factors regulations for design and certification (see table 2 for a summary of existing and future regulations). However we already know that some goals will not be achievable within this schedule because research efforts with be required from the Human Factors community.

Table 2   Main HF regulations related to design and certification in JAR 25 and JAR 21

Paragraph	Status	Content
JAR 25-145 and following sections	effective	Minimum flight quality requirements for end users
JAR 25-671and following sections	effective	Design requirements for warning and feedback systems when systems fail
JAR 25-1141 and following sections	effective	Minimum engine design requirements for end-users
JAR 25-1309	effective	System reliability, human response to system failure and human error
JAR 25-1322	effective	Color requirements for warning caution & advisory lights
JAR 25-1329	effective	Autopilot design requirements for end-users
JAR 25-1523	effective	Minimum system requirements for minimum crew
	expected 1999 from the results of the FAA/JAA HWG 23.1329/25.1335	Revisions of JAR/FAR 1329 and 1335 (aural and visual warnings appropriate to automatic flight control/guidance disengagement)

Paragraph	Status	Content
	expected 2000 from the results of the future FAA/JAA HF HWG	Ask manufacturers and operators to assert their automation philosophies and explicitly convey these philosophies to flight crews
	expected 2000 from the the results of the future FAA/JAA HF HWG	Regulation addressing human error in design and certification
	expected 2000 from the the results of the future FAA/JAA HF HWG	Regulations (or recommendations) on enhanced traceability in design and certification (including the place of end-users in the design and certification process)

Human Factors in aviation safety and data-bases

The needs

It is a constant feeling that Aviation Safety is a land of paradoxes. The safety level (less than one fatal accident per million departures in industrialized countries) is the best of all transportation industries but at the same time, the larger the activity, the higher the safety requirements. With 25 million departures per year, we will continue to see 20 major accidents per year. If the traffic is doubling, we will see 40 accidents per year. Is it too much? Can we improve? How?

The response to the statement 'Is it too much?' is not trivial. Most people consider that the perception of an increase in accident numbers (due to the increase in traffic) will not be acceptable. Such an attitude is probably true in western culture, but is not necessarily shared worldwide. If we must improve aviation safety, at least to maintain the current number of accidents, the next question is 'Is it possible?'.

Again the answer is complex since no other industry has reached such a good level of safety. The aviation safety players may be wrong in expressing their ultimate safety goal in terms of *50% less accidents* or even *zero accidents*. The true challenge for aviation safety may well be not to improve safety rates, but to maintain a stable safety level instead of the extreme worldwide competition, and to permit aviation to continue its growth with limited drawbacks (for a dedicated discussion see Amalberti, 1997; Sarter & Amalberti, 1997).

Since 70% of the accidents and incidents continue to be seen as caused by crew errors (and more than 90% if we include human error at the organization level), it is a worldwide recognized phenomenon that the safety priority is a systemic approach to individual and organizational error. The organizational approach to safety is not developed in this paper although they represent very important directions for safety improvement. The reader can find a summary of this approach in Reason at al, 1995.

The approach to individual human error is the other key area to improve safety. This approach has changed over time. Long restricted to the idea that human errors should be suppressed by all means, it is more and more accepted that human errors are part of normal human performance and cannot be eradicated. The goal is to avoid accident, not to eradicate errors. The safety efforts should minimize error consequences and their entry into an error chain.

Moreover, a series of studies (in-house IMASSA report, 1994, Amalberti, 1996, Wioland & Amalberti, 1996) show that humans are very good in error recovery, and that, contrary to expectations, the final risk of incident is higher when the crew spend all available resources to avoid errors (see figure 3). Indeed crews make less errors when the workload increases, thanks to the reinforced control of cognition, but recover a lower rate of the few errors they make. The final result is somewhere paradoxical since they have more incidents with fewer errors. Note that the optimal balance between the production and the detection of error comes with a busy condition (see Wioland & Amalberti, 1996) which corresponds to the ideal human-in the loop conditions.

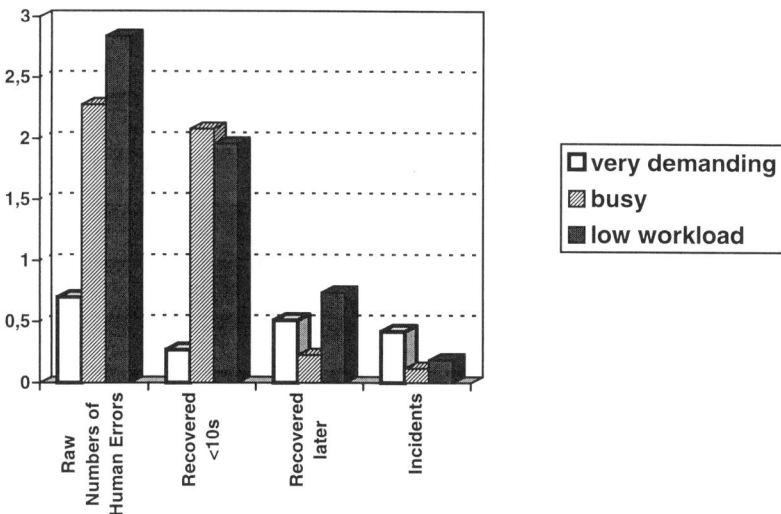

Figure 3   **Average number of crew errors per hour during a miminum crew certification campaign of a glass-cockpit aircraft (44 flight hours). Results are presented as a matter of task demand (in-house IMASSA report, 1994)**

The methods

The actions to improve safety policies are threefold. Firstly, shifting safety approaches from individuals to organizations. ICAO has played a central role in this new approach during the last ten years. Secondly, gathering more data on human errors. The Aviation Incident Reporting Systems are solicited to gather more data regarding errors and system deficiencies, but the problem remains what to do with the results. The available models for predicting accidents from these databases seem to be rather poor. Thirdly, designing the system according to a modern approach to human error. Error tolerant systems have replaced error repressive systems. Another challenge is now to enhance the visibility of errors to facilitate error detection and recovery.

In the end, the future directions for improvement in aviation safety depend on trust and beliefs more than on rational thinking. Do we believe that the future of safety will follow a linear extrapolation of the current logistics, or do we think the current system is close to its safety apogee. The history of technology tells us that technical systems have always been replaced by other technical systems once they reached an apogee, and safety has generally been improved through these major changes. Maybe we are close to the apogee of the aviation system. In this case the difficulty to progress beyond the current safety plateau that has been experienced during the last 20 years simply represents the asymptotic limit of the present system. If this is so, the Human Factors aspect of the current system will be of little use to anticipate the future system. For example, if the future of aviation is to be a fully automated system, based on a worldwide data-link network between ground based and airborne flight management computers, the safety efforts should rather be rapidly directed to more pertinent areas than Human Factors in the flight deck. But of course, nobody knows when the shift from one technology to the next will take place. Will this be after a particularly tragic accident (see the Zeppelin story) which could lead some people within the aviation community to think that the most important goal of aviation safety policy should be to avoid the 'big one'?

Conclusion

This chapter was intended to give a broad overview of Human Factors in crew training, aircraft design & certification, and aviation safety policies. Important aspects of Aviation Human Factors for the flight deck have not been developed. This is also the case for issues like vigilance, time on duty, stress management, co-operation with ground operational staff. Culture has also not been considered in this paper and needs a dedicated chapter. The Human Factors aspects of Maintenance and Air Traffic Controllers have also been deliberately left aside, because they deserve to be addressed as such. Future EAAP courses will be specifically devoted to these topics.

As we have seen in the historical overview, Human Factors in Aviation are not floating by themselves in a vacuum. They are embedded in a global aviation safety· system and reflect *specific theories* about risk and safety in the aviation transportation system. These theories are far from being mere rational constructions, consistent with all the available scientific evidence. They are also *historical and social outcomes*, conveying the current fears and faiths of the communities, the profession's interest, the weight and influence of the different nations and organisations. They result from a maturation of ideas from both the Academy, the Authorities and the Industry, recurrently catalysed by some accidents felt to represent major failures of the system and a growing need to meet new challenges. All along this process, the technocratic beliefs of the aviation 'technical' community have been slowly but firmly challenged. Human Factors are now recognized as a core discipline in aviation activities and the issue is now how to do the job and keep the commitments. This is the new challenge for Human Factors in aviation.

Appendix 1 summarizes some key milestones of the Human Factors evolution.

References

Basic books (basic courses)

Abbott C. Slotte S. Stimson D. (Eds, 1996) *FAA human factors team report on the interfaces between flightcrews and modern flight desks systems*, FAA: Washington DC

Amalberti R. (1994) (Ed): *Briefings, a Human Factors course for profesionnal pilots*, IFSA-DEDALE : Paris (French, English and Spanish versions) (contact IFSA to purchase tel (33)1 4495 2943 fax 2941) .

Billings C. (1997) *Human Centred Aviation Automation*, Hillsdale NJ: LEA

Maurino D. Reason J. Johnston N. Lee R. (1995) *Beyond Aviation Human Factors*, Ashgate-Avebury Aviation: Aldershot

Reason J. (1990) *Human error*, Cambridge University Press

Sarter N. Amalberti R. (Editors, on press 1977) *Cognitive Engineering in the Aviation*, Hillsdale NJ: LEA

Wiener E. Nagel D. (Eds) (1988) *Human Factors in Aviation*, Academic Press: NY

Wiener E. Kanki B. Helmreich R. (1993) *Cockpit Resources Management*, NY: Academic press.

Woods D. Johannesen D. Cook R. Sarter N. (1994) *Behind human error*, CSERIAC, WPAFB: Ohio.

To go beyond...(extended course)

Amalberti R. (1996) *La conduite de systèmes à risques*, Paris: PUF

Amalberti R. (1993) *Cockpit automation: maintaining manual skills and cognitive skills*, IATA Montreal, 8-10 octobre, 110-118

Amalberti R. (on press,1997) Automation in Aviation: A Human Factors Perspective, In (Eds) Garland D. Wise J. Hopkin D. (1997) *Aviation Human Factors*. Hillsdale: LEA

Anderson J.(1985) *Development of expertise in 'Cognitive psychology and its implications'*, Freeman, NY, 235-259

Aw Arona (1997) *Intermediary report on the experiment ARCHIMEDE 3*, APSYS research report, (in French)

Bainbridge L. (1987) Ironies of automation, In Rasmussen J., Duncan J. & Leplat J. (Eds), *New technology and human errors*, NY: Wiley, 271-286

Funk K. Lyall B. Riley V. (1995) Flight Desk Automation Problems, *Proceedings of the 8th International Symposium on Aviation Psychology*, Colombus, April 1995

Gras A. Moricot C. Poirot-Delpech S. Scardigli V. (1994*) Faced with automation : the pilot, the controller and the engineer*. Paris: Presse de la Sorbonne (condensed version of a book Face à l'automate: le pilote, le contrôleur et l'ingénieur, Paris: Presse de la Sorbonne

Lee J. Moray N.(1994) Trust, Selfconfidence, and operator's adaptation to automation*, Int. Journ.Human-Computer Studies*, 40,153-184

Layton C. Smith P. (1992) An Emperical Evaluation of Computerized Tools to Aid in Enroute Flight Planning, *Proceedings of the 1992 Annual Meeting of the Human Factors Society*,1194-2001, CSEL-92-CP-10

Helmreich R. Merritt A. Sherman P. (1996) *The flight management attitudes questionnaire : An International survey of pilot attitudes regarding cockpit management and automation*, Report of the University of Texas.

Hollnagel E. (1993) *Human Reliability Analysis, Context and Control,* London: Academic Press

Parasuraman R. Mouloua M. (1996, Editors) *Automation and human performance*, Hillsdale NJ: LEA

Pelegrin C. Amalberti R. (1993) Pilot's strategies of crew coordination in advanced glass-cockpits; a matter of expertise and culture. *Proceedings of th ICAO Human Factors Seminar*, Washington 12-15 April 1995, Circular OACI 217-AN/12

Plat M. Amalberti R. (in preparation) Crew training to automation surprises, *planned to be submitted June 1997 to Int J. Aviation Psychology.*

Rogalski J. Samurcay R. Amalberti R. (1994) Coordination et communication dans les cockpits automatisés, *(Coordination and communication in Advanced Glassockpit)* IMASSA-CERMA:Brétigny sur Orge, Rapport final convention de recherche DGAC

Rizzo A. Ferrente D. Bagnara S. (1994) Handling human error, In Hoc J.M., Cacciabue P., Hollnagel E.(Eds): *Expertise and technology*, Hillsdale: NJ. L.Erlbaum, 99-114

Sarter N. Woods D. (1992) Pilot Interaction With Cockpit Automation: Operational Experiences With the Flight Management System, *Int. J. Aviat. Psychology*, 2(4), 303-321

Sarter N. Woods D. (1991) Situation Awareness: a Critical but ill-defined phenomenom , *Int. J. Aviat. Psychology*, 1(1), 45-57

Sarter N. Woods D. (1995) *Strong, Silent and 'Out-of-the-Loop'*; Properties of Advanced Automation and Their Impact on Human Automation Interaction, CSEL Report 95-TR-01, Colombus University, Ohio.

Valot C. Amalberti R. (1992) Metaknowledge for time and reliability, *Reliability Engineering and Systems Safety*, 36, 199-206

Wanner J.C. Leconte P. (1989) *Etude Rachel-Archimède*, Rapport DGAC 89-52016

Wiener E.(1988) Cockpit Automation, In Wiener E. Nagel D. (Eds) *Human Factors in Aviation*, Academic Press: NY, 433-461

Wiener E.(1989) *Human Factors of Advanced Technology ('Glass Cockpit')* Transport Aircraft, Nasa Contractor report 177528

Wiener E. Chidester T. Kanki B. Parmer E. Curry R. Gregorich S. (1991) The impact of Cockpit Automation on Crew Coordination and Communication, NASA scientific report 177587.

Wioland L. Amalberti R. (1996) *When errors serve safety: towards a model of ecological safety, Cognitive Systems Engineering in Process Control*, November 12-15, 1996, Kyoto, Japan

Wise J. Abbott D. Tilden D. Dick J. Guide P. Ryan L. (1993) *Automation in Corporate Aviation*: *Human Factors Issues*, Final Report, ERAU, CAAR-15405-93

Appendix 1

Some milestones in the recent history of Aviation Human Factors

	USA & ICAO	Europe
40's War time	First Human Factors applications, anthropometry and perception (head up systems)	
50's to 70's	Development of extensive databases and compendium on 'classic' Human Factors Positive transfer to Aviation Industry (design offices)	Followers of US Medical and psychophysics approaches to 'classic' Human Factors problems: perception and rest
early 80's	Emergence of CRM. The focus is put on errors of front line actors (pilots, mechanists, controllers) Positive transfer to Aviation Industry (operators)	Followers of US in Aviation, Inovative in other industry: Birth of Cognitive Ergonomics and Cognitive Engineering (first book of Jens Rasmussen) Birth of Airbus
end 80's	ICAO asks for a mandatory Human Factors education of pilots (PPL and ATPL, annex 1) Some recommendations for the respect of human capacities and limitations are incorporated into FARs Wiener & Nagel publish Human Factors in Aviation	First generation glasscockpit (A320) First glasscockpit accident A few Human Factors specialists are trained and incorporated into the training and customer departments of the European manufacturer Birth of JAA The focus of human error is shifted from individuals to system approach (Jim Reason)
early 90's	Transfer from Europe to US and application of cognitive ergonomics concepts to aviation (Dave Woods & Nadine Sarter) US manufacturers hire a few Human Factors specialists in the design office	First European Glasscockpit CRM (Jean Pariès) More glasscockpit accidents occur
1992		Mont St Odile A320 accident
1993	ICAO asks for CRM being mandatory in pilot training (annex 6)	
	Human Factors groups are created in IATA and IFALPA	
1994	Nagoya A310 accident The FAA asks for a Human Factors audit of the interfaces between flightcrews and modern flight deck systems	
1995	Culture is emerging as a core topic for aviation safety (Bob Helmreich, Neil Johnston, Dan Maurino, etc)	The JAA forms the Human Factors Steering Group (JAA HFStG).
1996	The FAA HF team report is issued in June, 1996, and presented to manufacturers Positive welcome CRM is mandatory within the AQP program	The FAA joins the FAA HF StG to work in sync. European and US manufacturers participate to the design and certification sub-group CRM is mandatory in several European countries (e.g., UK, France)

	USA & ICAO	Europe
1997	ICAO asks for Human Factors being mandatory into design	
1997 continue	A JAA-FAA Harmonization Working Group for Human Factors in design and certification is planned to be formed The industry supports the action	
1998	CRM becomes mandatory for all pilots, cabin crew and dispatchers	CRM becomes mandatory for all pilots and cabin crew (JAR-OPS)
1999		JAR-FCL becomes mandatory
2000-2005	Expected HF regs & recommendations	for design & certification

Section 2

Selection

Course Manager & Section Editor:

Hans-Jürgen Hörmann

5 Basic concepts

Hans-Jürgen Hörmann
DLR - German Aerospace Center,
Aviation and Space Psychology, Germany

Introduction

Selection basically can be seen as a decision making process in which relevant information is gathered for the comparison of job-seeking individuals, in order to assess their suitability for a given training or position. Based on this information those applicants are chosen from the sample, that appear to have the most promising potential to fulfil the respective job requirements successfully. The quality of decisions in a selection process depends to a high degree on the appropriateness of the facts gathering methods and on the rationality of the algorithm for combining these facts into a predictive model.

From the point of view of the employer, selection is a comparatively inexpensive but powerful method for increasing the productivity of the staff members: Personnel selection can significantly reduce the attrition rate of the employees during career development, so training expenses can be saved, available training resources can be used more efficiently, and the whole personnel situation becomes more calculable.

However, the job-seeking applicants have to pass the selection filters more or less voluntarily by exposing personal, sometimes also private information in order to find a job. When facing a selection test, applicants might sometimes feel quite unpleasant since their fortune in terms of career progress can depend immensely on the result. Therefore the responsibilities of the professionals involved in personnel selection include not only ensuring scientific accuracy and fairness of the selection procedure to the highest possible extent, but also the prevention of misuse of the personal information. The selection procedure must be standardised, empirically justified, and free from subjectivity as far as possible. Decisions should be taken by an interdisciplinary team of highly qualified professionals who know how to handle the strengths and weaknesses of the diagnostic instruments as well as the present and future demands of the job at disposal.

This section is addressed to the practitioner working in the field of psychological selection. We omitted most of the scientific and psychometric background knowledge about test-construction because organisational psychologists are usually familiar with it. After the introduction of some elementary concepts three exemplary selection systems in aviation are described: First, a selection-system for civil aviation pilots is illustrated by *Hans-Jürgen Hörmann*. Especially the diagnostic of personality and social behaviour will be described in detail. *Per Byrdorf* is giving an overview of selection of military pilots in the NATO-countries in chapter 7. Chapter 8 is dedicated to the selection of air-traffic controllers. *Hinnerk Eißfeldt* describes the specific job requirements and selection methods in this area.

Job-analysis and interview techniques should belong to the standard repertoire of selection experts. However, in the practical field quite often they are conducted unstructured and intuitively which limits drastically the utility of these essential steps in the selection process. *Pieter Hermans* and *Hemmo Mulder* demonstrate several straightforward methods to job-analysis and interview.

The last part of this section contains a discussion of the legal and ethical issues. *Klaus-Martin Goeters* makes aware the legal situation for professionals involved in selection. This includes obligations for data protection as well as a discussion of the 'Psychological Requirement' for pilots described in the Flight Crew Licensing (FCL) part of the coming Joint Aviation Requirements (JARs). Afterwards he reviews the results from different empirical studies about the validity and utility of selection tests. *Hans-Jürgen Hörmann* concludes this section by giving some guidelines for how to combine diagnostic information into a selection decision. He also summarises some general recommendations and future perspectives for the field of selection.

Models and procedures of selection

In the history of pilot training aptitude testing was always regarded as an inevitable step to lower the risks of training failures and accidents. In their recent literature review Hunter & Burke (1995) report examples of pilot selection beginning with the early days of the Wright brothers. Especially in the case of "ab-initio" student pilots, that start flight training without having any prior experience in aircraft-flying, there is little alternative for the systematic assessment of basic flying abilities. Relevant job experience is not available, and gradings from high-school or another job training or a university degree have low predictive value for the special skills and abilities required to operate an aircraft safely. Let us assume that the base rate of people having the potential of becoming a safe airline pilot is about 30% in the general population of young adults, selection tests are working like filters that can only be passed by those individuals who show clear enough indications of the relevant aptitudes. Provided that the selection tests have the appropriate sensitivity the rate of successful candidates can be raised from the initial base rate up to 80 or 90% and even higher.

Of course the above picture of selection is simplifying the situation since it is based on a rather static view of the individual and the job demands.

With suitable training the potential of the students can be developed within certain limits. Thus the cut-off scores for the different selection tests have to be adjusted to the scheduled training intensity in the respective area. *Ideally, selection should focus on stable, job-relevant characteristics of the individuals, that vary substantially in the applicant's population, but cannot be compensated by training.* The situation becomes even more complex if one takes into account the dynamics of the job demands themselves. If the selection criteria are tailored too specifically to certain job-tasks which are critical today, they could loose their predictive power in the future in the event of a shifting task structure. For example pilot screening in a single engine aircraft with low complexity can have a high short-term prognostic validity but could loose its relevance for the working processes in highly automated cockpits and for crew coordination tasks.

Consequently, the benefits of selection, like lower drop out rates of trainees or higher safety standards can only emerge if selection itself is directly in tune with the training syllabi and the task design of the job under consideration. In other words a successful career development of the staff members does not only depend on the given potential of the individuals but also on the suitability of training opportunities and on a well-designed working-place and task-structure. These interconnections are illustrated in a systems approach of personnel development shown in figure 1. On the left half of this flow chart it is shown that analysis of the job tasks leads to a profile of required qualifications. From here the flow branches into two lines: Job qualifications that are not trainable will be secured via personnel selection. Qualifications that can be developed during the job training will be secured during training. After selection and training the performance of the job novices should be surveyed. This criterion information is compared in validity studies with the predicted performance and these results are fed back to the selection methods, the training syllabus, or if necessary also to the job design. This feedback loop on the right half of the chart, represents parts of the quality control for the personnel development system.

If the job profile includes a large variety of qualifications which have to be assessed for a larger sample of applicants, it is generally more efficient to follow a sequence of different selection steps. Generally it is advisable to screen a large number of applicants initially with relatively rough filters, such as the inspection of the persons files, and then to proceed with more in-depth methods for the most promising candidates after this pre-screening. Figure 2 shows a flow chart of an ab-initio pilot selection procedure, with fictitious pass-rates for the different stages. It starts with a check of the formal requirements (e.g. age, education), followed by paper-pencil classroom tests (40% pass-rate), and concluded by individual apparatus tests (50% pass-rate) and an interview (80% pass-rate). Overall, the selection rate would be 16% in this situation. The advantage of such a multi-stage selection is that the more cost intensive methods have to be administered only to a relatively small number of applicants.

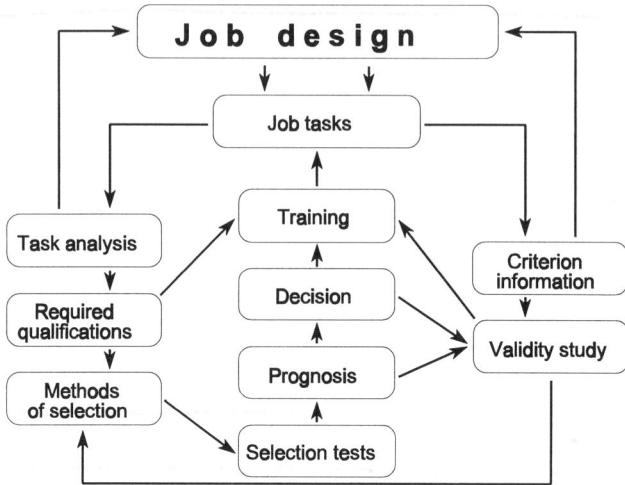

Figure 1   Interrelations of selection, training, and job design in a systems approach to personnel development

MULTI-STAGE SELECTION OF AB-INITIO PILOTS		
FAIL-RATE		PASS-RATE
RECRUITMENT OF CANDIDATES & CHECK OF FORMAL REQIREMENTS		
0%	⇓	100%
GROUP TESTING: BASIC OPERATIONAL APTITUDES		
60%	⇓	40%
INDIVIDUAL TESTING: PSYCHOMOTOR COORDINATION, MULTIPLE TASK CAPACITY		
50%	⇓	50%
INTERVIEW: PERSONALITY, SOCIAL BEHAVIOUR, BIOGRAPHY		
20%	⇓	80%
MEDICAL EXAMINATION		
20%	⇓	80%
FLIGHT TRAINING		
8%	⇓	92%
AIRLINES		

Figure 2   Example of a multi-stage selection procedure for ab-initio pilots with fictitious pass-rates for the different selection steps, selection methods and psychometric test criteria

What are the sources of information for a selection decision and how can the quality of this information be assessed? Cook (1988) has named the most popular methods in personnel selection the "classic trio": application form, letter of reference, and interview. Organisational psychologists have long known that these methods alone are not very effective and consequently they were looking for more advanced instruments (e.g. Goeters, 1995a). Many different methods have been developed and validated that cannot be reported comprehensively in this section. Summaries are given by Hunter & Hunter (1984), Cook (1988), Robertson & Smith (1989), or Landy, Shankster & Kohler (1994) for personnel selection in general. Hunter & Burke (1995) and Martinussen (1996) presented similar reviews for pilot selection.

In table 1 data reported by Hunter & Hunter (1984), Robertson & Smith (1989) for personnel selection in general is compared to results of pilot selection methods reported in meta-studies by Hunter & Burke (1995) and Martinussen (1996). In most cases methods have been validated against training criteria. Since the jobs for which the selection tests have been validated are very heterogenous this comparison is inevitably rather global. Keeping this limitation in mind the highest predictive accuracy seems to result from work sample tests (such as realistic simulations or job tryouts) and from ability composites (combined scores from several cognitive and psychomotor tests). Assessment centres (see chapter 6), ability tests, and biodata show moderate validities. References, interviews, personality, interest, and education provide low but still positive correlations with the criterion. In general the reported validities are lower for the selection of pilots than for other professions.

The sample sizes in these meta-studies are quite impressive. Nevertheless these results can only demonstrate broad trends for different classes of methods. They are not a substitute for the empirical validation of selection tests in a specific setting. For example the studies reviewed by Hunter & Burke and Magnusson cover the time period between 1919 and 1993. More then 90% of the data were collected in military pilot training mostly in the US. Consequently, the relevance for selection of civil airline pilots after their basic training has to be confirmed. The number of recently published reports in civil aviation is still too small to draw general conclusions (Stead, 1991; Bartram & Baxter, 1996; Hörmann & Maschke, 1987, 1996).

Table 1   Comparison of different methods for personnel selection in general and for pilot selection

Selection method	General selection		Pilot selection	
	Approximate sample size	Mean validities	Approximate sample size	Mean validities
Work sample	> 3,000	0.38 - 0.54	> 2,500	0.34
Ability composite	> 30,000	0.53	> 5,000	0.31
Assessment centre	> 15,000	0.41 - 0.43	-	-
General mental ability	> 30,000	0.25 - 0.45	> 15,000	0.13 - 0.29
Biodata	> 5,000	0.24 - 0.38	> 27,000	0.21 - 0.27
References	> 2,500	0.17 - 0.26	-	-
Interviews	> 2,500	0.14 - 0.23	-	-
Personality tests	> 20,000	0.15	> 22,000	0.10 - 0.13
Interests	> 1,500	0.10	-	-
Education	> 32,000	0.10	> 6,000	0.06
Handwriting	small	0.00	-	-

Validity is a crucial but not the only criterion for comparing the value of selection methods. Other methodological standards can have equal or sometimes even higher importance. Three classes of criteria can be distinguished:

Psychometric criteria:
- Objectivity: Degree of independence of measurement and interpretation from subjective factors
- Reliability: Degree of accuracy or repeatability of the measurement
- Validity: Degree to which a test really measures what it pretends to measure (construct validity). Degree of correspondence between test-scores and real job performance (prognostic validity).
- Utility: (Financial) gain of using method A for selection instead of method B or random selection

Practical criteria:
- Applicability: Specific facilities (e.g. simulator) being required or given environmental and time conditions can restrict the use of a test

- Availability: Test material with adequate norms must be available for the national language and culture of the applicant group under consideration.
- Qualifications of the user: Special expertise or training required for examiners have to be taken into account.

Social criteria:
- Acceptability: Applicants should accept the methods as adequate for determining their job qualifications
- Fairness: Methods are not in conflict with ethical norms (e.g. discrimination of minorities)

Compared to this catalogue the methodological recommendations of the JAR-FCL 3 (Section 2, Subpart A, B, C) for the psychological assessment methods seem to be incomplete. The JARs only focus on the psychometric criteria and do not even mention terms like test-fairness or acceptability. Also the aspect of validity is only understood by the JARs as construct validity. If tests are used for selection purposes, prognostic validity belongs clearly to the prime criteria. Some of the social and psychometric criteria are discussed in later parts of this section (chapters 10 and 11). For a thorough explanation refer to classical textbooks of test-construction such as Thorndike (1949), Cronbach (1970), or Nunnally (1978). Design and construction of psychometric tests is a genuine scientific task and is therefore beyond the scope of this section.

6 Selection of civil aviation pilots

Hans-Jürgen Hörmann
DLR - German Aerospace Center,
Aviation and Space Psychology, Germany

Following the introduction of advanced computer technology in the cockpit of modern aircraft job descriptions have often characterised the role of an airline pilot as being the manager of diverse technical systems and human resources in order to conduct a safe and efficient flight. Compared to the early days of flying nowadays the main piloting tasks consist to a lesser extent of pure manual control and coordination. Increasingly important are functions like monitoring and cross-checking of flight parameters and aircraft systems in relation to environmental conditions, integration of information from various channels, maintaining a broad view of the situation even under stress in order to timely recognise a need for decisions, to consult the involved crew members, and to coordinate the appropriate actions. Two critical safety-related interfaces can be distinguished in the working-place of airline pilots: a) the crew - aircraft interface and b) the crew - crew interface. Traditionally, pilot selection methods were focused on the primarily cognitive and motor tasks of the crew-aircraft interface. However, the efficiency of this interface depends to a high degree on the quality of the crew interaction. If the crew members do not cooperate as a proficient team, workload increases, productivity decreases and finally flight safety could be endangered. Taking this into account, modern selection test batteries do not only aim at the individual cognitive and motor skills of the applicants but also on their personality dispositions and competencies for positive social interaction.

A standard catalogue of operational aptitude tests for ab-initio pilot selection generally covers several of the following domains (see also the definitions in JAR-FCL 3, Section 2, Subpart A, B, and C):

- Mechanical comprehension and technical knowledge: Understanding and applying physical principles, understanding the functions of depicted technical systems.
- Number facility and numerical reasoning: Manipulating numbers quickly and accurately. Mental arithmetic, plausibility checks for given results, finding rules and applying them in sets of numbers and solving mathematical problems by means of logical reasoning.
- Short-term memory for auditory and visual information: Accuracy of storing,

retaining, and retrieving numeric, symbolic, or verbal information from short-term memory. Information can be presented through visual and/or auditory channels.

- Speed of perception: Speed of identifying and processing relevant information accurately and completely.
- Attention control: Ability to direct one's attention on a given task without being distracted by external or internal non-task related stimuli in order to maximise performance. If the task consists of several subtasks selective attention is required, that is the ability of switching one's attention focus quickly and goal-directed between subtasks.
- Spatial orientation: Ability to comprehend the spatial relations between multiple objects in two or three-dimensional space. Being aware of their position even if the viewpoint of observation is moving in relation to the objects.
- Choice reaction time: The time interval between the onset of a critical stimulus (pattern) and a correct response of the subject. Critical stimuli are often presented in random order as part of a larger set of different other stimuli.
- Psychomotor coordination: Ability to initiate and control movements of arms, hands, and feet smoothly in accordance to dynamic patterns of visual stimuli.
- Multiple-task capacity: Dealing simultaneously with at least two independent tasks. Ability to integrate different processes and activities into an effective working concept by setting appropriate priorities.

Depending on the applicant's population tests of English language, aviation knowledge, and others could be indicated for selection. Those domains listed above are primarily associated with the individual's capabilities to solve cognitive tasks fast and correctly. Most tests can either be administered as paper-pencil or as computer aided versions. Normally the applicants are working under time-pressure. Verbal abilities are rarely assessed during pilot selection except in form of language skills (e.g. Stead, 1991). An example of a typical paper-pencil selection test is shown in figure 1. Several other test examples are described in chapter 7.

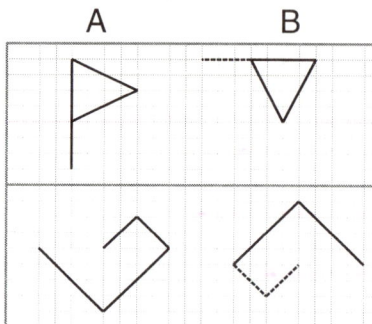

Figure 1   **Example item of a test of spatial orientation. Completion of rotated figures on the right side considering the correct spatial relations of the missing elements (source: DLR)**

Apparatus tests or PC-based miniature-simulations are generally required for the examination of psychomotor coordination and multiple-task capacity. Most of the classical electromechanical apparatus tests had been developed in the 1940ies for the US Air Force (Melton, 1947), like the Two-Hand Coordination Test (THCT), the Rudder Control Test (RCT), or the Complex Coordination Test (CCT). Some have nowadays been transferred to more (technically) reliable digital computer hardware, for example the CCT (eye-hand-feet coordination) and the THCT (see figure 2). In a recent review Griffin & Koonce (1996) concluded that the computerised versions of these psychomotor tests seem to be as predictive for pilot performance today as in the past. Besides their higher reliability computer-based psychomotor testing offers flexible possibilities of presenting dynamic scenarios or multiple tasks on one or more high-resolution monitors. Different tests can be administered with the same hardware equipment just by changing the software.

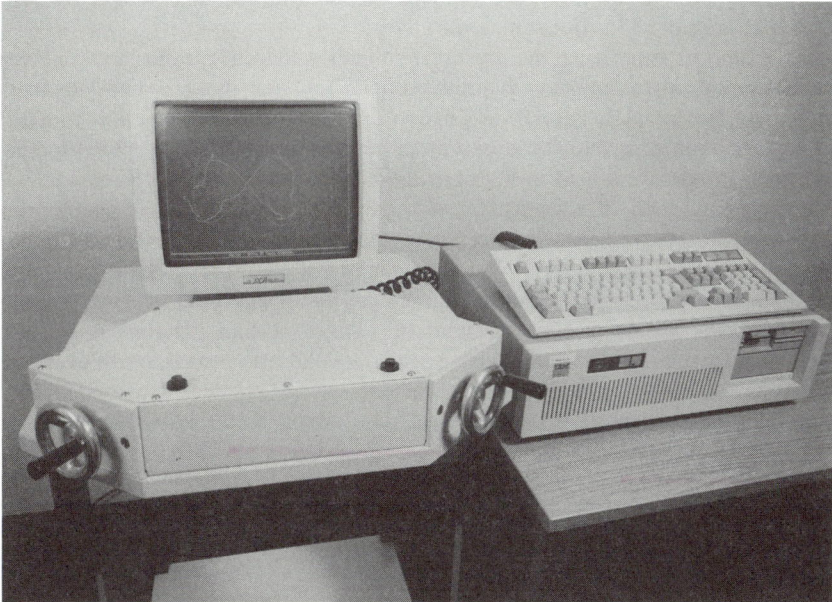

Figure 2   Computerised version of the Two-Hand-Coordination Test (source: DLR)

As shown in table 1 (chapter 5) and in table 2 (chapter 11) there is substantial empirical evidence that aptitude tests can significantly predict individual differences in flying performance during pilot training. By means of a thorough and consistent selection procedure Lufthansa German Airlines could reduce the attrition rate in ab-initio pilot training down to 3% (Hörmann & Maschke, 1996). While the utility of pilot selection based on aptitudes is commonly accepted among experts, the usage of personality instruments is discussed very controversially in the literature (e.g. Besco, 1995; Goeters, 1995b; Murphy, 1995). Besides the fact that there are conceptual misunderstandings even among psychologists about terminology, goals and methods of personality assessment, the often reported low validities of personality tests are in contrast to feedback information from the airlines about the behaviour of 'marginal pilots' and to findings from accident / incident investigations about cooperation deficits in the cockpit. A reason for the low validities could be that the job demands during initial pilot training and in line operations are discrepant to some degree. For the basic formation of adequate pilot skills operational aptitudes are more important than personality characteristics. Therefore flight instructor ratings in proficiency reports are primarily related to ability differences. The relative weight of personality increases if one shifts from training performance to performance in operational settings. During line operations with a multicrew environment, when the basic flying skills are already overlearned and so-called honeymoon effects are overcome, attitudes and personality traits become more important for the behaviour (Helmreich, Sawin & Carsrud, 1886; Houston, 1988).

From our experience the most difficult cases that the airlines are concerned about are not primarily pilots with ability deficits but those that repeatedly disregard company procedures, that are always in conflict with others, or show low initiative. While deficits in pure pilot skills can often be compensated by additional training, deficits in attitudes and personality traits are hard to correct within the company. In order to prevent such developments it makes sense to look for indications of critical behaviour tendencies as early in selection as possible. What methods are available to measure the pilot's personality? Which personality traits are regarded as relevant?

Generally *personality* can be defined as 'that which permits a prediction of what a person will do in a given situation' (Cattell, 1965). *Personality traits* are mechanisms within the individual that shape how (s)he reacts to classes of events and occasions. A trait summarises past behaviour and predicts future behaviour. Personality assessment tools include
- Standardised questionnaires (e.g. 16PF, NEO, OPQ, PCI, TSS)
- Projective techniques (e.g. Rohrschach, DMT)
- Graphology
- Clinical orientated methods (e.g. MMPI)

Besides these tools behaviour observation, interviews, or biographical analysis can be used to derive information about an applicant's personality traits. Clinical orientated methods or psychiatric interviews cannot generally be recommended to screen the average population of pilot applicants, since they have primarily been developed to filter out candidates with personality disorders. These methods do not directly identify candidates that have favourable predispositions for becoming a pilot in a multicrew environment. The utility of graphological and projective techniques depends to a very high degree on special expertise of the user that is very rare even among psychologists. Their validity in personnel selection is still not proven to be different from zero (Cook, 1988; Smith & Robertson, 1989; see also table 1 in chapter 5).

In personality psychology increasing consensus is emerging that the basic aspects of personality can be measured on five different dimensions: N - neuroticism, E - extraversion, O - openness to experience, C - conscientiousness, A - agreeableness. The NEO is a questionnaire developed by Costa & McGrae (1989) to operationalize this five-factor model. However, critiques of this model underline that the factors are too broad, so that specific information for description and prediction of human behaviour in job environments is lost.

Many organisations involved in civil-pilot selection are using a combination of questionnaires and interview in order to have comparable information about the applicants personality traits. For the above listed standardised questionnaires at least some publicised validity information related to civil-pilot selection and performance can be found: 16PF (Bartram & Baxter, 1996), NEO-PI (Dunlap & Pettit, 1995), OPQ (Stead, 1991), PCI (Chidester, Helmreich, Gregorich & Geis, 1991), TSS (Hörmann & Maschke, 1993, 1996). In general, validation studies indicate that the personality profile of successful pilots is marked by high self-confidence, emotional stability, and extraversion. Further information on these questionnaires or the underlying models can be found in the cited literature references.

As an example the TSS (Temperament Structure Scales; Maschke, 1987; Goeters, Maschke & Timmermann, 1993) is described here in greater detail. In the standard version it has ten different scales with about 200 yes-no items which are grouped under the following headlines:

Performance-related aspects:
• Achievement motivation: ambitious, hard-working, needs to succeed in competition
• Rigidity: methodical, correct, organised, principle-minded
• Mobility: ready to travel, to move, and to take risks
• Vitality: active in sports, looking for physical challenge, robust

Interpersonal-related aspects:
• Extraversion: sociable, lively, communicative, likes company of others
• Empathy: warm-hearted, helpful, feels affected by other's misfortune
• Dominance: decisive, ready for leadership functions and responsibilities
• Aggressiveness: aggressive, impatient, impulsive, complaining, distrustful

Stress resistance:
• Emotional stability: worried, insecure, low self-esteem, sensitive

Extra-scale:
• Social desirability: conformity, presenting oneself conform to social norms

One advantage of the TSS compared to other personality questionnaires is that it was developed within the same population in which it is now applied as a selection instrument. Some of the scales as well as the critical cut-off scores are directly based on experiences during flight training. In a comparison study by Hörmann & Maschke (1996) 274 airline pilots were classified on the basis of their training results into a group with standard career progress and a group with marginal progress. The TSS-profiles of both groups differed significantly in several aspects. First, the profile of the standard group showed more average scores for the different traits, whereas the marginal group had more extreme scores. Secondly, the marginal group appeared to be less emotionally stable, less vital, more aggressive, and more empathetic.

However, this is not to state that these traits are negative for pilots in general. Most of the traits have positive and negative aspects, depending on the situation. If necessary, a pilot can also be challenged for example to demonstrate a higher level of aggressivity. This adaptability to show situation adequate behaviour can best be achieved by a well balanced personality without predominant, one-sided behaviour tendencies. More results of this and other validity studies are also reported in chapter 11.

A common weakness of most questionnaires is that they are not sufficiently robust against faking when administered for personnel selection. The questions are often so transparent, that smart applicants can quite easily manage to give the examiner a positive impression. In part these validity-reducing effects can be compensated by comparing the questionnaire results with other information from structured interviews and behaviour observations. One of the most promising new approaches in applied psychodiagnostics has been the elaboration of systematic techniques for observing the actual behaviour of applicants in job-related social situations. The methods this refers to are called assessment centre methods in industrial settings. Usually, the term *assessment centre* (AC) is used to describe a process by which an individual or a group of individuals is observed and assessed by a team of well trained judges during different exercises like role-play, problem-solving games, or simulated job tasks. ACs should meet the following requirements (see also Ross, 1979):

- Multiple assessment techniques with at least one simulation
- Multiple trained judges to observe the applicants behaviour
- All behaviours assessed must be job-relevant
- All exercises must be designed as job-related
- Dimensions for assessment are determined by job-analysis
- Judges separate observation from evaluation of behaviour
- Overall judgements regarding an applicant are based on pooled information from different judges and different assessment techniques
- Overall judgements are not made until all AC tasks have been completed.

Different forms of exercises and tasks can be included in an AC:

Group exercises:

A group of applicants (usually between three and six) is involved in problem-solving games or negotiations.

- Assigned role exercises: The group is split into different parties or roles. In principal the task is to find collectively acceptable modalities to share limited available resources, though the needs of the different parties appear to be incongruent. Undesired behaviour is simply giving up one's position or bluntly overruling the others. The goal is to advocate the own position, to prove persuasiveness and negotiating skills, but also the ability to compromise when indicated by the situation.
- Unassigned role exercises: The task can be a group discussion to find conclusions or to solve a simulated problem under time pressure. Decisions have to be made based on incomplete information and changing conditions. The applicants have to prove tolerance of stress and uncertainty, analytic skills to structure a situation, and

adaptability to changing circumstances.

Individual exercises:

A single applicant is involved either in a simulation, a role-play, or a presentation.

- Simulation: Simulations are the central element of an AC. Like a work-sample the applicant has to solve a simulated critical job task. In pilot selection this could be to complete a flight-preparation or to solve a line-orientated scenario in a flight simulator. However, in a flight simulator more than one observer should be present to ensure greater objectivity of the assessments. Skills for planning, organising, decision making, or task delegation can be assessed among other dimensions.
- Presentation: The industry generally favours sales presentations which are of less relevance for pilots. It could for example make sense in form of an announcement to passengers that for example are upset because of a time delay or because of service problems. In this case it could be assessed whether the announcement is logically structured communicated credibly, and whether the applicant can understand and is willing to consider other peoples needs and points of view.
- Role-play: Role-plays are similar to simulations but played with an initiated human actor who, according to a detailed script, will lead the applicant into a social conflict situation. Conflict stability, assertiveness, and the flexibility to fluently integrate new information into one's own concepts can be observed.

Additional tools:

Standard selection methods like interview, ability tests, or questionnaires can be part of or supplemented to an AC.

During the exercises the behaviour of each individual is protocoled by at least two judges in order to reduce effects of observational bias. However, one judge can also observe more than one candidate at a time. Afterwards the observed behaviour is assessed by the respective judges on anchored rating scales.

In pilot selection this behaviour-based approach is still in it's infancy. Some airlines are using certain elements such as a group discussion or a problem-solving game in addition to standard selection methods. Unfortunately results of empirical evaluation studies are often not published. In 1994 Lufthansa German Airlines together with the DLR initiated an AC development programme for airline pilots. Since 1995 these techniques are integrated into the selection procedures of ab-initio and ready-entry pilots as follows: Day 1 - paper-pencil tests, day 2 - apparatus tests, day 3 - AC, and day 4 - interview. Based on the company's concepts on Crew Resource Management a taskforce of instructor pilots and aviation psychologists have developed several job-specific exercises and behaviour dimensions for the assessment of social skills (e.g. cooperation, conflict management) and performance-related skills (e.g. flexibility, decision making). First empirical findings of the reliability and validity were presented recently by Hörmann, Manzey, Maschke & Pecena (1997). The results of 30 ready-entry pilots who took part in the AC could be compared to training data of the type conversion course and the following route training. Though the sample size is quite small the consistency of the correlations between the AC-dimensions and the job-criteria is very encouraging. Especially the social skills dimensions are significantly correlated to instructor ratings of crew coordination behaviour and to the final check after the line-training. These validity coefficients vary between .30 and .60. A meta study by Smith & Robertson (1989) for selection in general shows a similar range of mean validity coefficients for AC techniques from .41 to .43 (see table 1 in chapter 5).

Nevertheless assessment centre techniques are time- and manpower consuming methods. Therefore it is indispensable to provide further empirical evidence for their utility in pilot selection. According to our preliminary results especially the dimensions for social competence seem to provide diagnostic information that show significant incremental validity for the prediction of training progress of ready-entry pilots. Provided these findings can be confirmed in other organisations as well, the AC together with standardised questionnaires and interview techniques can become a powerful instrument for the selection of the most suitable candidates for teamwork and cooperation tasks in airliner cockpits. The underlying principle of the AC-approach is prediction of future behaviour patterns through systematic observations of real behaviour in miniature simulated job-specific tasks. Applicants have a chance to prove themselves. This principle appears to be reasonable and if the other methodological standards as mentioned above are also fulfilled the acceptance of an AC by the applicants is generally higher compared to other personality or trait orientated methods. If more empirical research results on the predictive power of ACs in aviation were available, it could be possible to reduce time and costs of this methods by picking out the key elements with the highest validity.

7 Military pilot selection

Per Byrdorf
Institute of Aviation Psychology, Denmark

Introduction

Since 1918 psychologists in Europe have been occupied with pilot selection. Since that time both aircraft and operational environments have changed substantially, and the aircraft have turned into flying computers, which can provide the pilot with a tremendous amount of information. In spite of these changes, the purpose of the psychological examination is still the same: to select those pilots who will be able to successfully complete pilot training.

Jobrequirements, abilities and operator performances

Pilots have the task of controlling complex aircraft movements accurately and appropriately through certain stimuli and within a limited time frame. These tasks must be performed in combination with differentiated, integrated, and/or stepwise responses corresponding to visual, auditory, and proprioceptive stimuli received from inside and outside the aircraft. Furthermore, any mistake by these pilots could lead directly to a serious accident or at least a dangerous situation. Therefore, the pilot is considered to be under stress at all times. Not only is the pilot under mental stress but also physical stress as well, (i.e. changes in acceleration, atmospheric pressure, vibration, and temperature).

When creating a military pilot selection procedure it is necessary to have a scientific approach, and remember to go through all the steps in the process: Tasks for the pilot, his function, the training requirements, the training conditions, the job requirements, the job conditions, and individual qualifications. It is now possible to choose the selection method and the selection procedure. After the selection of pilot candidates there must be a follow up and a development of the procedure.

Principles behind selection

Pilot training and pilot function are so demanding, that it is necessary to make a special effort in the field of selection.

From knowledge of the specific training and working demands, a selection procedure can be worked out with a view to evaluating candidates prerequisites in exactly those fields that are essential in this context. The psychological model, or procedure, which is used in selecting military pilots can be described as a statistical/clinical method.

In order to make an evaluation of each individual personals prerequisites in areas which are of importance to the pilots function, several standardized tests and other information material are used. On the basis of the results and information available, a psychological dynamic overall evaluation is made, which as a conclusion contains a prognosis regarding the person's chances for completing the training applied for - and for his function in the service to follow.

Purposes for the psychological selection are: (1) to reduce failures, (2) to contribute to the development of a high degree of flight safety, regarding human factors, and (3) to support the efforts to develop a high individual satisfaction as well during training and in the working conditions - and in so doing, keeping constantly in mind the costs and the consequences.

Psychological selection method

A military psychological selection method and procedure must continuously be developed. The changes are the results of the continuous control of how the procedures work in practice, and a function of follow-up studies, which must continuously be carried out.

The military test battery must include:

Biographical data: (1) General life story. (2) Family. (3) Education. (4) Socio-economic status. (5) Occupational situation. (6) Critical behavioural incidents. (7) Diseases and accidents. (8) Delinquency.

Requirements: (1) Age between 18 and 27 years. (2) 10 years of ground school and 3 years of high school. (3) Citizenship in own country. (4) Unpunished by criminal laws. (5) Normal sight ability 20/20 and normal sense of colour vision. (6) Height between 163 and 190 cm. (7) Good physical condition.

Paper and pencil tests / Computer tests: Assessment of aptitudes and abilities.

Psychomotor tests: Assessment of psychomotor abilities.

Personality tests or psychological interview: Assessment of personal style and assessment of emotional pattern.

Psychological examinations: The military psychological selection procedure is normally based upon a statistical/clinical model, and as a consequence of that, the psychologist plays an important role as an 'instrument of selection'. Therefore, a psychologist working with pilot selection has to be carefully selected, introduced, trained, and steadily supervised and guided through feedback.

It takes about one year to educate and train a clinical psychologist to be able to work in the environment of aviation. The psychologists must go through the selection procedure themselves. This includes spending time at the Basic Flying Training School, at the Squadrons, at the Officers Academy etc. The psychologists must fly as passenger in all types of military aircraft, and experience some of the Air Battle Manoeuvre Program.

The job of a pilot is very complex, and the aviation psychologist must understand or interpret the situation, in order to act adequately. The job of the aviation psychologist is to select the right human material, to reduce failures, and to contribute to a high degree of flight safety.

After the psychological examination the psychologist makes a global, dynamic personality description and evaluation of the candidate. Variables taken into consideration include: motivation, emotional stability, panic resistance, action power and competence, awareness of possibilities and restrictions, dependability, social function, self discipline, leadership potential, intellectual resources, spatial orientation, stress coping, self confidence, reality testing, decisiveness, assertiveness, and cooperativeness.

The psychological interview can be very structured through fixed questions, but it can also be left to the psychologist's discretion, but the personality must be looked upon as a dynamic whole (gestalt).

A positive correlation between the psychologist's prognosis and the candidate's performance as operational pilot should be established.

Evaluation Conferences: After the selection process it is important to follow each students performance and progression throughout his/her pilot and officer training.

Normally the conferences could be placed (1) after the Basic Flying Training, (2) after the Advanced Flying Training, and (3) after one year as an operative Squadron Pilot.

The purpose of these conferences are: to give feedback to the selection centre, to advice the training system about strong and weak points of each student and to eliminate students with insufficient training marks.

Elimination: When students fail, they should be brought before an Elimination Board. If the student is eliminated from the training program, he/she should be referred back to the selection centre for an interview with an aviation psychologist. The purposes of this interview are: to get feedback from the students experiences with the training system, to give the student feedback about his strong and weak points, to help the student to cope with his failure, and to help him to begin a life outside the airforce in agreement with his personal resources.

Nato training

To reduce costs and to make pilot training more efficient NATO established the EURO NATO JOINT JET PILOT TRAINING (ENJJPT) program in September 1981 at Sheppard Air Force Base, Texas, USA.

Almost all NATO countries send their military pilot candidates through the ENJJPT program, and the countries have their own pilot instructors at the flying school.

Two years later, in 1983, the experience from the ENJJPT program made it necessary to develop a pilot selection procedure which could be used in all NATO countries. NATO therefore established an organisation with an Air Force Sub Group (AFSG), an Army Sub Group, and a Navy Sub Group. All sub groups have several working groups. AFSG has amongst other working groups an Air Crew Selection Working Group (ACSWG). The working group was renamed in 1993 to Air Crew Human Factors Working Group (AHFWG). The ACSWG was established in 1983. ACSWG is a multi-national group of appropriately qualified personnel formed to provide advice to the AFSG on the opportunities which might exist for joint action concerning aircrew selection techniques and methods. ACSWG delegates are aviation psychologists and operational pilots from the NATO countries. From 1987 to 1990 the ACSWG worked with identification, evaluation and implementation of ability tests which could successfully identify those pilot candidates having the greatest probability of being successful during their flying training.

In 1990, ACSWG Computerised Test Battery with ability tests and psychomotor tests were ready for trial. The test battery is now implemented in military selection procedures of several NATO countries.

During the research the ACSWG found 12 critical fast jet pilot tasks:

1. Perform systems / weapons checks
2. Manage on-board systems
3. Set up attack.
4. Perform tactical offensive flight manoeuvres
5. Avoid, evade or suppress threats
6. Monitor and control flight parameters
7. Perform weapons delivery
8. Perform formation tactics
9. Respond to aircraft emergency situations
10. Manage communications
11. Perform low level navigation
12. Perform tactical defensive flight manoeuvres.

During the research ACSWG also found 12 abilities of particular importance in fast-jet pilot performance:

SITUATIONAL AWARENESS:
The state of constant mental readiness in order to respond to situational changes.

TIME SHARING:
The ability to observe several sources of information, actions or tasks at the same time, to combine them, allot task priorities, and integrate them into actions that have to be performed.

SPATIAL ORIENTATION:
The ability to tell where you are in relation to the location of some object or to tell where the object is in relation to you.

VISUALISATION:
The ability to imagine the movement of objects in three dimensional space.

PSYCHOMOTOR CO-ORDINATION:
The ability to co-ordinate movements of two or more limbs, such as in moving equipment controls. Two or more limbs are in motion while the individual is sitting, standing or lying down.

MEMORISATION:
The ability to remember information, such as words, numbers, pictures, and procedures. Bits of information can be remembered by themselves or with other pieces of information.

REASONING:
The ability to combine separate bits of information and to apply general rules in order to derive logical answers or form conclusions.

PERCEPTUAL SPEED:
The ability to perceive quickly and accurately even small details in patterns and configurations.

SELECTIVE ATTENTION:
The ability to concentrate on a task one is doing.

RESPONSE ORIENTATION:
The ability to choose between two or more movements quickly and accurately when two or more different signals (lights, sounds, pictures) are given. The ability is concerned with the speed with which the right response can be started with the hand, foot, or other parts and the body.

AGGRESSIVENESS:
Having the incentive to accept challenge, to make daring decisions, to take initiative and to carry out actions in order to surmount difficulties.

ASSERTIVENESS:
Self assured (belief in one's own capabilities) and willing to defend one's own opinions.

EMOTIONAL STABILITY :
Emotional mature, stable, and having few neurotic symptoms.

CO-OPERATIVENESS:
Willingness to co-ordinate own activities with other or groups (example crew members).

LEADERSHIP:
Behaviour to structure other peoples tasks to sort priorities and motivate co-workers.

ACHIEVEMENT MOTIVATION :
A willingness and determination to work towards goals.
STRESS TOLERANCE:
To be able to cope with stressful circumstances (at short and/or long term) without significant degradation in performance.
DECISIVENESS: Ability to decide rapidly on an appropriate action and to carry out immediately.

Table 1   ACSWG computerised test battery

TEST NAME	Length mins	ABILITIES MEASURED
Test Battery Introduction	10	Biographical information
Vigilance	10	Situational awareness, time sharing, divided attention
Matrices	15	Reasoning (non-verbal)
Digit Recall	5	Memorization
Complex Coordination	10	Time sharing, psychomotor coordination (compensatory tracking)
Instrument Comprehension	20	Reasoning, visualization
Time Sharing 2	15	Time sharing, divided attention, control precision
Scheduling 2	6	Situational awareness, time sharing, divided attention
DTG	20	Selective attention, response orientation

Short description of the tests in the test battery

Vigilance

A 9 block grid appears on the screen. The numbers along the left side of the grid are the 'A' coordinates and correspond to the rows. The numbers along the top of the grid are 'B' coordinates and correspond to the columns. Each block in the grid can be identified by its row and column coordinates.

During the test, asterisks '*' appear within the blocks of the grid. The subject's 'routine task' is to cancel these asterisks as quickly as possible. An asterisk is cancelled (i.e. erased) by entering its row and column coordinates on the keypad.

In addition to the asterisks, arrows '^' may appear in the blocks of the grid. These arrows represent an 'emergency task'. The subject is instructed to respond as quickly as possible when an arrow (i.e. emergency) appears. This function is done by pressing the ENABLE key, then entering the row and column coordinates of the arrow (i.e. emergency). The subject is instructed to resume performing the routine task (i.e. cancelling asterisks), when no arrows are present. The measures of interest for this test are the number of routine and emergency tasks successfully completed and the average response time required to complete emergency tasks. The psychological factors assessed by this test include situational awareness, time sharing, and divided attention. The test requires about 10 minutes to complete.

Matrices

In the Matrices test, a picture of an incomplete geometric pattern appears on the screen. (The lower right-hand corner of the pattern is missing). The subject's task is to choose from several alternatives, which would correctly complete the pattern. The subject indicates his/her choice by entering the number of the chosen alternative on the response keypad.

The first 6 items are for practice only. The remaining 30 items are test items and are scored. The subject has the option to skip items, to review the items previously answered or skipped, and to change answers. This test has a 10 minutes time limit that begins when the subject starts the first test item. Response speed and accuracy are recorded on each item. The Matrices test assesses non-verbal reasoning and requires about 15 minutes to complete.

Digit recall

A string of number appears on the screen. After a few seconds, the number string is removed from the screen and is replaced by a string of empty boxes. (The number of boxes is equal to the number of numbers in the string). The subject's task is to enter the number string into the boxes.

The length of the strings vary from 7 to 12 numbers. Response time and response accuracy are recorded on each of the 30 test items. Response accuracy is calculated in 3 ways for each item: (1) correct or incorrect, (2) number of numbers placed in their correct position in the string, and (3) a weighted scoring algorithm that gives partial credit for numbers placed out of sequence. The test measures short-term memory and requires about 10 minutes to complete.

Complex coordination

In this dual-axis (right hand) control stick is used to control the horizontal and vertical movement of a cursor. Rudder pedals are used to control the left-right movement of a vertical 'rudder bar' of light at the base of the screen. The subject's task is to maintain the cursor (against a constant horizontal and vertical right bias) centred on a large cross fixed at the centre of the screen while simultaneously centring the rudder bar at the base of the screen (also against a constant rate bias). After receiving instructions, the subject completes a 3 minutes practice session and a 5 minutes test. The Complex Co-ordination test assesses psychomotor co-ordination and time sharing ability (i.e. compensatory tracking ability involving multiple axes) and requires about 10 minutes to complete.

Instrument comprehension

An illustration of an airplane in 5 different positions is shown on the screen. An artificial horizon indicator and a compass are displayed above these aircraft. The subject's task is to determine which of the aircraft agrees with the readings on the artificial horizontal indicator and compass. The subject indicates his/her choice on each item by pressing the numbered key that corresponds to the chosen alternative.

The test items begin after the subject has completed the instructions and practice items. As with the Matrices test, the subject may go backwards and forwards through the test, and may skip items, review items previously answered or skipped, or change answers.

The test has 60 items and a 15 minutes time limit that begins when the subject starts the first item.

Response speed and response accuracy are recorded on each item. The Instrument Comprehension test measures reasoning and visualisation. Total test administration time, including instructions, practice, and test items is about 20 minutes.

Time sharing 2

Two distinctly different kinds of tasks are involved in this test. The first is a measure of hand-eye co-ordination and the second is a measure of attention. The first three 1 minutes trials involve tracking only to provide a pure estimate of the subject's psychomotor co-ordination. During these trials, a 'stationary image' of an aircraft and a 'gunsight' that move to the left or right are displayed on the screen. The subject must manoeuvre the right-hand control stick to keep the gunsight centred on the airplane.

The next two 1 minute trials involve detecting and responding to missing numbers. The numbers appear one at a time in sequence on the lower part of the screen. The number sequence is 0,1,2,3,4,5,6,7,8,9,0,1,2, etc. Occasionally a number will be missing from the sequence (e.g. 0,1,2,3,4,6,7,... (5 is missing)). The subject's task is to type the missing number on the response keypad when it does not appear in the sequence. Subjects are scored on both response speed and accuracy.

The final five 1 minute trials involve both tracking and missing digits. While the subject is manoeuvring the right-hand control stick to keep the gunsight on the airplane, he/she also must monitor the number counter in order to be able to detect the missing numbers.

The test assesses the psychological factors of time-sharing, divided attention, and control precision. Test administration time is about 15 minutes.

Scheduling 2

In this test the subject is presented with 5 horizontal scales that can range in value between 0 and 10 points. Each scale increases at a unique, constant rate. Each scale appears on a separate screen and may be viewed by entering the scale number on the response keypad. (1,2,3,4, or 5). The subject 'scores' points equal to the current value of the displayed scale by pressing the ENABLE key. When the ENABLE key is pressed, the current value of the displayed scale is added to the subject's total score and the scale is reset to 0 (where it will start incrementing again). When the value of a scale reaches its upper limit, and the subject has not responded by pressing the ENABLE key, the value of the scale will return to 0 without the subject receiving any points for that scale.

The Scheduling 2 test measures the psychological constructs of situational awareness, time- sharing, and divided attention. This test requires about 6 minutes to complete.

Determinations Geraet (DTG)

The subject's task is to respond as quickly and accurately as possible to auditory (i.e. high and low tones) and visual signals (i.e. coloured lights) by pressing foot pedals and/or buttons. Subjects are presented with detailed instructions as to how to respond to different visual and auditory signals.

The scoring procedure for this test produces several response accuracy scores including the number of correct responses, and number of incorrect responses. The DTG is designed to measure selective attention and response orientation. The instructions, practice and test items require about 20 minutes to complete.

Data collection

It is important to collect data on a test battery. One method is to make an assessment form which can be used to collect data through the pilot training, and compare the data with the abilities measured in the selection procedure.

In the NATO training program all the abilities and personality traits which are covered in the test battery are included in the assessment form. The range of each scale is defined by two endpoints, which are expressed in terms of observable behaviour. The two endpoints reflect the positive and the negative behaviour.

The ACSWG Assessment Form is used at the ENJJPT program and at the national Flying Training Programs in order to perform follow-up and validation studies.

Conclusion

Since the ENJJPT program was started, NATO has emphasized the importance of developing a NATO Test Battery for pilot candidates. The purposes of a combined effort in the field of selection of military pilots are to reduce training costs, and to be sure to have the same standard of pilot training in all NATO countries.

8 The selection of air traffic controllers

Hinnerk Eißfeldt
DLR - German Aerospace Center,
Aviation and Space Psychology, Germany

Introduction

Compared to other professions in civil aviation air traffic control is relatively young. Its start can generally be located by the end of WW II, when experienced military pilots and navigators were trained for the control of civil air traffic. With the growth of civil air traffic and especially the appearance of modern jet aircraft in the 60s, in a number of countries actions were taken to select ab-initio air traffic controllers. The selection of air traffic controllers can be said to have a history of about 40 years.

Since the early days air traffic control has undergone several changes. The technical development in ATC is still in progress, this is typical for any job in a highly technical environment like aviation. New technical features have a high probability to be introduced. Primary and secondary radar, satellite navigation are some examples. Changes influence technical equipment as well as work routines, and an end of the technical evolution can not be foreseen. On the contrary there is a likelihood of an acceleration of the technical development. Above all, the steady increase of air traffic over the past years has put more and more demand on the daily work and it seems that this trend will continue.

The supply of new qualified controllers to the air traffic system is a challenging task for all air traffic control organisations. The number of internationally available trained controllers is rather limited and the validation for a new license in a different environment is time consuming and can in some cases become difficult. Therefore the intake of ab-initio controllers is the common approach to fill up vacancies. Among other aspects like manpower planning, recruitment, and training itself, the successful selection of applicants for ab-initio training is a major issue for all administrations.

What is special about selecting controllers?

At times the selection of air traffic controllers has been viewed as a derivate of pilot selection. This may reflect the historical roots of aviation psychology: it started with the selection of military pilots. For this task aviation psychologists have been in charge from the very start. Aviation psychologists got involved in air traffic controller selection at a comparatively late stage. When starting the selection of air traffic controllers most countries used civil servants test batteries depending on the institutional background of the ATC system. This sometimes lead to unsatisfactory results. Aviation psychologists have then been employed to improve selection because the special aspects of the profession limited the usefulness of civil servant tests. Trites (1961) provides an early example of an attempt to identify psychological tests as valid predictors for air traffic controller's training success. A lot of effort has been made over the years to rearrange and improve test batteries and to develop new job related tests.

The core argument why to deal with air traffic controller selection as a specific area of interest is the type of job that has to be performed. Air traffic control is a rather unique task. As many task analyses have stated, the dynamic process of collecting, processing and distributing information is the central aspect in air traffic control. For instance Seamster et al. (1993) have published a cognitive task analysis showing the two primary cognitive tasks in en route air traffic control to be 'maintaining situational awareness' (having the picture) and 'develop and revise sector control plan' (planning ahead). Typical for air traffic control is a high time criticality and the complexity of the task.

Another argument why to pay special attention to the selection of air traffic controllers is connected with costs. The training of an air traffic controller to full performance level (FPL) needs a high investment of time and money. After 3-4 years of training an ab-initio controller can receive a validated license, with costs for the professional education summing up to about 200.000,- ECU or beyond. Compared with the costs for training in other professions this is a remarkable amount of money that may even exceed the costs for ab-initio airline pilot training.

Also related to costs is the outcome of training: success rates in ATC training turn out to be limited. At present a pass rate of 80% for ab-initio controllers until license validation seems to be the limit of what can be achieved. However some air traffic control organisations have to face pass rates below 50%. In comparison the success in ab-initio pilot training is significantly higher, pass rates of about 95% and higher reflect the current state of the art.

Scientific issues

The selection of air traffic controllers has to deal with all aspects of psychological selection in general such as identification of required abilities, the development and evaluation of psychological methods, validation of the test system, the identification of relevant criteria to validate against etc (see Wing 1991). However, two questions shall be mentioned here being especially important for the selection of air traffic controllers. The first question is: can one really speak of 'air traffic control' as being one profession or is 'air traffic control' a term representing a set of professions with substantial differences in the abilities required (see Hopkin 1995, Bremer 1996, Eißfeldt 1997). Results of job analyses as well as results of studies on moderating effects of the type of training on the predictability of training success can answer that question. Presently the impression is that -may be due to the changes in the job environment during the last years- the differences between tower, approach and center positions do increase. If this can be proven to be substantial a reinterpretation of validity results and consequently adjustments of selection test batteries will become necessary.

The second question addresses training. Do we understand enough of how the process of skill acquisition in air traffic control works? It might be that the high failure rate of air traffic control trainees reflects a lack of understanding in this domain. This could affect training itself but it also could lead to the identification of deficiencies in the selection system.

An overview over some findings of cognitive psychology might be helpful to understand the process of skill acquisition in air traffic control. Starting with the work of Shiffrin & Schneider (1977) on automatic and controlled information processing, the theory was developed further by Anderson (1982) focusing on the term of knowledge. Anderson described the process of skill acquisition as being divided into the phases of declarative knowledge (knowledge of facts), knowledge compilation (learning to use knowledge) and procedural knowledge (know how to use knowledge).

Ackerman (1987, 1988) suggested certain aptitudes to be linked to the different phases of skill acquisition, namely: general aptitude or 'g' (in the domains of verbal, figural and numerical aptitudes) tied to the early phase of declarative knowledge in which processing of information is controlled and therefore slow, error prone and requiring almost all attention of a subject. In the second phase, perceptual speed has the highest influence on the effectiveness of the process of knowledge compilation and therefore on the process of automatization of more and more components of the task. According to Ackerman the third and final phase requires psychomotor abilities to allow a high degree of automatization of the task and thereby less attentional effort spent performing it. Underlying the whole process of skill acquisition are motivational processes relevant for the amount of attention paid to the task (effort) and for the individual's goalsetting process. The theory was validated in the ATC environment using a simulated ATC task for laboratory studies and training data of ATC trainees for a field investigation (Ackerman 1992).

According to Ackerman & Schneider (1985) 7 determinants of skilled performance in complex tasks can be described: limits in the physical system factors, the amount of controlled processing resources, motivation, automatic component availability, declarative knowledge availability, learning rate and strategy use. The same criteria (with personality as additional factor) will be determinants for the process of skill acquisition in air traffic control. It seems clear that air traffic control is a task which always requires a certain amount of controlled processing of information. Therefore the availability of controlled processing resources is a factor that limits performance in air traffic control. The amount of controlled processing resources invested in the task is restricted through the subject's relative capacity, moderated by motivational variables. It can be assumed, that the comparably high failure risk in ATC training results from the influence of one of the above factors or from a combination of them.

Two examples of how to improve a selection system

The following examples are taken from the work of the Deutsche Forschungsanstalt für Luft- und Raumfahrt DLR. The first example shows results of a job analysis using the Fleishman Job Analysis Survey (F-JAS) (Fleishman 1992) with air traffic controllers of the Deutsche Flugsicherung DFS. The second example shows predictive validity results of a new apparatus test. This test is in use for the selection of ab-initio controllers for DFS and for EUROCONTROL. The two examples were chosen because the job analysis discovered certain relevant abilities for which the apparatus test provides the measurement. However it must be stated, that - contradicting advise from the literature- the development of the test started years before the material of the job analysis was available.

Data for this analysis were taken from 54 controllers of DFS in 1995 in various places representing units of different sizes and different workload. Participation was voluntarily. The instrument F-JAS proved to be easy to administer. The main reason to conduct this task analysis was the preparation of a potentiality analysis at DFS (see Deuchert 1996 for details).

As figure 1 shows, time sharing and selective attention received the highest ratings, followed by visualization (only for center), speed of closure, problem sensitivity (mainly for approach), memorization and spatial orientation. Surprisingly low was the rating for mathematical reasoning, an ability which is represented in a number of test batteries worldwide. Even number facility was rated lower than expected.

One of the big advantages of the F-JAS is that it lists tests to measure the identified abilities. However only tests already existing and freely available are listed. In case of 'time sharing' the handbook states 'no standard tests of time sharing were identified' (Fleishman & Reilly 1992, p.94). So the most important cognitive ability for the selection of controllers seems not to be covered by any available test.

In 1989 a project started at DLR to develop a computerized apparatus test to measure the multiple task capacity of ATC applicants. This test should allow a better prognosis especially for success in the practical training than the test used before. It was decided to create a simulator-like work sample test according to the pre- and posttest design of a learning potential test. This requires a feedback provided by a well-trained test instructor. The test is called the Dynamic Air Traffic Control Test - DAC - . Several aircraft have to be guided through a defined airspace meeting the criteria of safety and economy. In addition acoustical information has to be processed. The DAC-Test is described in detail elsewhere (Eißfeldt 1995a, 1995b). It was first used with applicants in 1991 for research purpose before it became part of the test battery in 1992.

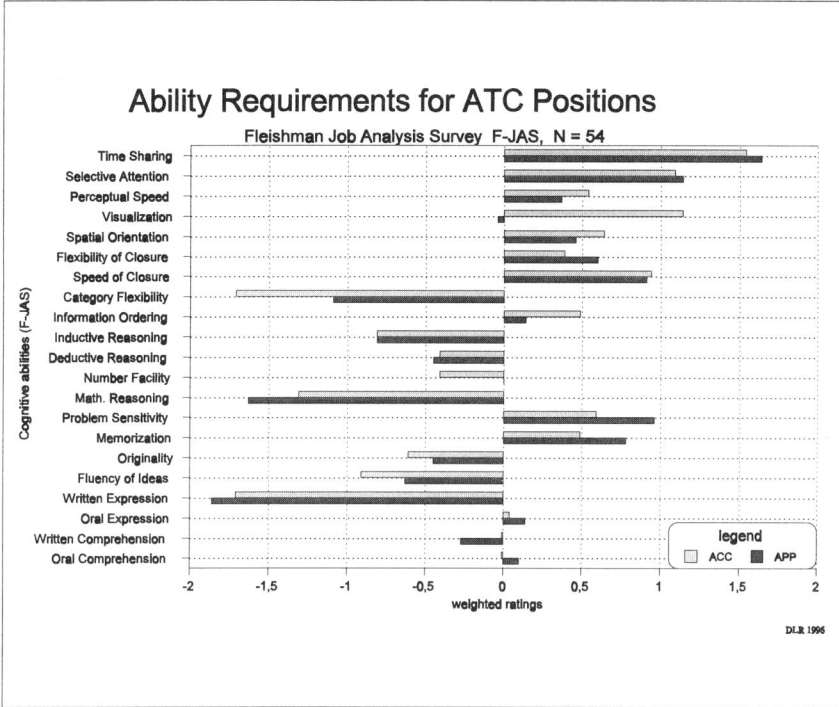

Figure 1 **Weighted cognitive abilities according to F-JAS. A rating of -2
would indicate that this ability was rated on the lowest level
compared to all other cognitive abilities. ACC = center controller
position, APP = approach controller position**

Table 1 presents results on the predictive validity of test scores obtained by 33
applicants of 1991 having meanwhile finished training. The criterion used is the
duration of the on-the-job training, which lasts between 12 and 24 months and is
done at the units. The duration was rated by an experienced training specialist as
being above, at or below average compared to the time required usually by trainees
to reach a license for that position. The test scores reflect the different aspects of test
performance like duration of separation conflicts 'CON', number of acoustical
questions answered correct 'QR', mean altitude of flights 'MA', length of flight track
representing the duration of flights 'MTM', precision on airway at handoff 'EXO' and
number of aircraft in incorrect state when leaving the airspace 'ERR'. These measures
are scored by the machine. In addition some of the ratings provided by the test
instructor are also listed in table 1.

Table 1   **Correlations between DAC results and duration of on-the-job training of ab-initio-controllers. Significant correlations are printed bold (p < .05, 1-tailed). Variable names are explained in the text.**

Correlations between DAC-Results and Duration of On-the-job Training		
N = 33	Duration	
Objective test data:		
1. Run CONflictions	.099	
Questions Right	-.247	
Mean Altitude	**-.314**	
Made Track Miles	-.021	
Offset of EXit	**-.312**	
ERRors	.221	
2. Run CONflictions	.199	
Questions Right	**-.391**	
Mean Altitude	-.006	
Made Track Miles	-.251	
Offset of EXit	-.269	
ERRors	**.400**	
Ratings by test instructor:		
Stress Resistance	**-.465**	(p < .01)
Learning Progress	**-.330**	
Overall Impression	**-.495**	(p < .01)

ˉInterpreting the results it has to be kept in mind that in 1991 applicants took the DAC test on a voluntarily basis, test results were not used for the selection decision. The criterion 'Duration of OJT training' shows different pattern of significant correlations for pretest and posttest. For the pretest 'mean altitudes' and 'precision on airway at exit', for the posttest 'number of acoustical questions answered correct 'QR' and 'number of aircraft in incorrect state when leaving the airspace 'ERR' correlate significantly. Besides for 'precision on airway at exit' the signs of all other correlations point into the expected direction. Taking into account the same correlation ('EXO') for the posttest there is a change of sign, although the correlation does not reach significance. This change of sign might indicate a change of strategy and thereby could reflect a learning process.

The ratings on 'stress resistance', 'learning progress' and 'overall impression' are done after the test is finished and therefore represent the whole test performance of an applicant. The high correlations between the ratings and the duration of on-the-job training indicate that the whole test situation can serve as a basis for valid observations by test administrators.

Issues for the work of the aviation psychologist

For the aviation psychologist a proper understanding of the work of an air traffic controller is essential for a professional selection work. A job analysis of the ATC work and information on ability requirements should be available as a basis for improvement of the test battery. This analysis ideally should be based on representative data collected at the institution the selection is done for and should cover the facets of different controller jobs.

The majority of European ATC organisations make use of external consultants for selection of ab-initio controllers. This can be due to the small size of an organisation as well as to other economical reasons that do not allow to fully employ an aviation psychologist. Recently national organisations can find recommendations for their planning of selection by guidelines for selection procedures and tests (EUROCONTROL 1996).

For the selection of ab-initio air traffic controllers the aviation psychologist often acts from outside the organisation. To be employed externally offers the advantage of being uninfluenced in the decision on individual cases, but it can lead to problems as well. Problems might be to gain insight to the field. As has been expressed earlier, the aviation psychologist has to gather knowledge of the ATC system, the work of controllers and the training structure as well. The more he/she knows about these aspects, the better the foundation of his/her decisions will be. Also he/she and his/her work will find more acceptance within the organisation.

Another problem might be to organise the follow-up process for the validation of tests. Often the pass/fail of a trainee is the only training criterion provided by operational units. This criterion is definitely the most important to be predicted and should therefore be part of any predictive validation. However for the purpose of validation more detailed training criteria are required to fully understand the true value of any test measure in the prediction of training outcome. Only a close cooperation with relevant partners inside the organisation can help to overcome such feedback problems.

How to improve?

For the aviation psychologist to improve selection results remains a challenging goal.

Failure rates of 20% or more indicate some space to improve the system and need to be tackled. In the view of the trainee a more valid prognosis can help to find an appropriate job not spending time and energy without final success. For the institution to reduce the number of failures by just one single trainee results in remarkable savings. Therefore the funding of work on improvement is a good investment for the organisation.

Although this chapter concentrates on selection it is important to bear in mind, that the supply of new qualified controllers is influenced by many aspects. Manpower planning, recruitment, selection and training structures as well as the quality of theoretical and practical training all contribute interdependently to the success of training. Not a single aspect as such can be tackled successfully when the others remain excluded. A good example for such a multi facet approach to improvement is the MRU Project by the Swedish CAA, which combines job analysis, development of psychological methods and training principles (see Haglund et al. 1996 for a description). From the perspective of the aviation psychologist this means, that a close cooperation of all the parts mentioned has to be established integrating expertise from the various fields.

If cooperation between the different departments mentioned above is missing, it is hard to improve the system. It is then likely that some useful energy will be absorbed in finding reasons why the other department is responsible for high failure rates. In such a case for the aviation psychologist it is a good position to take the lead in establishing an integrated approach in the institution. This can provoke some fundamental questions not always easy to answer. It also may create the need to make an effort to integrate different views of the matter. Finally such a cooperation will end in quality improvement and a high professional standard.[1]

---

[1] In order to bring forward these issues a working group focusing on ATC selection and training has been established within EAAP. For further information please contact the author.

9 Job analysis and the selection interview

Pieter H. Hermans *
Hemmo W. Mulder *
* SHL-PsychoTechniek, The Netherlands

Abstract

This chapter is about job-analysis, or work-profiling, and the selection interview. We will cover work-profiling and interviewing from a practical viewpoint. Under workprofiling, we will focus on ways to interview job-holders. To discuss the selection interview, we will actually prepare ourselves for an interview with an applicant. Hiring competent aircrew involves both activities; work-profiling provides us with a shortlist of psychological requirements, or criteria. Interviewing applicants may serve many different purposes. Doing it well can be learned, but many errors are still being made. Although scientists have proven that interviewing will often lead to false conclusions, applicants for jobs in aviation will be interviewed. Interviewers should know about the state of the art, and learn to interview using validated techniques.

Work profiling

Work-profiling is necessary whenever a selection-system has to be designed from scratch. When selection is the aim, it should preferably be taken care of by aviation psychologists. In this chapter, we will learn about two relatively fast, cut-and-dried methods, Critical Incidents (CI) and Repertory Grid (RG), applicable when computer-based systems or consultants are unavailable. CI and RG can be seen as interview methods. When you use them, as an aviation psychologist, you would interview job-holders about their job. Using two worksheets, contained in this chapter, you can familiarize yourself with the methods. The sheets provide instructions on a basic how-to-do-it level. Multiplying blank copies of the worksheets will enable you to practice extensively and to apply CI and RG in the field. Today, computer-based expert systems for work-profiling are available (SHL's work-profiling system); when work profiling has to be done at the organisational level, the use of such systematic approaches should be considered. However, the

Critical Incidents and Repertory Grid provide a first, and usually good shortlist of criteria for psychological selection.

Interviewing

The validity, and even the necessity of interviewing applicants has been righteously challenged by researchers; fully formalized selection procedures however, where applicants enter an organisation without having met anybody within, will never be reality. Interviews will remain to be part of the deal, anywhere in aviation. Interviewing, when done following a number of relatively simple guidelines, can be a valid technique, revealing assets and flaws of future personnel. Aviation psychologists should learn to be professional interviewers. They could and should also act as trainers, teaching company-staff (chief pilots) how to conduct selection interviews. The interview reaches its highest validity when its content is structured, straight, and situational. In this chapter, we will learn what structured, straight and situational mean, and how to prepare for an interview. Follow-up questioning is the second and final step toward getting what you want from an applicant: relevant information. Good follow-up questioning should be both pinpointing and enabling; good questioning actually helps the applicant to come across with relevant information. In this chapter, we will learn about content (the type of questions to ask), and about follow-up questioning. Especially for beginners, the main hurdles here are: What should we ask, and what to do with first answers, incomplete and/or vague answers? Good interviewing fits the triple S acronym, they are Structured, Straight, and Situational. After a first look at the bare skeleton of interviewing, we will step through three worksheets. We will work out a sequence of opening questions using a CCC-order (Curriculum, Criterion, Case). And we will practice with follow-up questioning, again using acronyms that bring each step into mind easily.

On using the worksheets

In this chapter, you will find 5 individual worksheets; each sheet has been designed to guide workprofilers and interviewers through relevant parts of the interview. Each sheet begins with an opening question, and then proceeds through follow up questions. At the bottom, there is room for making notes. These notes will later help the interviewer to summarize, categorize and evaluate what jobholders and candidates have said.

Work profiling

Producing a shortlist of criteria

Before running any kind of selection procedure, we should have a relevant shortlist of selection-criteria. Work-profiling, or job-analysis, can be a tedious and time-consuming job, involving systematic, consultancy supported, and computerized full analyses of tasks, stressors, and workload. The question might be: should we do it ourselves, as aviation psychologists, and if so, can we dip into the work that has been done already? In this chapter, we will point out that work-profiling will remain an item on our to-do-list for a while. Selection seems to shift its focus toward crew resource management, and toward its learnability. It is almost a cliché to point to cockpit-automation in this context; aviation psychologists have long been aware of the new work-environment created by information technology. But the broader employability issue provides a really new challenge; recruiters must increasingly look for applicants that have the potential and the willingness to learn new skills, among which using computers is only one.

Small scale methods

So we cannot skip work-profiling, nor make extensive use of existing material. There really have not been many sound job-analyses for aircrew. The good news is that there are practical small scale methods, that will do a good job at approximating the outline of a shortlist of relevant psychological selection criteria for selection. The more formal methods using exhaustive questionnaires and consultancy supported, software-aided workprofiling systems, should be considered when job-analyses are undertaken at the organisational level, for job-families, and for legal-contractual purposes. A good overview of all existing methods and instruments is provided by Greuter & Algera (1989)

Critical Incidents and Repertory Grid

In this chapter, we will discuss two so called small-scale interview methods where the work-profiler interviews job-holders or managers: Critical Incidents and Repertory Grid.

Critical Incidents

The idea behind the CIT technique is simple; if you want to know about the psychological requirements for a job, ask job holders for anecdotes of specific wrongdoings or heroic acts. Ask job-holders, for instance, for anecdotes of accidents and near accidents. Accidents may illustrate wrongdoings by people who do not meet certain requirements ('this second officer did not speak up'...). Near accidents may reveal the sort of behaviour one would look for in good professionals ('I sent the purser away, and afterwards apologised' ...). Worksheet 1 can be used to step you through a short Critical Incidents session with a job holder, or with a manager; getting your partner to come up with anecdotes may be difficult at first. The essential part, where most of the mistakes are made, is the follow-up-questioning. Using an old acronym for follow-up questioning, listed in the worksheet, you will learn to do a proper sequence. When properly done, it will enable you to distil two kinds of very useful information out of anecdotes; attributes and behaviour. Attributes are personality-traits to look for when selecting applicants; like decisiveness for instance, or assertiveness. Behavioural descriptions are more specific action-statements

Repertory Grid

The Repertory Grid technique is somewhat more complex. We will discuss and practice a somewhat simplified version of the technique. You, as an interviewer, ask job-holders to think of a poor performer he or she knows. You would then ask to think of a good performer too, and maybe to write down the initials for reference. This usually takes only a few seconds. You would then ask for significant differences, either in terms of attributes, or in terms of behaviour. Worksheet 2 can be used to step through a repertory grid session. Many people find the method somewhat difficult to understand in the beginning, but very easy to apply.

Convergence

CIT and Repertory Grid usually converge after about four sequences of each; what one has then is a list of about 8 relevant psychological criteria. No new requirements seem to pop up. In Sabaudia, at the first EAAP Tutorial, the authors did a massed group exercise, using the worksheets, and we arrived at a shortlist for pilots and air traffic controllers in about 2 hours (s. table 1 and 2).

Table 1   **Job requirement profile 'Pilot': Results of 1996 EAAP Conference practice session (using Critical Incidents and Repertory Grid)**

Behaviours *Listed*	Attributes *Tentative suggestions*
Carefully plan and prepare flight	Conscientious, detail conscious, forward planning
Welcome advice	Democratic, affiliative, caring, open to experience, agreeable
Accept advice	
Cooperate	
Inform passengers and others	
Divide attention	Intellectually capable, time sharing
Stay calm	Emotionally controlled, emotionally stable
Speak up	Assertive, decisive, controlling, extraverted
Control panic	
Decide	
Intervene	

Table 2   **Job requirement profile 'Air Traffic Controller': Results of 1996 EAAP Conference practice session (using Critical Incidents and Repertory Grid)**

Behaviours *Listed and suggested*	Attributes *Listed and suggested*
Visualise	Spatial Orientation
Manage information	Intellectually capable, forward planning, data rational, detail conscious, conscientious
Distribute attention	Time sharing
Control Workload	Forward planning, controlling, conscientious
Control yourself	Relaxed, emotionally controlled, emotionally stable
Co-operate	Democratic, affiliative, caring, open to experience, agreeable, extraverted
Adapt to circumstances	Adaptivity
Seek contact	Sociability

Interviewing applicants

Are interviews necessary?

Before deciding on hiring someone, one should at least meet the applicant face to face; that seems obvious. Scientifically however, the necessity and usefulness of interviewing applicants has been righteously challenged; interviewers make numerous errors and, on the average, they are bad predictors of future performance. Fully formalized selection however, where applicants enter an organisation without having met anybody within, is still hard to imagine, and hard to sell to the public. Interviews will remain to be part of the deal, anywhere in aviation. Interviewing, when done following a number of relatively simple guidelines, can be useful and valid as a selection-instrument. Aviation psychologists must learn to be professional interviewers. They will also be asked to train company-recruiters, such as chief pilots, to interview applicants effectively.

Effective interviews

Applied research points at three key-attributes of effective interviews. Good interviews are structured, straight and situational.

Structured, straight, and situational

Structure is necessary to avoid redundancy and to assure that more than just one or two items are discussed. Straightness, or criterion orientation in jargon, is necessary to ensure that the topics of discussion are relevant to the job at hand. Situational interviewing involves having applicants consider real dilemma's one could come across in the future job. It enables the interviewer to get a glimpse of the applicant's immediately available verbal and behavioural repertoire. When properly done, it steers the interview clear of vague intentions and hypothetical considerations.

Follow up questioning

Good follow-up questioning is the second cornerstone of modern interviewing. Even when the right questions are asked, applicants may be vague, too general, not factual enough with their answers.

Beyond vagueness

Very often, answers are intentional by nature. Modern interviewers should be able to provoke better answers, without having to adopt an interrogative style; they should be able to pinpoint the applicant, whilst at the same time maintaining a businesslike, open and even encouraging atmosphere. In this paragraph, we will discuss several AFQs, acronyms for follow-up-questioning, that can help you achieve this combination of pinpointing and encouraging. Good interviewers are really curious listeners, actually interested in hiring good personnel. Follow-up questioning sequences and episodes of pinpointing should be interspersed with occasional resets, remarks or ending statements that enable the applicant to catch his breath and start from scratch. Typical examples are the appropriate use of humour, a short summary of an answer, a request for alternative answers (what else could be done), or an open invitation to brainstorm on both advantages and disadvantages of a choice of action; resets are really important intermezzo's, in between pinpointing sequences of follow-up questioning, that carry applicants through the interview, and keep them available for you.

Stepping through the worksheets

We will step through three worksheets, that will show us the state of the art of modern interviewing. Each worksheet covers a particular opening question.

A step by step guide through a modern interview

As a way to practice it is a good idea to follow the bare skeleton for a modern interview. Here again, it may help to consider the acronym SSS, for Structured, Straight and Situational, as below. Step through the instructions, using the worksheets as indicated.

Structured
1 Make a shortlist of the criteria to be covered (max 4)
2 Set a CCC-order (Curriculum, Criteria, Case)
3 Allot about 10 minutes for the curriculum
4 Allot about 10 minutes for each criterion
5 Lay aside a simple description of a difficult situation (case)
6 Take out a blank copy of worksheet 3 and a pencil
7 Open the interview with a short review of the curriculum
      Here we have a first opportunity to avoid long, irrelevant and free-floating discussions; make sure that you have read the curriculum, confirm its readability, allow for some initial freedom and divergence in the discussion, and then, as soon as a job-relevant episode turns up, ask for specific information Situations, Tasks, Actions, and Results (we will meet the appropriate acronym, STAR, many times again). Even better when you are experienced: take 5 minutes for the curriculum, give full freedom to speak, show genuine interest and curiosity, and then close the subject, and get straight on to the next part of the interview; straight-in questioning on relevant criteria.

Straightness
1 Immediately after reviewing the curriculum; get straight
2 Inspect your shortlist of criteria
3 Pick the next criterion on the short list
... for instance ... decisiveness
4 Take out a blank copy of worksheet 4 and your pencil
5 Mention the criterion, define it if necessary
... for instance ... pilots should be decisive
6 Ask if the candidate meets the criterion
... are you decisive?
7 If the answer is yes, be curious for evidence
... could you illustrate that with an example?

The follow-up questioning starts now; asking for the situation, the applicants task, the applicants actions, and the result. We have already seen this old sequence acronymed as STAR. You find two more acronyms on the worksheet, MMM, one Man, one Moment, and one (fine) Mess. When your applicant illustrates a situation, what you want is an anecdote, involving one Man, one Moment, and one (fine) Mess; some real difficulty). And secondly, GNAW, for Gimmick Names and Actual Wordings. When the applicants illustrates what he did in a situation, you do not need the actual names of the persons involved, but you want are actual wordings; you want to hear exact, literal sayings. You help your applicant to use literal phraseology, his or her own verbal repertoire, by allowing the use of a gimmick name (lets say, your chief-pilot was Jim, now what did you say to Jim). Do a reset after running through the STAR-sequence. Summarize what you have heard, ask for any alternative actions (or wordings!) the applicant might have considered, ask for possible advantages and disadvantages of a chosen course of action. If a particularly difficult situation has been discussed, you might share a laugh or some sympathy about the whole thing. It is also very effective to ask for lessons learned, because this is exactly what applicants very often, for good reasons, would like to add to a candid recollection of some wrongdoings of their own 'nowadays, I act differently'. You can always restart your STAR here ... Applicants tend to be very eager to share this type of information, and very often for good reasons; people do have reasons to make certain decisions, and the circumstances may have been exceptional (I fired this guy because he had a detrimental effect on the team-spirit, in other episodes I stood up for employees)

Situational

Finish the interview with a case; a sketch of a simple, but difficult situation one could really come across in a job like the one your applicant is applying for. Take out a copy of worksheet 5 and your pencil

1 Describe a simple, but difficult dilemma, one liner ..

... colleague impolitely orders coffee
2 You give your applicant some time for brainstorming
... Take some time
3 Help to specify the situation more exactly (S)
... Yes, the purser is very busy ...
4 Help to specify the applicants task (T)
... Yes, lets suppose you're the captain
5 Supply gimmick names
... Its Harry ...
6 Ask for possible actions (A)
... What could you do
7 Ask for actual wordings
... How would you address Harry
8 Ask for expected results (R)
9 Ask for (dis-)advantages & alternatives

Some interviewers even do some role playing while discussing cases. If properly announced (I'm Harry, ok?) and ended (thanks for the role playing!), this introduces the strength of assessment-exercises in the interview. It also helps to avoid the often mentioned trap of intentionality in the situational interview. Candidates may make sweeping intentional, hypothetical statements. Asking them to really talk to someone makes it far more difficult for the applicant to remain vague and intentional. Do a reset. Summarize what you have heard, ask for possible advantages and disadvantages of a chosen course of action, and for any alternatives.

Order variations

Modern interviews are always structured, usually the curriculum is discussed for a limited amount of time, usually there is straight in questioning about criteria, ('I fired this guy because he had a detrimental effect on the team-spirit, in an other episode actually stood up for a guy, usually the follow up questioning is being done with STAR'). and usually one or two situations are discussed and the end. The order may vary however. CCC is good (Curriculum, Criteria, Cases) but experienced interviewers have their own variations.

The seemingly obvious

Prior to beginning with the practising, also do the seemingly obvious; arrange for time, space, make sure that you really have the allotted time, and make sure that you can really remain uninterrupted, make sure that you do have a shortlist of criteria, say, decisiveness, teamplayership, and ability resolve conflicts among crew-members, and make sure that you are curious, even after having interviewed others.

Worksheet 1	Critical Incidents
What is ...	Asking job holders ...... for striking examples of model behaviours, wrongdoings ...
Probing Question	Tell me about some crucial event ... that recently happened...
Situation	Situation, tell me about it ... who was the hero, or the fool ...
Task	Task, what was his role, pilot flying ... in command?
Action	Action, what was *actually* done, or *actually* said ... *actions, wordings*
Result	Result, how did the story end ...
Action Taken *Interviewer Take Notes!*	Example (*Shouted Go Around!*)
Behaviour	(E.g. *Deciding*)
Attribute	(E.g. *Decisiveness*)

Worksheet 2	Repertory Grid
What is ...	Comparing job holders, one good, one bad ...
Probing Question	What makes them different ...
Illustrate	*Illustrate* that with an example ...
Situation	Situation, tell me about it ...
Task	Task, what was his role, pilot flying ... in command?
Action	Action, what was *actually* done. What was *actually* said ... *actions, wordings ...*
Result	Result, how did the story end ...
Action Taken *Interviewer Take Notes!*	Example (*Carried her bag ...*)
Behaviour	(E.g. *Supporting passengers*)[1]
Attribute	(E.g. *Service-orientation*)[2]

---

[1] Write here, using a noun, what behaviour is demonstrated by the action taken
[2] Write here, using trait-names, what attribute or personality-trait could be connected to the behaviour.

Worksheet 3	Reviewing Curriculum
What is ...	Reviewing education, training, assignments, achievements, and lessons learned ...
Probing Question	Tell me about an achievement, regret, lesson learned ...
Situation	Situation, when *exactly* did it happen ...
Task	Task, what was your goal ...
Action	Action, what did you *actually* do, or *actually* say ... *actions, wordings* ...
Result	Result, how did the story end ...
Action Taken *Interviewer Take Notes!*	Example (*Said ... go and apologize now!*)
Behaviour	(E.g. *Taking corrective action ...*)
Attribute	(E.g. *Firmness*)

Worksheet 4	Probing Criteria
What is ...	**Direct path**
Probing Question	**Pilots should be able to ...** Describe an important competency **Closed Question ...** Can you ...?
Illustrate	*Illustrate* that with an example ...
Situation	Situation, tell me about it ...(MMM)[3]
Task	Task, what was your role, captain? ... PNF? ...
Action	Action, what did you *actually do, or actually* say .. *actions, wordings* ... (GNAW)[4]
Result	Result, how did the story end ...
Action Taken *Interviewer Take Notes!*	Example (*Carried her bag ...*)
Behaviour	(E.g. *Supporting passengers*)

---

[3] Using MMM with the S in STAR

Follow-up question really begins to bring results when you apply MMM, one Moment, one Man, one fine Mess; *tell me about one particular incident, where you had to deal with one particular difficulty.* As long as an applicant keeps remembering many situations, he will keep being general, intentional or philosophical in his answering. At times, such intentionality may be informative in itself, but very often, the interviewer will feel stuck when given intentional answers. MMM helps the applicant to come across with an anecdote that really illustrates his of her behaviour under difficult circumstances.

[4] Using GNAW with the A in STAR

Gimmick Names, Actual Wordings; GNAW really helps to remove the last bit of intentionality and vagueness in answers; when the applicant reveals his intentions, ('I tried to explain to this guy that he was doing it wrong ... I tried to make him realise that ...'), ask for the actual wordings. Introducing a gimmick name usually helps here; you do not want to know the real name of the person involved, but you do want to hear the applicant speak, because here, in the choice of words, the applicant has to dip into his available behavioural repertoire. Not always, but very often, applicants will come across with what they really said, probably, his actual words are most readily available in memory. Attributes like impatience ('can't you try to'...), empathy ('sorry Jim, I know this is a hard time in training'...), underdog ('you are making it difficult for me Jim'...) often surface here.

Worksheet 5	Discussing Cases
What is ...	Discussing a simple, but difficult dilemma ...
Probing Question	Consider this dilemma ...[5] What would *you* do?
Pinpoint Force Choice	Actual doings ... Actual wordings please ... Kindly refuse intentions ... *Fake* Name, *Actual* Wordings ...
Reset & Brainstorm	Ok, I understand ... Your Considerations ...? Any Pros and Cons ...? Any Alternatives ...?
Action Taken Words spoken *Interviewer Take Notes!*	Example (*You'd really better consult Jim ...*)
Behaviour	(E.g. *Waving responsibility ...*)
Attribute	(E.g. *Irresponsibility*)

---

[5] Share the situation with the applicant, make it a one-liner, and check for clarity of recognition ('do you really see the situation in front of you'). Welcome questions for particulars, do fill in any details ('yes, in this case, you are in charge, or, no, in this case, the purser refuses to help that passenger any longer'), or build two cases when the applicant answers with it depends ... welcome that remark, ok 'so it depends on your seniority, lets discuss both cases, first, assume you are new' ... or ... build both cases ...

Checklists	Modern Interviewing
SSS	**Interviews should be** Structured Straight Situational
CCC	**Starting questions** Exploring Curricula Probing Criteria Discussing Cases
STAR	**Follow up questioning** Situation Task Action Result
MMM	**Situational anecdotes should be about** One Moment One Man One fine Mess
GNAW	**Action anecdotes should be contain** Gimmick Names, Actual Wordings

10 Standards of selection: Legal and ethical issues

Klaus-Martin Goeters
DLR - German Aerospace Center,
Department of Aviation and Space Psychology, Germany

The selection of new personnel for an industrial or governmental organisation is primarily concerned with the question: who of the applicants can cope successfully with the work demands of a particular position or job for which one seeks personnel. Industrial psychology offers methods by which the capabilities of applicants can be assessed so that valid predictions with regard to job success of future employees can be made. The assessment of the capabilities of applicants is based on data collection from:

- Biography
- Psychological tests for aptitudes and personality
- Observations of behaviour
- Proficiency ratings

The data which enters into the psychological files of applicants is of high sensitivity since it consists of very personal information. According to the civil rights of the applicants it is necessary to prevent the abuse of such data samples. The prevention of abuse is regulated by:

- Respective laws
- Code of ethics

Legal situation: All modern societies have established Codes of Civil Law which usually also regulate in a very general manner the use of personal data. For special fields of application more precise laws have been introduced:

Data Protection Law (e.g. 'Bundes-Datenschutzgesetz' in Germany) regulates the handling and storage of personal data (primarily by electronic media and systematic file systems). Law regulating the professional work of psychologists (e.g. 'Psychologengesetz' in Austria). Legal requirements which directly regulate the application of psychodiagnostics in aviation (e.g. JAR-FCL 'Psychological Requirements').

Code of ethics: The professional associations of psychologists set standards with two different purposes:

1. the regulation of inappropriate behaviour, and
2. the promotion of optimal behaviour

Large variety of national codes exist in Europe, but the European Federation of Professional Psychologists' Association (EFPPA) has developed a Meta-Code. All psychological associations in Europe are requested to harmonized their code of ethics with this meta-code (see Lindsay 1996).

Select-In vs. Select-Out: In personnel selection one has to differentiate between the recruitment process of an organisation and the identification and rejection of problem cases. The recruitment of an organisation is looking for the most suitable applicants for the free positions for which new employees are needed (Select-In-Situation). Usually the number of free positions is limited and much lower than the number of applicants. This fact often implies that applicants have to be rejected because all free positions have already been occupied and not because these applicants are principally unsuitable. The question of unsuitability of persons for a certain kind of work is the central problem of the psychological evaluation of problem cases (Select-Out-Situation). Here one is interested in an answer to the question whether an applicant is acceptable or not. It is not surprising that the Select-Out-Situation is very common in safety related areas of work like traffic in general and aviation in particular. Here a public interest exists that persons who mean a latent risk for the system can be rejected.

In both the select-in and select-out situation it is of utmost importance that the psychologist as a professional establishes a climate of confidentiality and respect in his contact with the applicant. Only in such an atmosphere the psychologist can expect to receive unbiased, objective and even critical information.

A solid basis for the creation of an atmosphere of confidentiality is that the psychologist follows a set of legal and ethical rules. These are reviewed and described in the next paragraphs.

Which legal aspects have to be conformed in both the recruitment procedure (Select-In) and the evaluation of problem cases (Select-Out)?

The protection of individual data is the key issue. Therefore the psychologist has to inform the applicant before psychological testing about:

1.   Purpose of testing (e.g.: Finding applicants who can be recommended for basic pilot training.)
2.   Kind of data to be collected (e.g.: Tests for relevant aptitudes such as memory functions, spatial orientation, ... are applied and test results will be reviewed.)
3.   Use of data for the selection decision (e.g.: Only data with some relevance for the selection decision are collected and used for this purpose.)
4.   Storage and use of data after the selection (e.g.: Data are stored in order to perform psychometric checks, validity studies etc.)
5.   Protection and access after the selection (e.g.: Later access to the data for a third party is always dependent on a written permission of the applicant.)

It is important that the applicant takes notice of the procedure as described by the 5 points mentioned above. He also has to agree by signature. If he does not agree, he must have the possibility to step back from the selection before the testing and data collection starts.

Which ethical aspects have to be covered in both the recruitment procedure (Select-In) and the evaluation of problem cases (Select-Out)?

The psychologist is obliged to work according to professional standards like:
1. Only psychologists have the full responsibility to apply and interpret psychological tests.
2. Only tests for factors/traits which are relevant for the respective occupation are permitted.
3. Only scientifically proven tests can be applied.
4. The right of the applicant must be respected in being informed about the test results and receiving an explanation of the decision taken by the selection board.
   Sometimes it will be necessary to defend these 4 principles against intentions of the psychologist's employer or contractor. However, the psychologist in selection has a similar position as for instance a flight surgeon who is responsible for the medical checks.

Which additional (legal) aspects have to be followed particularly in aviation?

In Europe the Joint Aviation Requirements (JAR) for Flight Crew Licensing (FCL) are introduced on 1 July 1999. JAR-FCL/Part 3 which describes the medical certification, also includes 'Psychological Requirements'. These requirements are a non-mandatory part of the medical assessment of pilots. Due to these regulations a psychological evaluation of a pilot applicant can only be requested if significant doubts exist with regard to his personal reliability. Therefore the issue of a Class I (commercial) or Class II (private) pilot medical certificate can depend on the psychological assessment of a pilot applicant. This is a typical select-out situation.
   JAR-FCL 3.240 (for class I) and 3.360 (for class II) was adopted on 22 May 1996 by the European States and reads as follows:
a) '... A psychological evaluation may be required by the AMS where it is indicated as part of, or complementary to, a specialist psychiatric or neurological examination...'
b) '... the AMS shall utilise a psychologist approved by the Authority'
c) 'The psychologist shall submit to the AMS a written report detailing his opinion and recommendation.'
AMS stands for the Aeromedical Section of the respective national Civil Aviation Authority. Paragraph a) describes a typical view of the medical branch. It seems as if a psychological evaluation is only feasible in combination with a psychiatric or neurological examination. That this is not an adequate position will be explained below.
   Up to now the approval of psychologists by the national authorities is not regulated. In many cases those psychologists who already did such a work in their

national aviation environment will probably get this approval under the JAR conditions. EAAP is helping aviation psychologists to receive this approval by the installation of a register. Psychologists listed in this EAAP register have passed official EAAP courses, which is a guarantee for the authority that an appropriate standard of know-how in aviation psychology is met.

In JAR-FCL/Part 3 the Appendix 17 gives more information with regard to the Indication (1) and Criteria (2) of the Psychological Evaluation:

1. 'A psychological evaluation should be considered ... when the authority receives verifiable information from an identifiable source which evokes doubts concerning the mental fitness or personality of a particular individual. Sources for this information can be accidents or incidents, problems in training or proficiency checks, delinquency or knowledge relevant to the safe exercise of the privileges of the applicable licences.'
2. 'The psychological evaluation may include a collection of biographical data, the administration of aptitude as well as personality tests and psychological interview.'

In the published manual which is adjacent to JAR-FCL/Part 3 the psychological criteria are listed and described by exact definitions. Besides biographical data the following aptitudes and personality factors will be investigated:

Operational aptitudes
1. Logical reasoning
2. Mental arithmetic
3. Memory function
4. Attention
5. Perception
6. Spatial comprehension
7. Psychomotor function
8. Multiple task abilities

Personality factors
1. Motivation and for Class I: Work orientation
2. Decision making
3. Social capability
4. Stress coping

Which are the advantages or disadvantages of the 'Psychological Requirements' under JAR-FCL/Part 3?

The advantages are:
•   clear guidelines, how to deal with cases of psychological relevance
•   precise code of reference with regard to the content and the methodology of a psychological evaluation.

The disadvantages are:
The connection with a psychiatric/neurological examination is often inappropriate because:
-   It means double effort in administration, time and money, if the applicant has

only a psychological indication (Examples: A trainee consistently failing checks or a pilot with a history of orientation problems in the airspace. In Germany an annual rate of 30-40 of such cases can be observed. Most of them come from general aviation or the private sector, where the control mechanisms are weaker than in the airline business).

- Cases which have already been mentioned as examples become 'psychiatrized' if they are also submitted to a psychiatric/neurological examination.
- It reflects an old hierarchical position by the categorization of Aviation Psychology as an auxiliary science of Psychiatry/Neurology.

Fortunately there is a solution for this problem, since psychological evaluation can be requested by the national aviation authority via a second way. If the authority refers to JAR-FCL 3.105 (f) an additional examination of every kind (e.g.: also a psychological evaluation) can be ordered. JAR-FCL 3.105 (f) 'Additional examination' reads: 'Where the authority has reasonable doubt about the continuing fitness of the holder of a medical certificate, the AMS may require the holder to submit to further examination, investigation or tests. The reports shall be forwarded to the AMS'.

It is expected that in the future cases with a primarily psychological indication will be handled primarily via JAR-FCL 3.105(f) in order to keep this work practical.

11 General standards of selection: Validity and utility analysis

Klaus-Martin Goeters

DLR - German Aerospace Research Establishment, Aviation and Space
Psychology, Germany

Methodological aspects of validity research

Psychological testing is applied in order to receive an assessment of the capabilities and personality structure of applicants so that behaviour in real life situations can be predicted. By validity studies it is checked whether the intended predictions can be observed. In personnel selection the validity of tests is determined by comparing the test scores with future training results and occupational success. The cohesion between the predictor X (=tests score) and the criterion Y (=training and job success) is described by coefficients of correlation. Coefficients of correlation vary between 0 (=no relation) and +/- 1.0 (=max. cohesion).

Training and job success are concepts of a very general nature. They can be defined by different indicators (or criteria). The following list summarizes global criteria of job success:
- Successful job training (pass-fail)
- Total record in job training
- Duration of training
- Success in probation (pass-fail)
- Rating of the general qualification by superiors
- Rating of the general qualification by colleagues
- Objective results of work
- Demand for additional training
- Special job positions (yes - no)
- Job satisfaction
- Involvement in incidents .
- Involvement in accidents
- Early retirement

It is obvious from this list that different criteria refer to different aspects of professional behaviour. This directly implies that a certain test may be a good predictor for criterion A, but not valid for criterion B. Or stated in another way: For a given test there are as many validities as there are criteria. Therefore it is important in practical validity research that criteria are grouped into meaningful categories with particular relevance regarding a certain professional setting.

Not only the diversity of criteria is a problem of validity research but also the fact that the observed validity is always diminished compared to true validity. This effect of correlation statistics is based on the following factors:

- Low reliability of predictor and criterion: In practical selection only the reliability of the criterion is relevant .
- Poor psychometric precision due to a dichotomization of predictor and criterion
- Attenuation of variance of
  - ➥ the predictor due to selection and of
  - ➥ the criterion due to a systematic group shrinkage

What are expected statistics of empirical validity research? From summary studies the following data are available:

- Mean sample size of 406 validity studies is N=68
  (see Lent, Aurbach and Lewin, 1971)
- Mean reliability of criterion: Estimated at R=.60
  (see Schmidt and Hunter, 1977)
- Mean attenuation of variance by selection: Estimated at S:s=10:6
  (see Schmidt and Hunter, 1977)

The consequences under these conditions are: Given a true validity of Rho_{xy}=.50 correlation statistics predicts an observed validity in the population of R_{xy}=.38 (due to the limited reliability of the criterion) and an observed validity in the selected group of r_{xy}=.24 (due to the attenuation of variance). This example is calculated by the application of statistical formula and shows very clearly how a true validity coefficient of a reasonable value is diminished to relatively low coefficients for which it sometimes becomes hard to prove the significance of the difference from zero. That such a shrinkage happens to observed validities could be shown in an 'experimental selection' in the US Army Airforce Aviation Psychology Program during World War II (Thorndike 1947). In this program a total number of 1,036 applicants for military pilot training were tested in various aptitude tests. The results of these tests used to calculate a composite score which was called 'Pilot Stanine'. After having been tested all applicants were submitted to pilot training (without any selection). Training results were correlated with the previous test scores and led to substantial validity coefficients (see table 1). In an 'experimental' selection only the best 13 percent of the applicants in the variable 'Pilot Stanine' were included in the determination of 'observed validities'. As can be seen in table 1 this shrinkage of variance resulted in clearly diminished validity coefficients (some not even significantly   different from zero). These results show that in practical selection significant validities are not easily received. But if they are received their low value stand for a much higher correspondence between variables than the observed coefficients seem to indicate. This fact should always be kept in mind if validity results in aviation psychology are discussed, because usually only validity coefficients from selected and not from unselected groups exist.

Table 1   'Experimental Selection': Validity coefficients for selective tests and a composite score for the selection of student pilots with and without restriction of range (AAF Aviation Psychology: Thorndike, 1947)

Variable	Correlation in the total group (N = 1,036)	Correlation in the selected highest 13 per cent (N = 136)
Pilot stanine	.64	.18
Mechanical principles	.44	.03
General information	.46	.20
Complex coordination	.30	-.03
Instrument comprehension	.45	.27
Arithmetic reasoning	.27	.18
Finger dexterity	.18	.00

If one tries to identify the most relevant predictors in a certain area, meta-analyses should be performed. The meta-analyses collect data from different validity studies and calculate mean observed validity coefficients. These means are based on relatively large sample sizes and therefore can be seen as representative. They enable good assessment of the relative importance of predictors; but it should be remembered that the true validities are significantly higher than the observed values. In a study of Hunter & Burke (1991) a table was published which report mean validity coefficients for various psychological test categories and other variables as predictors of pilot training (see table 2). If values of approximately .2 are taken as a limit the following areas seem to be good predictors: High standards of knowledge and interest (see: General and Aviation Information as well as Bio-Inventory), fast perception and working speed (see: Perceptual Speed and Reaction Time), good spatial comprehension (see: Spatial and Mechanical Ability), good performance in tests for psychomotor and multiple task capabilities (see: Job sample (=simulators) and Psychomotor Coordination).

Validity studies in pilot selection: From the ab-initio to the ATPL level

DLR has developed test programs for pilot selection which are adapted to the level of proficiency which the applicant holds.

Table 2 Validity coefficients for specific sets of predictors for pilot training (adopted from Hunter & Burke 1991)

Predictor Measure	Number of r_{xy}	Total Sample	Mean r_{xy}
General Intellect	12	7,927	.1294
Verbal Ability	14	20,756	.1244
Quantitative Ability	31	44,799	.1036
Spatial Ability	35	47,247	.1851
Perceptual Speed	41	29,732	.2001
Manual Dexterity	11	2,547	.1044
Reaction Time	7	6,854	.2953
Mechanical Ability	37	38,708	.2890
Aviation Information	18	21,196	.2324
General Information	14	27,480	.2536
Education	8	5,495	.0456
Age	8	13,142	-.0964
Job Sample	16	2,822	.3272
Bio-Inventory	22	27,962	.2646
Psychomotor Coordination	73	42,893	.3035

On Level I which is the lowest level no flight experience is necessary. These candidates apply for an ab-initio training program. The test program for ab-initio applicants is the most extended since the broadest spectrum of risks with respect to training and line operation has to be covered. The test program (see Goeters, Hörmann & Maschke 1989) therefore includes the largest number of tests. Due to the principle of redundant measurement more than one test is often used to assess the relevant performance and personality dimensions listed in table 3.

Level II is for those applicants who are PPL holders. Here the basic structure of Level I is still used, but the number of tests is reduced (e. g. in the area of psychomotor and multiple task capabilities).

Level III is for holders of commercial pilot licences who have not much professional experience (e. g. no ATPL, only prop operation, low number of flight hours). Here the test program is reduced further. Basic operational aptitude tests are still used, but knowledge tests are completely cancelled. Besides the assessment of proficiency personality assessment gains importance. Therefore, the test program is supplemented by a simulator check.

Table 3 Basic knowledge, operational aptitudes and personality traits relevant for the psychological selection of ab-initio student pilots

Performance
Basic Knowledge:
- English
- Technical Knowledge and Comprehension
- Mathematic-Logical Thinking

Operational Aptitudes:
- Memory (Auditory/Visual)
- Perception and Attention (Auditory/Visual)
- Spatial Orientation
- Psychomotor Coordination
- Multiple Task Capacity

Personality
Achievement-Oriented Traits:
- Motivation
- Rigidity
- Mobility
- Vitality

Interpersonal Behaviour:
- Extraversion
- Empathy
- Aggressiveness
- Dominance

Stress Resistance:
- Emotional Stability

Level IV is for experienced ATPL holders with sufficient experience in jet operation. Here the major components in the assessment of applicants are the proficiency check in a simulator and an extensive personality evaluation. Depending on the contract with the particular airline a small number of tests for basic aptitudes can also be administered. These aptitude tests are used more for control than selection purposes.

In the last years validation studies were performed at DLR for Levels I, III and IV (Hörmann & Maschke 1993). A validation study for Level II was completed but not published since it revealed similar results as the Level I study. In all studies a variety of criteria for training and occupational success was used. Besides training records or scores from rating scales the DLR always used a classification of the subjects into successful versus problematic cases. The latter comprise those subjects with problem reports such as failing of checks, dismissals, incidents or accidents and other negative behavioural events indicating some personal unreliability. It is of great advantage for airlines if such problem cases can be identified early enough and then will be rejected.

Level I: Prediction of failures in ab-initio training

In a representative validation study, 393 student pilots of a major European airline were followed up after their acceptance in the psychological selection program for ab initio training (Hörmann & Maschke 1987; Maschke & Hörmann 1988). When flight instructor ratings (aircraft and simulator) were used as training criteria, tests of mathematical reasoning, mental concentration, perceptual speed, and spatial orientation reached the strongest validities. Some personality factors correlated with training results, too. When failures had to be predicted, tests of complex psychomotor coordination and multiple task capacity were identified as especially powerful: Student pilots with low performance on these tests have a significantly higher probability of failing in their later flight training. Differences of average performance in five complex apparatus tests are reported in figure 1 where candidates, who failed in pilot training, were compared with successful students. The test performance is expressed in STANINE scores which can vary between 1 (=lowest performance) and 9 (=highest performance) with an average of 5. This scale is based on the distribution of test scores in the population of all applicants.

The psychomotor tests applied in this validation study were the Complex Coordination Test (CCT), the Two-Hand-Coordination-Test (THC), the Test of Multiple Task Performance (TOM), the Instrument Coordination Analyser (ICA), and the LINK Simulator (SIM). The majority of failures happened in the advanced flight training (IFR, Multi-Engine) when the task structure becomes more complex. Obviously, tests for psychomotor coordination and multiple task capabilities are able to predict the cases who become unsafe under these demands due to their personal performance limits.

Level III: Prediction of problem cases in line acceptance (pilots with limited experience)

What about applicants who already have commercial pilot licenses? The hypothesis could be that, contrary to the conditions for unexperienced ab initio pilot trainees, some aspects of flight experience (e. g. flight hours, class of license) might be more valid predictors than psychological tests. This hypothesis was tested in a validation study where licensed pilots applied for employment in a commuter airline. The criterion of professional success or failure was given by a proficiency rating during the first line check. In this phase, pilots still could be rejected from employment. Psychological aptitude and personality test scores which were collected in the preceding selection program correlated significantly with the criterion, whereas aspects of flight experience did not show any correlation (Maschke & Hörmann 1989).

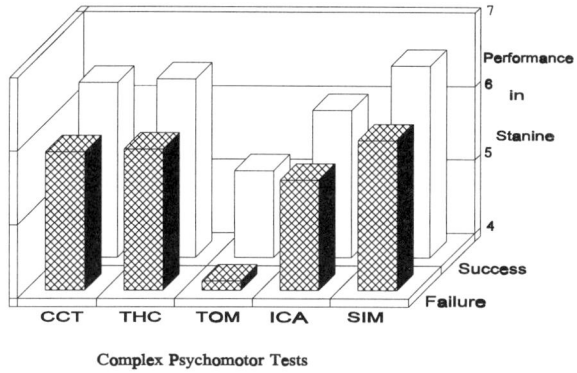

Complex Psychomotor Tests

Figure 1 Average performance in five complex psychomotor tests: Comparison of successful and unsuccessful airline pilot students (Training result: Success N = 343, Failure N = 50)

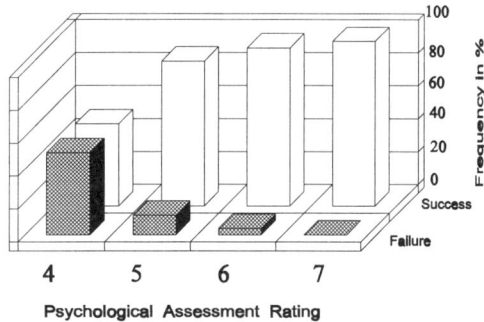

Psychological Assessment Rating

Figure 2 Licensed pilots as applicants for a commuter airline: Comparison of the distributions of the psychological assessment ratings for pilots with different results in the first line check (N = 88)

The validity of psychological prediction can be visualized by comparing the distributions of a global assessment during selection for pilot groups rated differently in the line check. For simplicity, figure 2 only reports the distributions for the pilots who failed and those who succeeded in the check. The global assessments were given by the members of the selection board on a nine-point rating scale similar to the STANINE system. Usually candidates with a mean rating of 4 and below are rejected, but in some cases of 4 a waiver was given. So for the selected pilots the distribution of ratings started with 4 and ended at the level of 7 because scores of 8 or 9 were not chosen by the selection board. For applicants who were assessed as more qualified in the psychological evaluation, significantly fewer problems were revealed in their cockpit work. The rate of failures reached its maximum (nearly 50% failures) at a global assessment of 4. It decreased gradually to 0% at the assessment level of 7. These results clearly show that psychological evaluation methods can provide a valid diagnosis of problem cases even for trained pilots.

In the Level III validation no single group of tests can be identified as the most relevant predictor. It seems it is more the integration of critical information from various areas that gives the best predictive power.

Level IV: Prediction of problem cases in line operation (experienced ATPL holders)

193 licensed airline pilots were followed up after passing the selection for an European charter airline (Hörmann & Maschke 1993, 1996). Most of the subjects (95%) had at least 1000 flight hours (mean 6,695 hours). The selection was based on a proficiency check in a jet simulator and on an extensive personality assessment by the Temperament Structure Scales TSS (Maschke 1987, Goeters et al. 1993), by the Cockpit Management Attitudes Questionnaire CMAQ (Helmreich 1984), by biographical data and finally by a psychological interview.15% of the selected pilots developed some problems. In 3% these problems were so severe that the pilots had to be dismissed. The problem cases could be classified into 4 major categories:

Low knowledge standard	14%
(e. g. lack of knowledge of aircraft systems and procedures)	
Low flying abilities	34%
(e. g. performance deficits under time pressure, being overloaded or mentally tunnelled in simulator exercises)	
Poor crew coordination	26%
(e. g. lack of command ability, sloppy habits using procedures and checklists)	
General behavioural problems	26%
(e. g. lack of openness for feedback and opinions of others, rude behaviour towards colleagues and staff)	

All these four categories indicate potential risk factors. Nearly half of the problem cases were concerned with performance, the other half dealt with interpersonal aspects. So it was not surprising that the simulator check records as well as the personality evaluation correlated significantly with the development of problems. Personality assessment was as well a good predictor as the simulator results although both methods covered different sources of interindividual variance.

For the topic of this paper it is of particular interest how the personality assessment worked as a predictor. Especially the well-developed scales of the TSS correlated significantly with the probability of becoming a problem case.

The TSS incorporates scales for all the personality traits reported in table 3. Scales of stress resistance and of interpersonal skills were found to be the best predictors (see figures 3 and 4). Even in the group of experienced pilots there is obviously enough variation with respect to critical behavioural dispositions.

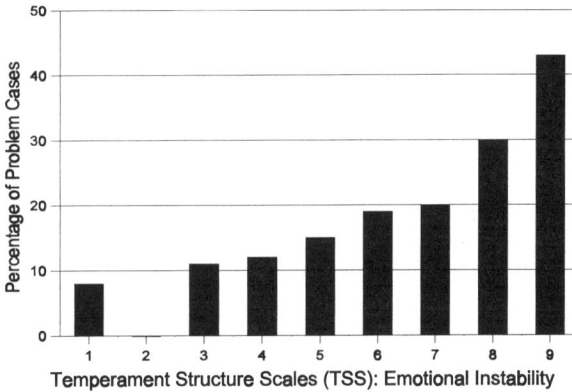

Figure 3   **Selection of experienced ATPL holders: Probability to become a problem case as a function of the score in the TSS-Scale 'Emotional Instability'**

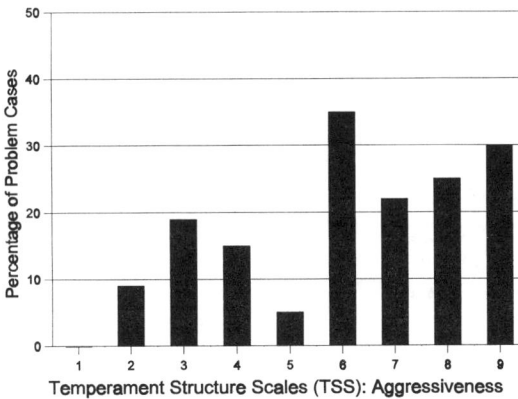

Figure 4   **Selection of experienced ATPL holders: Probability to become a problem case as a function of the score in the TSS-Scale 'Aggressiveness'**

It is well established that the more conventional tests for operational aptitudes and personality traits are valid predictors for problem cases not only in flight training, but also in line operation. The early identification of such critical cases in selection programs will significantly reduce the risk of unsafe cockpit management. The relative importance of personality factors compared to aptitudes increases from the selection of ab-initio student pilots to the screening of experienced pilot. The results of validation studies reported in this paper include only those subjects who were not rejected by the established psychological selection programs. Thus much stronger effects can be expected to exist in the large group of unselected applicants. Therefore, airlines are well advised to use the diagnostic know-how of aviation psychologists when employing new cockpit personnel.

Utility

If a test system is valid it is usually implied that its application shows utility in financial terms. This fact may be clarified by a simple hypothetical example. Provided that validity studies show that a certain test system is significantly predicting the duration of ATC training which is needed. And given the reasonable assumption that the duration of training usually has a direct influence on the training costs: The longer the training the higher the costs. Then, if one only selects those ATC applicants for whom the test scores would predict a reduced training duration this could result a substantial benefit by saving training costs.

Valid test systems have benefits for the organisation as well as for the individual applicant. For the organisation the utility of the selection of aviation personnel lies in aspects like these:

- Benefits by saving investments for ab-initio training: Low rate of failure is a financial advantage
- Benefits by saving costs for recurrent training: Low rate of additional training / rechecks is a financial disadvantage
- Improvement of the safety standard

For the applicant the utility can be expressed in such benefits:

- Diminishing the risk of false personal investments of effort, time (and money if self-financed training)
- Increasing personal security during a long term career
- Promotion of job satisfaction and mental health

The last example shows that utility may not be restricted solely to financial aspects.

12   Diagnostic decisions

Hans-Jürgen Hörmann
DLR - German Aerospace Center,
Aviation and Space Psychology, Germany

After having administered a state-of-the-art test-battery to a number of candidates the goal is finally to choose the most suitable applicants for the job. At the first glance this might seem to be an easy decision: just hire the ones with the highest test-scores. However, there are two problems with this approach: One is that simply hiring the best applicants does not mean that all of them really have the potential of becoming successful jobholders in the future. If there is no clearly pre-defined cut-off score as a reference for the test performance the suitability of the candidates cannot be determined. The second problem is that with an increasing number and diversity of tests things become complicated because it is often not possible to integrate the different test-scores into one total score.

Psychometric theory offers a statistical procedure known as *multiple regression* to 'automatically' combine test-scores for a prediction. In a regression equation each test is weighted according to how well it predicts the chosen job-criterion. The limitations of this procedure are that only one job-criterion can be predicted at a time. If this is not representative for the whole profile of job demands the predicted job performance could have a narrow scope of generality, which means it covers only a few of the desired job elements. Furthermore, multiple regression assumes a linear relationship between the test-scores and the criterion. That is, the higher the test-scores the better the performance on the job. Usually the linearity assumption is fulfilled for the achievement tests but not for personality variables. In diagnostic decisions personality variables are often handled like age or physical variables (e.g. height, weight). In general, the average scores comprise the best prognosis for job success. Extreme low or high scores are equally regarded as less positive. This is clearly contradicting to the linearity assumption.

Because of these shortcomings of purely statistical decision models, diagnostic decisions in practice are usually made by an experienced psychologist or even better by a board consisting of experienced jobholders and organisational psychologists. In order to evaluate the direct raw-scores from different test-methods it is necessary to convert the individual results on a standard scale with the same units. Otherwise the data are not comparable, as for example reaction times and number of solved numerical problems. The JARs recommend for this purpose the Stanine-scale. The Stanine-scale is a standardised nine-point scale with a mean of 5 and a standard deviation of 1.96 (see figure 1).

All tests and questionnaire scores can be converted into stanines provided a normal distribution for the respective variable can be assumed. This procedure is called *standardisation*, it follows three steps:

1)   Determine the distribution of the test in a representative sample of the applicant population under consideration (norm sample). The norm sample and the future applicants must correspond in important characteristics like age, education, culture, prior job experience etc..

2)   Generate a norm table. According to the percentages shown in figure 1 stanines are assigned to discrete intervals of test-scores

3)   Convert test-scores of real applicants according to this norm table into stanines

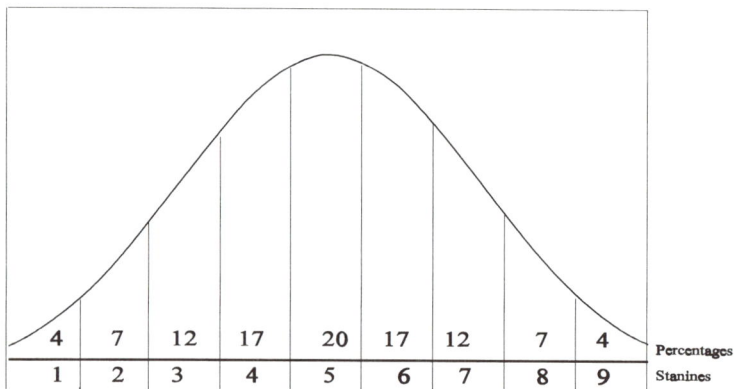

| 4 | 7 | 12 | 17 | 20 | 17 | 12 | 7 | 4 | Percentages |
| 1 | 2 | 3 | 4 | 5 | 6 | 7 | 8 | 9 | Stanines |

Figure 1   Stanine-scale ('Standard Nine')

The first step in the standardisation process is to determine the distribution of the test-scores in the relevant norm group, which means that the test has to be administered to a representative sample of at least 100 or 200 subjects. Based on this distribution a norm table is generated in which a specific interval of raw scores is assigned to each stanine as follows: the lowest 4% of the test-scores are assigned to stanine 1, the next 7% are assigned to stanine 2, the next 12% are assigned to stanine 3 and so on (refer to figure 1 for the percentages). Referring to this norm table all scores collected during subsequent selections with the hereby standardised test, can be converted into stanines. This procedure has to be completed for all tests and questionnaires in the selection battery.

The advantage of the standardisation process is not only that the results of every test-method can be compared on the same nine-point scale independently of their inherent metric. Furthermore the conversion into stanines directly offers an evaluation of individual test results compared to the 'average candidate' in the applicant's population. An individual stanine of 7 for example means that this applicant's test-score is as high or higher than the test-scores of 77% of all other applicants in the population. A stanine of 5 represents exactly the average candidate. Stanine 2 means 89% of the applicants in the population score higher than the respective candidate. This description of how to generate norms and how to standardise a test might seem very academic. However, a basic understanding of these steps is essential for conducting selection professionally according to the methodological recommendations of the JARs.

When all individual test results have been converted into standard scales the selection-board members can inspect the data-profiles of the candidates in order to identify their suitability. First each board member should make up his own opinion. In a subsequent discussion agreement can be found regarding the final recommendation about an applicant's qualifications. To reduce effects of subjectivity these decisions should be based on specific rules, for example:

(1) In regard to the aptitudes those test-scores are critical that are clearly below the average of the norm sample. Suitable applicants should not have clear deficiencies in any of the required aptitudes. Whenever possible each aptitude should be measured by at least two different methods. This possibility for cross-references improves the decision quality.

(2) The whole profile of aptitude-tests is relevant. It should be average or better compared to the norm sample. A deficiency identified for one aptitude cannot be compensated by high scores for another aptitude if these two areas are not strongly interrelated (e.g. spatial orientation and number facility). This rule also excludes that all aptitude scores are simply summed up to a total score as a basis for decision.

(3) In regard to personality the applicants should be examined for the relevant traits with more than one method. For most traits extreme high and extreme low scores can both be critical. In order to ensure maximum flexibility for changing social and operational working conditions suitable applicants should not have extreme personality traits compared to the norm sample.

(4) Furthermore certain types of the personality profiles can be significant during selection (e.g. low extraversion together with low self-confidence). However, to understand how to identify critical personality types based on more than one trait requires more knowledge about personality theories which is beyond the scope of this chapter.

Similar rules are recommended by the JARs when a pilot or would-be pilot is examined for the psychological requirements. To illustrate how these rules can be applied in selection four different cases with their data records are presented. The test results are taken from real applicants for ab-initio pilot training (source: DLR). All data are given in stanines. The personality information is omitted, except observer ratings of stress tolerance that are collected during the apparatus tests.

These four cases can be used to illustrate how the respective selection board decided. Decisions were taken in three different steps according to the multi-stage selection concept (see figure 2, chapter 4): 1) after the paper-pencil classroom tests, 2) after the individual apparatus tests, 3) after the interview. Case 1 was rejected after step 1 because of below average performance in tests of number abilities and of memory. Mechanical comprehension is also weak but here at least one of two tests is average. The higher than average scores in perceptual speed and attention control do not compensate the mentioned deficiencies. Case 2 was accepted after the paper-pencil tests though some deficiencies are obvious especially for the memory functions. Such generous evaluation can be adequate, if one wants to collect more information before the final decision is made. In the second stage this candidate scored two times below average in the coordination tests and was rejected afterwards. Case 3 was accepted during all three stages though he showed some weak performance scores in different areas. The decision was nevertheless positive since the second test-score in each of these areas was at least average. Case 4 passed the selection without deficiencies. One marginal score in English is compensated by good performance in the second English-test.

Both cases 3 and 4 also passed the pilot training successfully and got type-rated in the airline's entry-fleet. Case 4 completed all hurdles without any re-checks in minimum time. Case 3 was also successful but received several recommendations by his flight instructors that correspond to some degree to his performance during the selection. Six different flight instructors commented literally on different grade sheets as follows: 1) 'standard', 2) 'always trying hard', 3) 'generally good performance, in abnormals possible consequences (speed limits, performance restrictions) should be anticipated in time', 4) 'continuous progress during this phase up to satisfactory and good performance; trim technique and anticipation should be improved', 5) 'good performance, quite professional working style, no problems', 6) 'descent-planning should be more judicious, good progress finally leads to standard and above performance'. These comments seem to indicate that this pilot simply needed slightly more efforts to reach the expected standards, which is not serious if everything is safe.

The examples should also demonstrate that successful trainees do not necessarily have to have high scores in every selection test. Isolated weak performances are not always a reason for rejection if the respective aptitude in total can be seen as uncritical. However, if the selection test-battery does not contain redundancies diagnostic decisions become quite difficult. If each aptitude is measured with only one test-method, compensation and cross references within one aptitude area are not possible and decision quality drops substantially.

Once the decision has been made whether or not to hire an applicant, the applicant must be informed about the result of the selection. In case of a positive decision this is a pleasant task. However, if an applicant is rejected care should be taken that the reasons for the negative result are communicated tactfully. It should be understood that a selection test does not evaluate the person in total. It just covers a sample of certain abilities or personality aspects which are evaluated in relation to a specific profile of job requirements.

Table 1   Illustration of data profiles of real applicants for ab-initio pilot training. Underlined scores are below the average of the respective norm sample.

Aptitude Area	Case 1	Case 2	Case 3	Case 4
PP-Tests (Step 1):				
English Language Skills	9, 5	6, 5	6, 6	7, *4*
Mechanical Comprehension	5, *1*	7, *4*	7, 8	7, 6
Number Facility and Reasoning	*3, 2*	7, *4*	6, 5	5, 7
Memory Functions	*4, 2*	*3, 4*	8, 7	6, 6
Perceptual Speed	7, 7	7, 5	*3*, 8	9, 9
Attention Control	7	7	*4*, 5	9
Spatial Orientation	5, 5	5, 5	5, *4*	8, 7
Apparatus Tests (Step 2):				
Psychomotor Coordination	-	*3, 3*	8, 7	8, 9
Multiple Task Capacity	-	-	8, *4*	6
Stress Tolerance (Observation)	-	-	7, 7	8, 8
Interview (Step 3):				
Interview Grade	-	-	6	7

This has no implications for qualifications for other positions. The way applicants are being treated by a company significantly contributes to the company's public image. Rejected applicants are welcomed as customers or future applicants for other positions and should always be treated with respect. Bearing this in mind the literature gives some suggestions for the contents of *rejection letters* (see Aamodt & Peggans, 1988):

- the applicants should be notified of the result without delay after the decision is made so that they can continue job-search
- the letters should be personally addressed and signed
- the company's appreciation for the application should be emphasised
- qualifications of the applicant should be praised

- high qualifications of other applicants should be mentioned
- wish of success for further career should be expressed
- if true, it can be promised to keep the resume on file

These suggestions might seem self-evident. However, those who have practical experience with selection can probably confirm that when sifting through hundreds of applications or conducting job-interviews several days in a row until late in the evening, things can get slightly hectic. Then it is time to watch out for unwilling degradation of style.

13 Recommendations and future perspectives

Hans-Jürgen Hörmann
DLR - German Aerospace Research Establishment, Aviation and Space
Psychology, Germany

In a systems approach to personnel development in organisational settings the selection process has strong ties to job design and training. The required qualifications to cope successfully with specific job tasks can often be secured either via selection or via training. If for example none of the available applicants has the desired qualifications either the job tasks have to be redefined or those qualifications have to be developed through suitable training curricula, which however is not always possible. If some but not all of the applicants already have the right qualifications, selection is indicated, especially if these qualifications are not trainable, like certain aptitudes or personality traits. For larger numbers of applicants a multi-stage selection procedure should be considered especially for a job-profile that includes a variety of qualifications that cannot be inferred from the 'classic trio' of selection methods: application form, letter of references, and interview.

The chapters on air-traffic controller and on military and civilian pilot selection illustrate examples of how selection is conducted in different occupational fields in aviation. The methods utilized for these positions include traditional paper-pencil tests, computerised apparatus tests, questionnaires, behavioural exercises, simulations, and interviews. These methods focus on certain knowledge factors, aptitudes, skills, motivation, personality, and social competencies. Whether the selection criteria are really relevant for the position under consideration has to be determined in advance by job-analysis techniques that are described by means of ready-to-use worksheets within this section. The role of the aviation psychologist and the corresponding legal and ethical responsibilities are also described as guiding principles for the work in selection.

One basic goal of selection is certainly the reduction of failure rates and problem cases throughout job training and following career. By means of a well arranged selection system, that meets the basic scientific criteria like objectivity, reliability, and validity, this can normally be achieved for many positions. There is sufficient empirical evidence that the application of selection methods has contributed significantly to achieve and maintain a high standard of the operators that manage todays air-traffic and flight decks in civil and military aviation.

Recommendation

Several recommendations were given in the subparts above about how to ensure that selection will be an efficient tool for personnel development in the aviation industry. Five important notions shall be summarised here again:

1) Job-task relatedness: The diagnostic methods shall be clearly related to the job requirements otherwise their validity and acceptability will be insufficient. New technological and conceptual developments, like the glass-cockpit or aircraft-to-ground data-links, can cause significant changes of job tasks that have to be carefully taken into account in the selection procedure. However, it is not always possible to foresee such developments over a longer time period, therefore, selection departments are more in a position of reacting to such changes. In fact, we are predicting future performance on the basis of todays requirements. This is only reasonable if the selection methods are not too specific. The narrower the scope of predicted behaviour is, the sooner it might become irrelevant through changes in the job tasks. Major modifications to an otherwise functioning test battery should be well considered and planned some time ahead, since validation and standardisation processes have to be completed before a new test instrument can be fully used.

2) Redundancy of measurement: Every test-method has its own bias of measurement. In order to reduce the probability that selection decisions are based on errors of measurement at least two independent methods for the same aptitudes or personality characteristics should be included in the test-battery. For example statements about an applicant's personality should not be based on a questionnaire alone but whenever possible cross-checked with information from real behaviour observations or from an interview.

3) Validity: All selection tests without exceptions have to comply with the basic psychometric standards. Empirical studies and analyses undertaken by professionals to prove this compliance should be thoroughly documented. The validation of a new test-principle is a quite difficult and often time-consuming process. Therefore it should be encouraged here to make the findings from such studies available to the scientific community in this field. International conferences or working groups are providing an ideal forum for straightaway exchange of new ideas and research results. Especially for civil aviation pilots and air traffic controllers published validation studies are rare.

4) Social validity and fair testing: Complementary to the psychometric validity, which is certainly the prime criterion for selection tests, the notion of social validity (e.g. Schuler & Stehle, 1985) is discussed in the literature as a criterion for the selection situation in total. Organisations increasingly value applicants as customers. The application is the first contact between an employer and its potential future employees. Therefore, organisational attractiveness can be significantly affected by the perceived fairness and acceptability of the applicant-employer relationship. Popularity of selection practices from the applicant's point of view can be increased by the transparency and job-relevance of the selection criteria, the opportunity to discuss questions with competent company representatives, the chances of being reconsidered if rejected, and the form of the given feedback about test results. Quite unattractive it appears, if the selection department is working like a 'sausage factory' in which 'human potential' is screened by self-made professionals in order to supposedly increase profitability and productivity one-sidedly for the company.

5) *Autonomy:* Diagnostic decisions and standards should be independent of economical pressure and momentary demands. Interdisciplinary working teams of jobholders, training experts, and aviation psychologists together should define appropriate standards and guidelines for accepting or rejecting applicants. For the credibility of the selection department it is important to have the sovereignty of implementing and maintaining those guidelines and not being overruled and without prior consultation by direct interventions of a superior department in the company.

Perspectives

Although aviation psychologists have been involved in selection of pilots and air-traffic controllers already for many decades their job is still far from becoming routine. Several vital challenges for their successful work have to be faced in the future:

- Attrition of candidates: Over the last few years the number of applicants especially for the pilot career has shown a decreasing trend. The reasons are probably rather complex: Rapid ups and downs of pilot demand in the major airlines, different conditions for financing the costs of training, decreasing job security and many other factors have lead to uncertainty among the younger generation in regard to vocational choices. Related to these influences are shifts in the vocational motivation of the applicants. External aspects are getting a higher weight when choosing the pilot career. Selection departments could be forced by a continuous lack of applicants and economical pressure to increase the pass rates of the different selection filters. If the validity of the test-battery is weak and flying an aircraft has not become easier, this will inevitably lead to an increase of problem cases and failure rates in training. Therefore a thorough monitoring of such developments as well as a better planning of personnel recruitment strategies is needed.
- Problem of adequate performance criteria: Studies of prognostic validity are mostly based on the pass-fail criterion during initial training phases. This criterion has many shortcomings, since training failures are rare and the reasons often do not represent whether someone could become a strong or weak employee. What is that, what we are going to predict during selection? Efforts to better elaborate the technical and non-technical criteria of job success as a pilot or controller are long time overdue. These criteria have to fulfil the same psychometric standards as the selection tests. If for example instructor ratings or ratings by superiors are used, the raters have to be trained before in making reliable judgements. Until now the research on performance criteria for pilots and controllers is lagged far behind the

results of research already done on the selection tests themselves. In order to prove the often mentioned argument that selection increases individual satisfaction and mental health, since the positive candidates are more capable to cope with the job demands, indicators of job satisfaction and personal well-being should also be considered as validity criteria. Many experts would agree that motivational factors are important precursors of human error and therefore indirectly linked to flight safety.

- Test-faking: Many test-principles utilized in selection tests are known to the applicants, so that they can prepare themselves quite carefully before they go for the real examination. This is not a negative trend in general since it shows that the applicants are willing to take own efforts for the job. However, it could become a severe problem if the quality and the amount of foreknowledge differs uncontrolled and to a greater extent among the applicants. Selection tests should not simply measure differences in preparation but the strengths of abilities that underlie the test-scores. In order to avoid unfair testing the selection department has to take care that the test-information is distributed equally among the applicants. This can be achieved for example by changing the test-principles from time to time or by systematically providing official test-training booklets to all applicants. In case of test repetition the time interval between test and retest should be long enough to minimize memory-effects. Also empirically based correction formulas for the retest-scores should be used.

- Computer-based assessment (CBA): Rapid developments in the power of personal computers and their software have made them extremely useful tools in selection. The appeal and the face-validity of CBA is very high for the applicants and for the customers as well. As Hunter & Burke (1995, p 44) pointed out: 'The obvious strength of CBA combined with models of cognitive psychology is to move towards more fluid, dynamic, and perhaps more validatable measures of cognitive abilities'. Tests can be presented with dynamic item-material (e.g. for spatial orientation), the difficulty level can be continuously tailored to the candidates performance, reaction or decision times can be measured during an applicants problem solution process, and manual control devices (e.g. joysticks) can be added to the periphery for psychomotor testing. The scope of potential benefits from CBA is immense and by far not limited to the test administration itself. It reaches from automatic item generation, via online data-scoring to computer-guided decision making and so on. The variety of possibilities is so large that a proper balance between the application of traditional validated methods and a new generation of partly experimental assessment methods has to be found. If we do not want to end up with a couple of highly sophisticated and expensive computer games then further efforts must be taken to transfer proven psychodiagnostic concepts as a basis for a new form of aptitude testing.

- Intensified personality research: There is little doubt that job proficiency as a pilot or as a controller is not only a function of abilities, but also of motivation and temperament. However, the question is, why selection still does not go far beyond the measurement of cognitive abilities? As we have described in the chapter 6 on pilot selection, problems with the employees are more often related to personality and interpersonal behaviour than to pure abilities. Research is urgently needed here to improve the quality of personality testing in selection. It is not only the individual personality per se that should count in selection but also the interpersonal effectiveness and the benefits a team can get from the characteristic contributions of the individual.

References

Aamodt, M.G. & Peggans, D. (1988). Tactfully rejecting job applicants. *Personnel Administrator, 33*, 58-60.

Ackerman, P. L. (1987). Individual Differences in Skill Learning: An Integration of Psychometric and Information Processing Perspectives. *Psychological Bulletin, 102*, 3-27.

Ackerman, P. L. (1988). Determinants of Individual Differences during Skill Acquisition: Cognitive Abilities and Information Processing. *Journal of Experimental Psychology: General, 1117*, 288-318.

Ackerman, P. L. (1992). Abilities and Individual Differences in Complex Skill Acquisition. *Proceedings of the 36th annual meeting of the Human Factors Society*, 921-925.

Ackerman, P. L. & Schneider, W. (1985). Individual Differences in Automatic and Controlled Information Processing. In R. F. Dillon (Ed.), *Individual Differences in Cognition* (Vol. 2, pp. 35-66). Academic Press.

Anderson, J. R. (1982). Acquisition of Cognitive Skill. *Psychological Review, 89.* 369-406.

Bartram, D. & Baxter, P. (1996). Validation of the Cathay Pacific Airways pilot selection program. *The International Journal of Aviation Psychology, 6*, 149-169.

Besco, R.O. (1995). The potential contributions and scientific responsibilities of aviation psychologists. In N. Johnston, R. Fuller & N. McDonald (Eds.). *Aviation Psychology: Training and Selection* (pp. 141-148). Aldershot, United Kingdom: Avebury.

Brehmer, B. (1996). Issues in the selection of air traffic controller candidates. *Recruitment, selection and training of air traffic controller students, 24.*

Chidester, T., Helmreich, R., Gregorich, S. & Geis, C. (1991). Pilot personality and crew coordination: Implications for training and selection. *The International Journal of Aviation Psychology, 1*, 25-44.

Cattell, R.B. (1965). *The scientific analysis of personality.* Penguin, Hammondsworth,Middlesex.

Deuchert, I. (1996). Controller Selection. *Paper presented at the ATC Training and Simulation Conference Langen 29-31 October 1996.*

Cook, M. (1988). *Personnel selection and productivity.* New York: John Wiley & Sons.

Costa, P.T. & McCrae, R.R. (1989). *The NEO-PI/NEO-FFI manual supplement.* Odessa, Fla: Psychol. Asses. Res.

Cronbach, J.A. (1970). *Essentials of psychological testing* (3rd ed). New York: Harper & Row.

Dunlap, J.H. & Pettitt, M.A. (1995). A comparison of personality characteristics for freshman entering a university professional pilot program with third-year students and airline pilots. In N. McDonald, N. Johnston & R. Fuller (Eds.). *Applications of Psychology to the Aviation System* (pp. 315-320). Aldershot, United Kingdom: Avebury.

Eißfeldt, H. (1995a). Dynamic Assessment of vocational aptitudes in Air Traffic Control. *European Journal of psychological Assessment*, 11, Supplement No.1, p. 82-83.

Eißfeldt, H. (1995b). The Dynamic Air Traffic Control Test (DAC). In N. Johnston, R. Fuller & N. McDonald (Eds.), *Aviation Psychology: Training and Selection. Proceedings of the 21st Conference of the European Association for Aviation Psychology (EAAP)* (Vol. 2, pp. 130-136). Cambridge: Avebury Aviation.

Eißfeldt, H. (1997). Ability requirements for different ATC positions. Paper presented at the *Ninth International Symposium on Aviation Psychology* (April 27-May 1, 1997), Columbus, Ohio.

EUROCONTROL (1996). *Guidelines for Selection Procedures and Tests for Ab-Initio Trainee Controllers. HUM.ET1.ST04.10000-GUI-01.*

Flanagan, J. C. (1954). The Critical Incident Technique. *Psychological Bulletin*, 51, 327-58.

Fleishman, E. A (1992). *The Fleishman Job Analysis Survey (F-JAS)*. Palo Alto:Consulting Psychologists Press, Inc.

Fleishman, E. A. & Reilly, M. E. (1992). *Handbook of Human Abilities. Definitions, Measurements, and Job Task Requirements..* Palo Alto: Consulting Psychologists Press, Inc..

Goeters, K.-M., Timmermann, B. & Maschke, P. (1993). The construction of personality questionnaires for selection of aviation personnel. *The International Journal of Aviation Psychology*, 3, 123-141.

Goeters, K.-M. (1995a). Personalauswahl. In K. Steininger, S. Fichtbauer & K.-M. Goeters (Eds.) *Personalentwicklung für komplexe Mensch-Maschine-Systeme.* Weinheim, Psychologische Verlagsunion.

Goeters, K.-M. (1995b). Psychological evaluation of pilots: The present regulations and arguments for their application. In N. Johnston, R. Fuller & N. McDonald (Eds.). *Aviation Psychology: Training and Selection* (pp. 149-156). Aldershot, United Kingdom: Avebury.

Goeters, K.M., Hörmann, H.J., & Maschke, P. (1989). The DLR test system for ab-initio pilot selection. *Proceedings of the 5th International Symposium on Aviation Psychology*, Columbus, Ohio: OSU.

Greuter, M. A. & Algera, J. A., (1989). Criterion Development and Job Analysis, in: Herriot, P. *Assessment and Selection in Organisations*, John Wiley, ISBN 0471916404.

Haglund, R., Backman, B. & Brehmer, B. (1996). A review of new interimistic selection procedures concerning applicants for air traffic controller training and training of On-the-Job-Training instructors. *Recruitment, selection and training of air traffic controller students, 20.*

Helmreich, R.L., Sawin, L.L. & Carsrud, A. (1986). The honeymoon effect in job performance: Temporal increases in the predictive power of achievement motivation. *Journal of Applied Psychology, 71*, 185-188.

Helmreich, R.L. (1984). Cockpit management attitudes. *Human Factors* 26, 583-589.

Hörmann, H.-J., Manzey, D., Maschke, P. & Pecena, Y. (1997).

Behaviour-orientated assessment of interpersonal skills in pilot selection: Concepts, methods, and empirical findings. In R.S. Jensen & Rakovan, L. (Eds.), *Proceedings of the Ninth International Symposium on Aviation Psychology*. Columbus: The Ohio State University.

Hörmann, H.-J. & Maschke, P. (1987). *Bewährungskontrolle eines eignungsdiagnostischen Auswahlverfahrens für angehende Verkehrsflugzeugführer* [A validity study of a selection procedure for student airline pilots]. DLR Research Report no. DFVLR-FB-87-34. Hamburg, DLR.

Hörmann, H.-J. & Maschke, P. (1993). Personality scales as predictors of job success of airline pilots. In R.S. Jensen (Ed.), *Proceedings of the Seventh International Symposium on Aviation Psychology* (pp. 450-454). Columbus: The Ohio State University.

Hörmann, H.-J. & Maschke, P. (1996). On the relation between personality and job performance of airline pilots. *The International Journal of Aviation Psychology, 6*, 171-178.

Hopkin, V. D. (1995). *Human Factors in Air Traffic Control*. London: Taylor & Francis. Houston, R.C. (1988). Pilot personnel selection. In S.G. Cole & R.G. (Eds.), *Applications of interactionist psychology: Essays in honor of Saul B. Sells*. Hillsdale, NJ: Lawrence Erlbaum.

Landy, F.J., Shankster, L.J. & Kohler, S.S. (1994). Personnel selection and placement. *Annual Review of Psychology, 45*, 261-296.

Lindsay, G. (1996). Psychology as an Ethical Discipline and Profession, European Psychologist 1, 79 - 88.

Maschke, P. (1987). Temperament Structure Scales (TSS). Technical Report ESA-TT-1069.

Maschke, P., & Hörmann, H.J. (1988). Zur Bewährung psychologischer Auswahlverfahren für operationelle Berufe in der Luft- und Raumfahrt. Zeitschrift für Flugwissenschaften und Weltraumforschung 12, 181-186.

Maschke, P., & Hörmann, H.J. (1989). Vorhersage der Berufsbewährung bei lizensierten Flugzeugführern: Die Validität von fliegerischer Vorerfahrung im Vergleich zu standardisierten psychologischen Eignungstests. DLR Research Report DLR-FB 89-53.

Melton, A.W. (Ed.). *Apparatus tests* (Army Air Forces, Aviation Psychology Program, Research Report 4). Washington, DC: US Government Printing Office.

Murphy, E. (1995). JAA psychological testing of pilots: objections and alarms. In N. Johnston, R. Fuller & N. McDonald (Eds.). *Aviation Psychology: Training and Selection* (pp. 157-164). Aldershot, United Kingdom: Avebury.

Nunnally, J.C. (1978). *Psychometric theory (2nd edition)*. New York: McGraw-Hill. Ross, J.D. (1979). A current review of public sector assessment centers: Cause for concern. *Public Personnel Management, 8*, 41-46.

Schuler, H. & Stehle, W. (1985). Soziale Validität eignungsdiagnostischer Verfahren: Anforderungen für die Zukunft [Social validity of selection methods: Future requirements]. In H. Schuler & W. Stehle (Eds.), *Organisatinospsychologie und Unternehmenspraxis. Perspektiven der Kooperation* (pp. 133-138).

Göttingen: Verlag für Angewandte Psychologie / Hogrefe.

Seamster, T. L., Redding, R. E. Cannon, J. R., Ryder, J. M. & Purcell, J. A. (1993). Cognitive Task Analysis of Expertise in Air Traffic Control. *The International Journal of Aviation Psychology*, *3*, 257-283.

Shiffrin, R. M. & Schneider, W. (1977). Controlled and automatic human information processing: II. Perceptual learning, automatic attending, and a general theory. *Psychological Review*, *84*, 127-190.

Stahlberg, G., & Hörmann, H.J. (1993). *International application of the DLR test system: Validation of the pilot selection for IBERIA*. DLR Research Report DLR-FB 93- 42.

Stead, G. (1991). A validation study of the Quantas pilot selection process. In E. Farmer (Ed.), *Human resource management in aviation*. Proceedings of 18th WEAAP conference. Aldershot, Avebury Technical.

Trites, D. K. (1961). *Problems in air traffic management: Longitudinal prediction of effectiveness of air traffic controllers.* (Vol. 61-1). Oklahoma City: FAA.

Thorndike, R.L. (1949). *Personnel selection*. New York: Wiley.

Wing, H. (1991). Selecting for Air Traffic Control: The State of the Art. In J. A. Wise, V. D. Hopkin & M. L. Smith (Eds.), *Automation and System Issues in Air Traffic Control* (pp. 409-427). Berlin: Springer Verlag.

Section 3

Training

Course Manager &
Section Editor:

André Droog

14   Introduction

André Droog
Human Factors Department, KLM Flight Academy, The Netherlands

In 1930 Francis Chichester flew solo from London to Sydney in his Tiger Moth. Before that, he planned a trip round Europe for the purpose of some navigation practice. As he still owed some money on his plane, he felt he could not leave England unless it were insured. '..some countries are regarded as a bad insurance risk, furthermore my aeronautical status was that of a mug pilot'. He found Captain Lamplugh willing to underwrite the risk '..provided I took with me Joe King, an experienced 'B' License Pilot who had done a lot of aerial survey work in Bolivia'. From the word 'go' on October 25th that trip around Europe was 'great sport'.

> *'Let her go,'* says Joe King, pushing the throttle full open. He being an experienced pilot, I assumed he wished to take the plane himself, so I dropped the controls altogether. We seemed a long time leaving the ground and then only just cleared the trees on St. George's Hill by a foot or two. However, I didn't bother, as that was in keeping with Joe's style. 'Hey!' roared a voice through the telephone, 'what on earth are you doing?' 'Doing,' I said indignantly, 'why, I'm not touching any of the controls.' 'Nor am I,' says he.

After full throttle (by the Pilot Not Flying!) the plane took off all by itself. Flying together with an experienced pilot for extra safety turned out to be not safe at all. In this case, errors like the ones illustrated above (no co-ordination, no clear statement of who would be flying the aircraft, no verification of (false) assumptions, maybe even over-courteousness towards an 'ace') were the result of Chichester's changed situation: he was no longer single in the cockpit. Chichester, after a minimum of flight instruction, took his license and endlessly practised his flight techniques (especially all kinds of landings) as preparation for his long and hazardous trip. But his plane and plan nearly crashed as soon as he was backed up by a second person. The simple complexity of flying together requires a different behaviour pattern.

One wonders if Chichester still would have thought of the trip as 'great sport' if they had actually hit the trees. Had they arranged for some rules of co-ordination and practised these, the near miss could certainly have been avoided. Now this we have learned: Standard Operating Procedure for all kinds of situations and tasks have been trained and practised for many years by now. And as we know that most often the human factor is decisive in piloting activity, we also introduced Crew Resource Management training, to control for this factor. After several 'CRM-generations' (Helmreich, 1996) we even are at the point that 'human factors training' is going to be prescribed by European regulation and law.

This part of the book is about training, in particular about training of aircrew in the domain of Human Factors. It aims to layout general principles of training for those who want to become skilled as trainer in the field of aviation. We will consider training to be:

the systematic development of the attitude/knowledge/skill behaviour pattern required by an individual in order to perform adequately a given task or job.

Training activity takes place in all kinds of contexts, be it occupation, leisure time or game. Here, of course, we concentrate on the occupational context of aviation, which in itself hosts a wide variety of subcontexts and of jobs and tasks.

Table 1   Aviation contexts of training

- *jobs*, for example: atc controllers - cockpit crew - cabin crew - designers - ground crew - investigators - maintenance crew - managers - researchers - regulators - etc.

- *subcontexts*, for example: civil aviation - military aviation (airforce, navy, army) - general aviation -

- *cultural contexts*, for example: organisation - country

For a better understanding of the activity of training, it helps if we are aware that training is not the only solution to the problem of performing tasks and jobs. If a task poses a problem to a performer, we actually have three potential solutions:
1. to *select* the people who through their aptitudes, abilities or previous training can deal with the particular task demands;
2. to *train* people to deal with these demands;
3. to *design*, or redesign, the job situation in order to *reduce* the task demands. (Stammers & Patrick, 1975)

Training, therefore, should be seen as being part of a process or system which also includes design and selection. The triad of design, selection and training must ensure effectiveness of job behaviour.

Given a certain design of job situation and given well-selected trainees, we need (like psychologists occupied with selection) an exhaustive and concise task- or job description in order to be able to design training for the given tasks. From such a description we can derive training objectives. However, although this may sound very logical and sensible, the making of a good job description and the extraction definition of training objectives is a difficult task. The problem lies in defining the objectives in terms of behaviour that can be trained and assessed, the latter with view to evaluation of performance.

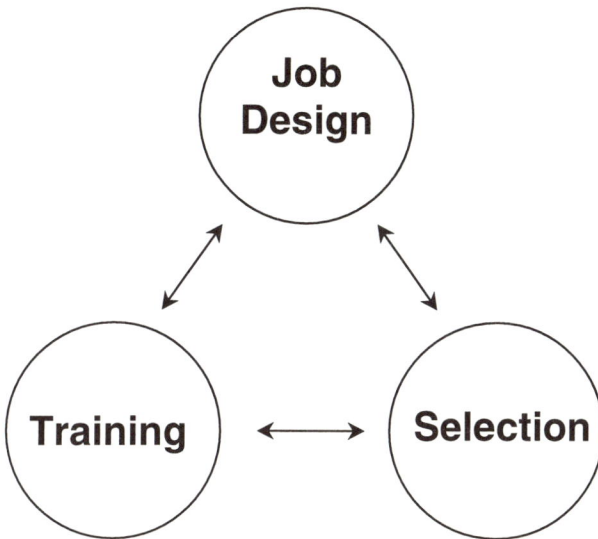

Figure 1   Design, selection and training are interdependent

The definition of training objectives is the first step in the development of a particular training programme. From this we develop criterion measures which, after training, will indicate whether someone has obtained the objectives,. Deriving the training content (what should be trained?) is the second step. The next stage involves the devising of training methods and equipment to present to the trainees. Trainees and material come together in the training programme, at the end of which the trainee's performance is measured against the criterion measures.

The underlying chapters on training of aircrew cover the stages of the process outlined in Figure 2. However, before directing our attention to the specific elements of the training system, there is a chapter on the regulation of 'Human Factors Training' in Europe. In due time, knowledge of human factors issues and the training of 'Non-Technical'- or 'Crew Resource Management'-skills will be a mandatory part of the pilot's licensing process and of his training during his professional career. This chapter, called 'JAR-FCL and JAR-OPS', informs the reader about the coming regulation in Europe and serves to give him an overall picture of how training programmes for human factors issues may look like.

After the chapter on JAR-FCL and JAR-OPS we will address some specific training system issues: pilot skills and attitudes (content of training); the trainee;

134 *Aviation Psychology: A Science and a Profession*

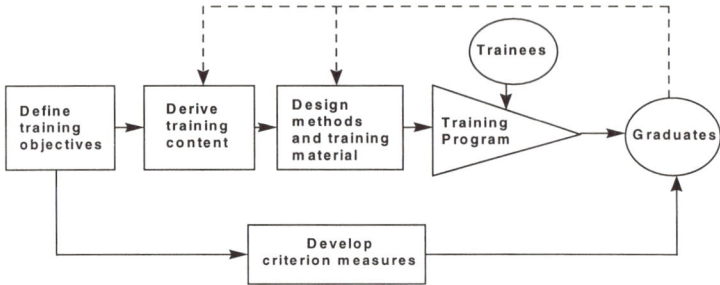

Figure 2   Training system

integration of CRM in pilot training (training programme philosophy). The success of a training programme not only depends on the content of the programme and the training materials used. There is strong evidence that the person and skills of the trainer or facilitator of the learning process are a very influential factor in the result of any training. Therefore, attention is given to the necessary qualifications of the human factors trainer or facilitator in the chapter on development of skills and attitudes (Chapter 2). After these chapters, human factors training for ab initio pilots will be highlighted (training programme).

Much has been written about CRM, but the hot topic is the effectiveness of CRM-training. Can it be measured? Can it be proven? And how? These questions will be addressed in a chapter on evaluation of training programmes. Also the role of the management of the organisation in success of CRM-training will be addressed.

At the end of a training programme we measure or assess the performance of the trainee against the developed criterion standards. Flying skills have been assessed from the beginning of aviation, but the task of flying an airplane has dramatically changed over the years. Indeed from 'flying the airplane' to 'managing the flight'. How to assess the levels of the skills involved in managing the flight? This is also a hot topic, as we are now entering the relatively new domain of assessing the so called 'non-technical skills' (although, as we will see, this term will not do any longer when CRM will be fully integrated with in flight training). The participants of the EAAP Conference of 1996 in Sabaudia, Italy, will find the results of the working groups in all these chapters.

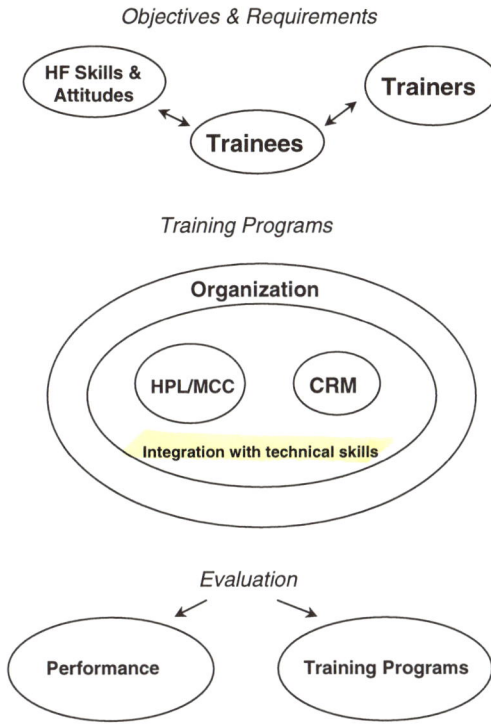

Figure 3   Human factors training overall picture

15   JAR-FCL and JAR-OPS

Werner Naef
Human Aspects Development, Switzerland

An introduction into future European aviation regulations influencing 'Human Factors' training topics

Since 1970 European civil aviation has been increasingly coordinated by a number of then still loosely cooperating individual European national state civil aviation authorities. Step by step the initially loose cooperation turned into a more solid regulatory network and 1974 the first regulations under this new regulatory structure have been published concerning construction of new airplanes. 1983 the first aircraft certification according to these new European regulations took place.

The process of harmonization of European regulations continued steadily and starting in 1998 European aviation will have a pan-European regulatory structure ruling on all aspects of civil aviation operations. Under the umbrella of JAA (Joint aviation authorities) and within the structure of the new JAR (Joint aviation requirements) all aspects of civil aviation will be dealt with on this supra-national regulatory level. Memberstates will have to comply with all the requirements and a specific quality system will make sure that the standards will be met as required.

Starting in 1999 also all training aspects of civil aviation personnel will be under strict JAA rules. Finally this regulatory structure will be divided into a part JAR-FCL (Joint aviation requirements Flight crew licensing) and a part JAR-OPS (Joint aviation requirements Operations). JAR-FCL will regulate everything that has to do with any licensing at any stage of a flight crew member. JAR-OPS will regulate everything that has to do with the operation of aircraft, including e.g. training and recurrent training of crew members.

Both, JAR-FCL and JAR-OPS will furthermore be specified into requirements and regulations that apply for e.g. airplanes or helicopters, for commercial airtransport, agricultural flying, helicopter operations etc. Each field will have its own published set of requirements.

Generally JAR-FCL as well as JAR-OPS are structured into 'Section 1' and 'Section 2'. The first section will always state the requirements, 'what' has to be

137

done, and the second section will always describe the 'Acceptable Means of Compliance' including interpretative and explanatory material - in other words: 'how' the requirements should be met.

'Human factors' as a topic in general will be included in JAR-FCL and JAR-OPS in several aspects: Under the heading 'Human Performance and Limitations' in the JAR-FCL as a basic introduction into 'Human Factors' influencing flying solo and/or in a crew, under the heading 'CRM' (Crew Resource Management) in the JAR-OPS as dealing with Human Factors issues that are being introduced, trained, applied and assessed during a crew member's career.

JAR-FCL

Structure of 'Human Factors' issues within JAR-FCL

The huge amount of information/regulations within the JAR-FCL is being structured into a numbered paragraph system. 'Human Factors' are dealt with under the heading 'Human Performance and Limitations' (HPL) as follows:

040 00 00 00　Human Performance and Limitations
040 01 00 00　Human Factors: Basic Concepts
040 02 00 00　Basic Aviation Physiology and Health Maintenance
040 03 00 00　Basic Aviation Psychology

Whereas the first and second paragraphs are rather general headings, the third and fourth paragraphs are full of relevant issues. 040 02 deals with medical requirements and 040 03 finally deals with 'Human Factors' in the sense of 'Human Behaviour'. This 040 03 00 00 chapter has to be of special interest for training institutions since it will regulate all psychological / human factors / behavioural training of future flight crew in Europe.

The goals

Considering goals within the frame of 'Human Factors training' it must be said that such training will mostly focus on behavioural training efforts. Therefore goals have to be addressed on three different levels as shown below. It can be said, that on each goal level, the participants of such training under JAR-FCL should:

- whilst aiming at cognitive goals: learn, comprehend and get competent to explain the major influencial factors in human mental performance, limitations and interrelations,
- whilst aiming at affective goals: get concerned and identify with the issue at hand - become owner of the issue,
- and whilst aiming at psychosocial goals: modify behaviour in order to improve flight safety, customer service and the well-being of all team-members involved.

The topics

Table 1

The topics within '***Basic aviation psychology***', that are of our special interest, are these:

• 040 03 01 00	:	Human information processing
• 040 03 02 00	:	Human error and reliability
• 040 03 03 00	:	Decision making
• 040 03 04 00	:	Avoiding and managing errors: Cockpit management
• 040 03 05 00	:	Personality
• 040 03 06 00	:	Human overload and underload
• 040 03 07 00	:	Advanced cockpit automation
• 040 03 08 00	:	Company matters.

These topics then are divided into subtitles; details can be seen in the JAR-FCL documentation that is available from your national civil aviation authority.

As an example, the subtitles of 040 03 07 00 : 'Advanced cockpit automation' are shown here:

040 03 07 01 :   Advantages and disadvantages
040 03 07 02 :   Automation complacency
040 03 07 03 :   Working concepts.

That's the JAR-FCL so far. The rest, means the buildup of a real training program that takes these topics and subtopics into consideration, is now up to the industry! The individual training goals, the program, the syllabus, the methodology, the didactics, the evaluation - all this has to be developed by training developers, human factors specialists, psychologists and training managers.

Also the 'train-the-trainer' courses for future HPL-facilitators have to be designed by the industry. It finally just has to comply with all the topics put into the regulation by JAA!

Since we are now having the overall goals by methodological experience and the topics by JAA, the next questions are: 'how to implement this, by what means, when and by whom?'

The first steps will most probably be to design training modules that focus on one specific issue each. To give an example how such a modular HPL-system could look like, being arranged strictly according to the hierarchy of the JAA topics, I may present here the beginning part of the Swissair HPL-program as it has been in use now for the last two years.

The list shows the JAR-FCL paragraph on the left, the respective paragraph title in the second row, the JAA subtitles in the third column and to the far right you find the HPL training modules that have been designed to cover this specific topic during HPL training. Such a training module can consist of several steps, a multi-lesson package or just one single individual video with groupwork. This depends largely on the specific topic; its contents, impact and relevance. This list, which in reality is much longer since all 8 topics have to be covered (on this one list here, there are only the first three topics shown as examples), can contain several modules per topic. Under 040 03 04 00 'Avoiding and managing errors; cockpit management', for example, there are 9 training modules to cover this important issue. This list of course has nothing to do yet with training syllabus; it just shows the JAR-FCL paragraphs plus how many training modules have been designed to meet the relative importance of the topic. The next task after completing the list will then be to arrange these modules into a systematic build-up of such knowledge and know-how during the basic pilot training from ab initio up to the ATPL stage, including the MCC phase.

Criteria for implementing HPL modules into basic training

The modules shown in the table above have to be implemented in an appropriate way into the training syllabus of pilot training. Principles of adult learning have to be considered as much as the relative relevance of specific training modules to practical training issues.

For example: It does not make any sense to position an HPL training module dealing with 'Risk' into any theoretical part of pilot training. Such a topic has to be brought in at the time, when the trainee starts to fly solo for example.

In this context there are some criteria that have to be considered when implementing HPL training into basic pilot training as follows:

- spread the HPL program over the whole period of the basic training; it must by all means become a regular topic being applied as a recurrent issue and not as a 'one-time-flight-safety-shot'.
- topics of a specific HPL training module have to correspond with specific Human Factors issues and Human Factors needs at that stage of pilot training
- HPL should be covered within a total of some 70 hrs of instruction
- the availability of adequately qualified HPL-trainers must be assured
- all three levels of goals (as indicated above) have to be addressed in each training module
- proper evaluation technique and adequate measures should ensure optimal acceptance of such training; this is the first and very important goal to be achieved by the training managers.

Table 2   Structure of JAR-FCL 1, Section 2, Subpart J

Paragraph number	Paragraph title	Subtitles	Swissair Module
040 00 00 00	HUMAN PERFORMANCE AND LIMITATIONS		
040 01 00 00	Human Factors: basic concepts		
040 02 00 00	Basic aviation physiology and health maintenace		
040 03 00 00	BASIC AVIATION PSYCHOLOGY		
040 03 01 00	Human information processing	01 01 Attention and vigilance	
		01 02 Perception	01 02 S01 Perception basics
		01 03 Memory	01 03 S01 F. Vester
		01 04 Response selection	01 04 S01 Learning Strategy 01 04 S02 Dealing with critique
040 03 02 00	Human error and reliability	02 01 Reliability of human behaviour	02 01 S01 Filters of Perception
		02 02 Hypotheses on reality	02 02 S01 How real is reality?
		02 03 Theory/model of huuman error	
		02 04 Error generation (2 case studies)	02 04 S01 'Stadlerberg' accident 02 04 S02 'Riahd'
040 03 03 00	Decision making	03 01 Decision making concepts	03 01 S01 Hierarchy 03 01 S02 Risk-Management 03 01 S03 CMN-ZRH case study 03 01 S04 Judgement and Decision making

An example of combination and implementation of specific topics into one single HPL training day, according to the specific situation of training at this stage

This example will deal with *Day 2* of the whole 9 days HPL program. This *Day 2* is situated in the flight training phase where the student has just begun to fly solo. These criteria are of importance during this critical pilot training phase:

- Low flying experience, but just flying solo.
- Student has to cope with an instructor and therefore with gradings, qualification, assessment and critique.
- The student flying solo has also to cope with another student on board flying as an observer. The student therefore has to cope with attitude and with behaviour.
- The student has to cope with autonomously learning on the job and with risk management.

Therefore, this 2nd HPL course day should focus on:

1. Basic attitude,
2. choosing behaviour,
3. chain of events,
4. critique and qualifications,
5. risk management, and
6. learning strategy.

Table 3   Such a Day 2 could look like this

Time	Duration	Sequ Nr.	Topic	JAR-FCL HPL Swissair module nr.
08.30	15'	2/1	Bang, Welcome and Recap	
08.45	55'	2/2	**Individual differences in personality**: Basic Attitudes	**040 03 05 02 S03**
09.40	30'		Coffee Break	
10.10	60'	2/3	**Personality and Attitudes**: Choosing Behaviour Video 'If looks could kill' (28')	**040 03 05 01 S01**
11.10	10'		Break	
11.20	50'	2/4	**Safety awareness**: Chain of Events	**040 03 04 01 S01**
12.10	20'		Break	
12.30	90'		Lunch	
14.00	60'	2/5	**Response selection**: Dealing with critique and	**040 03 01 04 S02**

Time	Duration	Sequ Nr.	Topic	JAR-FCL HPL Swissair module nr.
			qualifications	
15.00	10'		Break	
15.10	60'	2/6	**Decision making concepts**: Risk Management Video 'Risk' (35')	**040 03 03 01** S02
16.10	15'		Coffeebreak	
16.25	35'	2/7	**Response selection**: Learning strategy	**040 03 01 04** S01
17.00			Closure of the day	

An individual lesson out of 'Day 2'

Let us now concentrate on one specific topic item like '040 03 04 01', Safety awareness, topic *'chain of events'* and its structure as a lesson.
This lesson should be planned including at least these generic, methodological items:
- Lesson topic and contents
- Lesson goal
- Method of instruction
- Social form, and
- Teaching aids:
Such might therefore look a syllabus of one specific lesson before going into the detailed lesson buildup step by step:

Table 4

Time	Min.	Topic/Content	Goal	Method	Social form	Teaching aids
17.40	30	'Chain of Events' Role of feelings and emotions in my own warning system Role of awareness in my own warning system Breaking up the chain of events: - by assertiveness - by selfesteem - by communication	Analyze the chain of events, emphasize the 'internal law' Cite the role of subjective elements like: feelings/emotions/awareness influencing my own warning system	Teaching	Plenum	OHP: - Chain of Events

Time	Min.	Topic/Content	Goal	Method	Social form	Teaching aids
		- by taking a decision				

JAR-OPS 1

Structure of 'Human Factors' issues within JAR-OPS 1

'CRM is the effective utilisation of all available resources (e.g. crew members, aeroplane systems, and supporting facilities) to achieve safe and efficient operation' (JAR-OPS 1, IEM OPS 1.945, p. 2-N-4).

As in JAR-FCL requirements and means to comply with these regulations are being structured into an equal system of numbered paragraphs. 'Human Factors' are dealt with under the heading of 'CRM'. In the JAR-OPS 1 several sorts of CRM can be found:

- Recurrent CRM
- Transition CRM
- Command CRM, and
- Joint CRM, including cabin crew.

In order to get CRM started as a new cluster of training contents, goals and methods the industry applied a very practical mode of CRM: 'Introductory CRM' which combines topics, methods and goals of both the future HPL and CRM together.

Some operators (airlines, airforces, ATC and others) have introduced a condensed CRM course of one to more days duration, covering the most important issues in HPL training plus transferring this directly into a daily operation context, thus reaching 'CRM' status.

Other operators have introduced a multi-modular system of Human Factors training, including a series of recurrent CRM courses covering one specific topic in depth in each course.

All operators have recognized the importance of introducing 'on the job' Human Factors training during e.g. simulator training. Some, including some national authorities went even to the point of assessing Human Factors-related performance of crew members.

The objective of CRM

Is clearly defined in JAR-OPS 1, Subpart N (Flight Crew), section 2, para IEM OPS 1.945(a)....:

'The objective of CRM is to enhance the communication and management skills of the flight crew member concerned. The emphasis is placed on the non-technical aspects of flight crew performance'.

Together with the statement about what 'CRM' means (see at top of para 2.1 of this paper) it becomes quite clear that CRM cannot be something isolated just within one single professional group. CRM is much more overlapping and combining forces and interactions between different professional groups. Therefore 'Joint Training in CRM' will be seen combining flight crew and cabin crew, ATC and maintenance workforce.

JAR-OPS 1 makes already clear statements in this context referring to 'combined training for flight crew and cabin crew' (p. 2-N-4).

The topics

According to the JAR-OPS 1 CRM training should include:
- Statistics and examples of Human Factor related accidents,
- Human perception, learning process,
- Situational awareness,
- Management of workload, tiredness or fatigue, and vigilance - management of stress,
- Operator's Standard Operating Procedures,
- Personality type, delegation, leadership, effective communication skills,
- *The CRM loop (notion of synergy)*
  - *Inquiry (or explore, examine, scrutinise)*
  - *Advocacy (support a cause; present a view)*
  - *Conflict resolution*
  - *Decision making*
  - *Critique*
  - *Feedback.*
- Effective communication and co-ordination within the flight crew, and between crew members and other operational personnel (ATC, maintenance personnel etc)
- Error chain and taking actions to break the error chain; and
- Implications of automation on CRM.

Training Modules

The characteristics of such training modules depend very much on the mode of training that has been chosen by the operator. One single CRM course followed by purely Simulator-related Human Factors training looks very different from a system that builds on dedicated recurrent CRM training modules. Therefore a general layout cannot be presented in this area. CRM will develop during the next years and different forms of implementation of CRM will be observed.

Examples of implementation on CRM

Swissair followed the path of recurrent CRM with each crewmember passing a two-day CRM seminar every two years. The topics of these seminars have been:

1993/94	:	Communication
1995/96	:	Conflict - Task and Chance
1997/98	:	Decision making
		Joint CRM with Pursers: Behaviour in Emergencies

Other airlines have built up CRM programs of e.g. three days covering the major topics all at once.

CRM facilitator training

In all JARs it is stated that Human Factors Issues have to be instructed by 'specifically qualified personnel'. However it does in no way say what exactly this means.

In the near future EAAP should take the initiative to forward proposals of such appropriate CRM facilitator training. In close cooperation with JAA it should be defined what exactly the requirements are to handle HPL and / or CRM issues and how the initial training and recurrent training of such specialised trainers / facilitators should look like.

Conclusion

JAR-FCL and JAR-OPS offer a great opportunity to bring Human Factors training onto a professional and appropriate platform. It bears the great potential for not only increased flight safety, but better service to the customer through improved well-being by better communication and teamwork. However a close coordination between professionals like psychologists, human factors specialists, training designers on the one side and the users like crewmembers, unions and companies on the other side is of utmost importance when it comes to the implementation, to the assessment and to quality assurance of and within Human Factors training.

A great chance for quality growth!

16 Developing the pilot's skills and attitudes

André Droog
Human Factors Department, KLM Flight Academy, The Netherlands

Introduction

We have defined training as: the systematic development of the attitude / knowledge / skill behaviour pattern required by an individual in order to perform adequately a given task or job. How can we describe the pilot's job? What skills should be trained in pilot training? What are the required attitudes? To what extent can these be trained, changed or shaped, and how? And who should be the trainer? This chapter will deal with these questions and also review some basic definitions.

Job description and training objectives

A job consists of all the tasks carried out by a particular person in the completion of his prescribed duties. We can conclude from this, that the job of the pilot (or any other job of aviation personnel) can, at least to a certain degree, be described by summarising and describing all tasks he has to perform. (A task is a major element of work or a combination of elements of work by means of which a specific result is achieved). However, there are numerous tasks to perform and the task of describing the job may seem endless. Some structuring should take place, so that a taskstructure emerges.

An example of this comes from Mintzberg. He was unsatisfied with the vagueness of job descriptions which were written in terms of duties and responsibilities. Therefore he observed managers of different organisations, environments and organisational levels performing their jobs during a certain period of time and registered all they actually did. Thereafter he grouped the tasks into what he called 10 general managerial roles, and thus clarified the nature and structure of managerial work (Mintzberg, 1973, see Table 1).

Table 1   Mintzberg's managerial roles

Role	Content of role
Communication roles	
monitor	Monitors the activities of his unit and its environment. Detects problems, risks and chances.
disseminator	Sends information (facts, preferences, values) to the people within his unit
spokesman	Sends information (results, explanations) to people outside his own unit e.g. higher management or the public
Decision making roles	
resource allocator	Allocates time, people, and money to tasks. Sets priorities, aligns and times decisions (=co-ordination), pays attention to people etc.
disturbance handler	Diagnoses situations and threatening stimuli (internal conflicts, environmental threat, expected loss of resources). Solves problems and takes measures.
Leadership / Relational roles	
leader (his most important role)	Integrates his unit's objectives and the personal needs of his people. The leader's core activities are: keeping his people alert and motivate them.
figure head	Because of his formal status he is seen as a symbol representing his organisation.
liaison	Gathers useful information from outside his unit by means of his network of contacts.
negotiator	Negotiates with other units or organisations
entrepreneur	Initiates and designs change; sets goals.

The manager's job and style will vary as to the level of his position in the organisation, the kind of organisation and the kind of environment (e.g. stable, dynamic, crisis etc.). So, when describing a job, we should also describe the essentials of the organisation and of the environment.

Another very important element of job description is the description of the critical situations that most likely will arise for someone performing the job. Someone's effectiveness strongly depends on his behaviour in critical situations or high risk situations. The critical incident technique may help here to get the right picture of effective and not effective behaviour and the skills required for effectiveness.

Mintzberg compares the manager to the nerve centre of his unit, be it a department or a whole organisation. The use of metaphors like 'nerve centre' may clarify the content of a job a lot, for example if we have to explain someone what is expected of him.

It is quite common nowadays to speak of the pilot (especially the airline pilot or captain) as a 'manager of the flight' and a 'manager of resources'. Droog

(1986) applied the Mintzberg categories to the function of airline captain and concluded that most of the managerial roles mentioned in Table 1 apply to the airline captain's job as well, taking into account the specific unit (aircraft and crew) he leads and the environment in which he operates. The captain is teamleader, disseminator, spokesman (for example when performing the Passenger Address), decision maker (resource allocator, disturbance handler), figure head (ambassador of his airline). The captain directs his 'system' (aircraft + crew + passengers) towards its destination in a safe, efficient, comfortable and satisfying way.

What 'attitude / knowledge / skill behaviour pattern' should he develop during training? By attitude / knowledge / skill behaviour pattern we mean: the essential determinants of effective performance in terms of attitude, knowledge and skill - the attitude to perform, the knowledge required to take the right attitude and the skills to do it (see Table 2).

Table 2   Skill pattern of airline pilots (but many similarities with military pilots)

SKILL DOMAIN	SKILL	SPECIFIC SKILL
Information processing	perceptual	visual/spatial judgement
		spatial orientation
	attentional	vigilance
		multitasking
	psychomotor	psychomotor co-ordination
		reaction speed
Situational awareness	monitoring	
	error detection	
Problem solving	collect information	
	analyse information	
	logical reasoning	
	generate alternatives	
Decision making	exhaustive inquiry	
	complex judgement	
	evaluate resources	
	priority setting	
	time management	
Planning	anticipation	
Co-operation	listening	
	communication skills	
	conflict resolution	
Leadership	assertiveness	
	authority	
	task orientation	
	teambuilding	motivate
		conflict resolution
	representation	
Stress management	stress recognition	
	coping techniques	

Attitudes

We are not born with attitudes. Attitudes are acquired and learnt. Since we all have attitudes there must be some *need* to acquire them because of some function they serve. When we possess an attitude related to some object or person, although it may be subject to change, it has a fixed quality about it; it is enduring rather than temporary.

Attitudes are related to values but values and attitudes are not synonymous. Values are less specific than attitudes. Having an attitude implies the existence of some object towards one has it. This is not the case with values. Another important distinction is, that values serve as standards ('safety', 'honesty') and they also have a motivational function: values are like ideals for which we strive. Attitudes and behaviour can be seen as outcomes of value orientations.

Attitudes should also be distinguished from 'personality'. 'Personality' refers to the general principles and organisation of internal psychological functioning, while attitudes relate to objects outside the person.

In 1935 Allport defined an attitude as 'a mental and neural state of readiness, organised through experience, exerting a directive or dynamic influence upon the individual's response to all objects and situations with which it is related'. Later on attitudes were defined, for example, as '...enduring systems of positive or negative evaluations, emotional feelings, and pro or con action techniques with respect to social objects' or '.. a predisposition to experience, to be motivated by, and to act toward, a class of objects in a predictable manner'.

Modern definitions of attitude emphasise, that each attitude has an affective, cognitive and conative (that is a 'tendency to act') component. If we like someone, we *know* positive things about him or her, we feel positive towards him or her and we *tend to act* positively towards him or her as a consequence.

As research has shown, values and attitudes have strong intrapersonal consistency. Which means, that from the values we can predict the attitudes. Also, differences between individuals in value orientations are good predictors of specific attitudes.

The link of values and attitudes to behaviour is not always as consistent as that. From someone's intentional behaviour towards an object it is relatively easy to deduct what his attitude and values are towards that object. But to predict someone's specific behaviour by knowing his values and attitudes is more difficult. Why? Firstly, because there may be other motives or personal dispositions which clash with the behavioural expression of an attitude. For example, a person with the value 'honesty', verbally expressing the attitude of 'always telling the truth', may some day not tell the truth in a certain matter because he feels it to be socially unacceptable to do that, given the specific situation. The 'need for social acceptance' is the motive clashing with being honest. Secondly there may be situational factors which intervene between the value-attitude orientation and the expression through action. For example, a pilot with a very responsible attitude may one day act irresponsibly (for example by taking a risk) under conditions of fatigue.

Abelson once wrote: 'we are well trained and very good at finding reasons for what we do, but not very good at doing what we find reasons for'. Nevertheless he suggested some strategies to strengthen the attitude-behaviour link. One method he suggests is through 'encouragement cues', which increase the probability that one will express one's attitudes behaviourally. Encouragement cues may be:

1. social modelling
2. self-perception as a 'doer'

Modelling may be the most powerful of these: the 'model' (for example an instructor or facilitator) translates intention into action and thus validates the proper behaviour for the trainee, who is observing the model.

The second encouragement is by planting the idea in a person that he is the kind of person who is a 'doer'. This method can also be very effective in shaping or changing attitudes.

Another method of strengthening the attitude-behaviour relationship is by 'facilitating' the behaviour, that is by creating favourable conditions or by spelling out for the person specific forms of action (tell him exactly when, where and how to use the desired behaviour). When the person finds his new behaviour to be effective and satisfying some central need of him, the probability that he will repeat this behaviour has increased.

Attitudes should be addressed during training, but the starting point lies in addressing behaviour. If the behaviour of trainee in some stage of pilot training matches the needs of the aviation system for safe, responsible, respectful, communicative etc. behaviour (to mention some), we can reinforce this behaviour by positive feedback and reinforcements. However, if the behaviour does nót match (mismatch) the needs of the aviation system, we tell the person to behave differently, for example by describing the expected behaviour, by explaining it to him, by modelling, encouraging, facilitating, coaching and adequate feedback.

What if the behaviour persistently mismatches the requirements of the safety culture?

Argyris (1988) says that learning occurs under two conditions. First, when a person achieves what he intended to achieve. In that case there is a match between a plan for action and the real outcome. Secondly, learning occurs when there is a mismatch between intention and outcome and when this mismatch is identified and corrected: then the mismatch is turned into a match. Whenever an error or mismatch is detected and corrected without questioning the underlying values of the system (be it individual, group, or organisation), the learning is single-loop. 'Double-loop learning occurs when mismatches are corrected by first examining and altering the governing variables and then the actions. Governing variables are the preferred states that individuals strive to satisfice when they are acting. These governing variables are not the underlying beliefs or values people espouse. They are the variables that can be inferred, by observation, to drive and guide their actions' (see Figure 1).

In case of repeatedly inadequate safety attitudes or behaviour (be it the working attitude, the decision making behaviour, the leadership behaviour, the

TMA23

stress coping behaviour, the team behaviour, etc.) behavioural change and attitude change may be achieved by using this double-loop learning concept, which results in the following *intervention-strategy* (see Figure 2).

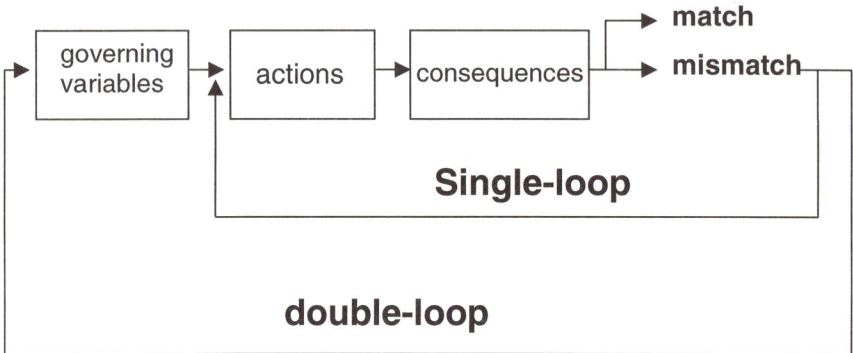

Figure 1   Single- and double-loop learning

Trainers and facilitators

Human factors trainers try to enhance the competence and effectiveness of their trainees in the human factors domain. They train skills and try to install in the trainees values and attitudes that in the end should all contribute to flight safety and the prevention of error. From research into the effectiveness of trainers there is strong evidence that the success of any training, especially when behaviour, attitudes and interpersonal skills are involved, strongly depends on the skills and personality of the trainer.

The JAR speak of 'suitably qualified HF-facilitators'. What requirements should they fulfil? It may be clear that also for trainers or facilitators there are knowledge, skill and attitude requirements. Trainers must be accepted and respected by the pilots who participate in their training courses. Essential qualities of trainers are shown in Table 3.

Under what conditions do HF-trainees learn most? Argyris (1973) identifies a number of conditions causing individuals to behave most competently. The more training courses approximate these conditions, the greater the probability that the trainees will learn and benefit from the content. The conditions are:

- *Self-acceptance*: this is the degree to which a person has confidence in himself and regards himself. The higher the self-acceptance, the more he values himself, the more he will value others.
- *Confirmation*: a person experiences confirmation when a trainer can give positive feedback. Confirmation is needed to validate one's view of one's self. The more frequent the confirmation, the greater the confidence in one's potential to behave competently.

• *Essentiality*; this means that the more the trainee is able to use his central abilities and express his central needs, the greater will be his feelings of essentiality to himself and to the training. The more essential he feels, the more committed he will tend to be to the organisation and to its effectiveness.

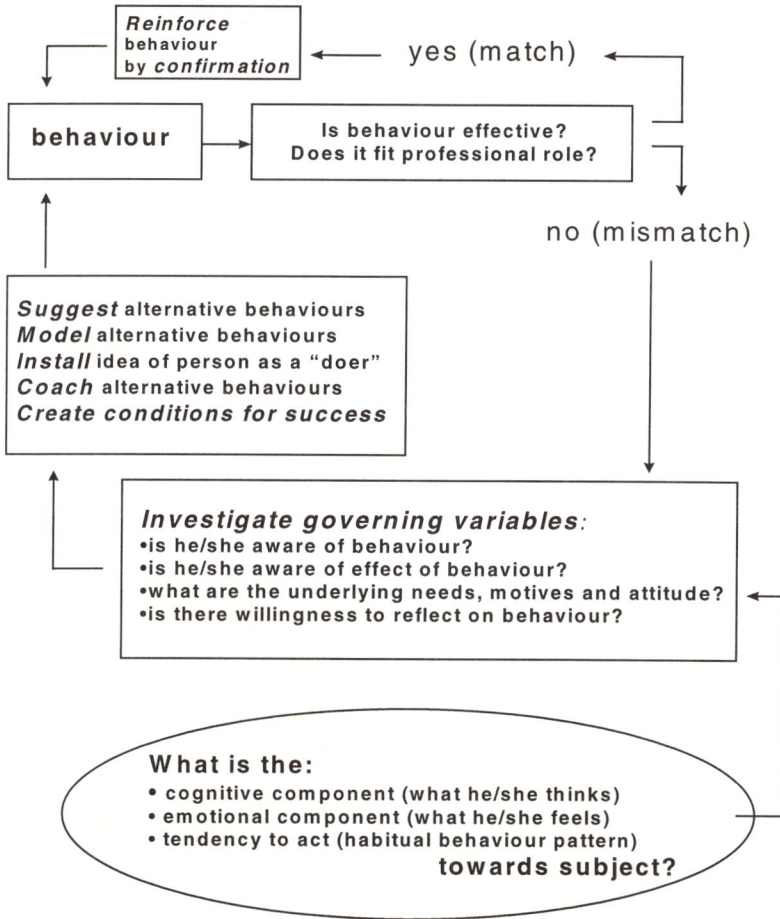

Figure 2   Intervention strategy for behavioural change

Table 3   Some of the essential qualities of the 'suitably qualified HF-trainer / facilitator'

Knowledge	Skill	Attitude	Personality
broad human factors knowledge	communication skills	listening, seeks interaction	open
familiar with aviation	presentation skills	empathetic attitude	warm, expressing feeling
familiar with language, values and norms of target group	can clarify and bring structure to unstructured brains	gives trainees responsibility	reliable & honest no manipulator
human sciences framework of understanding	empathy and flexibility towards all kinds of persons	motivation, enthusiasm	emotionally stable
	can lead groups	good relations with management	relation builder
relevant experience i.e. some flying exp.	intervention skills	positive to norms of aviation	punctual
has undergone HF and CRM training	role model for trainees	encouraging	authority

One of the most effective ways to help individuals increase their self-acceptance, confirmation, and essentiality is to create conditions for psychological success. This is the essence of the task of the trainer or facilitator (see Figure 3). Psychological success occurs when:

(a)   the individual is able to define his own goals,

(b)   these goals are related to his central needs, abilities and values,

(c)   the person defines the path to these goals, and

(d)   the achievement of the goals represents a realistic level of aspiration, which means a challenge or a risk that requires hitherto unused, untested abilities.

When working with groups, trainers can stimulate that trainees develop their potential abilities and their interpersonal competence by encouraging the following behaviours:

• being open to ideas and feelings of others and those from within themselves

• experimenting with new ideas and feelings, and helping others to do so.

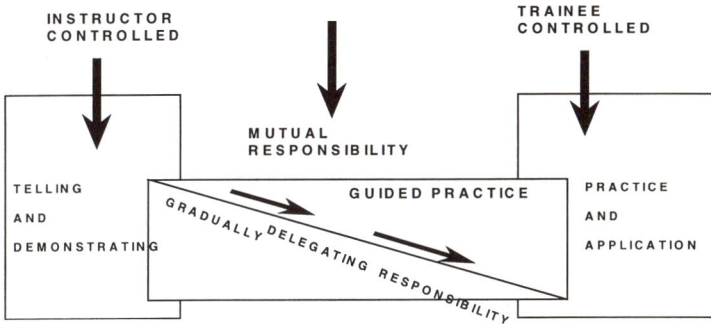

Figure 3   Changing roles of HF-facilitator and HF-trainee: developing responsibility (Pearson & Gallagher, 1983)

Conclusion

Many skills as mentioned in Table 2 can be trained, provided the person who wants to be a pilot has the potential to develop these skills. This potential will be largely determined by general intelligence, specific aptitudes, and the motivation to learn the skills. Can attitudes also be trained? The answer is yes: Behaviour rooted in attitudes can be addressed during training. This requires special skills and attitudes of the trainer or facilitator, because we must think here in terms of strategies of intervention as outlined in Figure 2. 'Essentiality, self acceptance and confirmation' as defined by Argyris are essential conditions for behavioural change.

17 Human factors training in aviation: The trainee

Karsten H. Severin*
Patricia Antersijn**
* Lufthansa Flight Training GmbH, Pilot School, Germany
** KLM Flight Crew Training Dept., The Netherlands

Introduction

Accident and incident analyses clearly show again and again that Human Factors- (HF-) training in the broadest sense of the word, is a necessity in todays aviation community. However, it does not only need to focus on the civil or military flight crew but is to be aimed at the whole aviation industry.

This of course is easily stated. Why don't human factors specialists just give a HF-training to every relevant person in the aviation organisation and the problem will be solved. Unfortunately it is not that simple. Training as an enhancement of knowledge and skills can only be one aspect of the solution. The preceding aspect is the often neglected matter of personal attitude: The whole organisation with every single member - from management to ancillary staff - needs to be human factor centred. It is always surprising, that so called well introduced Total Quality Management- (TQM-) programmes hardly take this basic aspect into serious consideration. These kinds of programmes will only succeed when proceeding through the organizational levels from the top down. The motivational question 'Why should I care?' needs to be addressed and convincingly answered before quality improvement guidelines might have a chance to develop into fruitful processes. Keeping this in mind, we will now concentrate on the training aspects.

Training considerations

For training to be effective there are several critical factors to be considered for a successful outcome, e.g. quality of the trainer, quality of the training material, established acceptance and promotion of the training within the organisation and - last but not least - the trainees themselves. Again, here we will restrict ourselves and focus on the *trainee*. It is our intention to establish an understanding of 'how to approach' the trainee effectively.

Let us start with some commonly known 'bold facts':

- Every trainee is different.
- Groups of trainees do vary.
- Effective training must take these points into consideration.

Effective HF-training, i.e. task-sufficient knowledge and adequate resource management skills, delivered in easily digestible chunks, is more than merely task-oriented information exchange. Therefore it has to include behavioural training techniques, administered by qualified trainers [1]. Task-oriented means specified operational performance to be expected on the job, a well defined standard to be met by commercial pilots. The didactical goal of the HF-training should be to allow for an individual learning progress for each trainee. Since trainees do have different needs, an effective training has to be trainee-centred. Therefore trainers must get to know as much as possible about their trainees and adjust their programme according to the individuals' needs.

What different kinds of trainees do we find in the field of aviation? Based on the authors' experience you will encounter a wide variety of differences between trainees, mainly depending on their different backgrounds (e.g. military, civil, ATC, maintenance), different previous experience with HF-training (e.g. ab initio-pilot students, flight crews, flight instructors, flight inspectors, management). Other variations are because of differences in a person's

- personality, gender, age;
- role / task within the organisation, e.g. F/O, F/E, Vice President,
- educational background,
- cultural background, e.g.nationality, previous company philosophy.

Trainers also need to take further factors into consideration which may differ between members of one occupational group, for instance:

- Motivational situation of a trainee; is the person reaching his/her own decision, because of a management decision, or regulatory decision.
- Present psychological and physical condition.
- Individual learning style.
- Personal attitude towards subject at hand.
- Personal needs, ranging from pure entertainment to philosophical enrichment.
- Level of skills regarding intra- and interpersonal behavioural aspects.
- Individual task-oriented needs, e.g. practical job-counselling/coaching.

---

[1] There are different opinions in the aviation industry regarding the suitable qualifications, background and experience needed to be a successful pilot trainer. The authors came to believe that neither a pilot nor a licenced psychologist or other behaviour expert would automatically qualify because of their profession itself. There needs to be a common ground and consistency in the field of HF-training. Therefore pilots have to obtain at least some appropriate basic academic training, while professionals need to gather as much insight as possible into the pilots' world - preferably by becoming a pilot themselves. Ideally an appropriately rated pilot with a degree in psychology or another behaviour science would be most suitable for this task.

Indeed there are a lot of things for a trainer to consider when designing an effective training programme. And these items only refer to the trainees. Other important aspects are e.g.,

- targeted goals of the course,
- regulatory requirements,
- time and money available,
- instructional tools at hand (slides, video, CBT, real life demonstrations, simulator, etc.),
- physical environment available, e.g. inhouse- vs. external training,
- required results of the individual's behavioural assessment,
- co-operation level between the company departments involved.

How can HF-trainers transfer all these factors into a manageable and realistic training?

Although it is not our intention to offer a comprehensive overview of instructional or didactical principles to be taken into consideration here, we would like to point out some helpful facts which have been proven to be beneficial:

- First of all, create an open and safe atmosphere. A helpful way to do this is to give the training course somewhere outside the company catchment area.
- Be flexible in your approach by using different methods, e.g. group-discussions, role-play, lectures, 'games', case-studies (analysing an incident or accident), guided brainstorming.
- Use different instructional aids like video, overheads, flipboard, handouts, music, etc.
- Design a training in such a way that different learning-styles and temperaments are addressed.

Therefore instruct

- from specific to abstract (induction),
- from observation to active participation by the trainees themselves.

For example, do an exercise (specific / self-involvement), discuss what happened (specific / observation), why it happened (specific / guided brainstorming), what can we learn from this in relation to what we already know (deductive / group discussion), what rules we can take from this that will be useful in day to day practice (abstract / self-involvement).

Use different communication channels, e.g. visualize your message (video, slides, overheads, etc.), use figurative examples (anecdotes, metaphors, parables), stimulate self-experience (demonstrate, provoke responses, relieve the tension, mediate insight).

- Structure your content in a logical and learning friendly way.
- Use the trainees' own language.
- Be practical. The trainees' question 'How can I use this tomorrow?' should not even arise because the anwers should be obvious.
- And if necessary, choose the 'right' (co-) trainer. However, this decision very often depends on the organisational philosophy and the political particularities within a company.

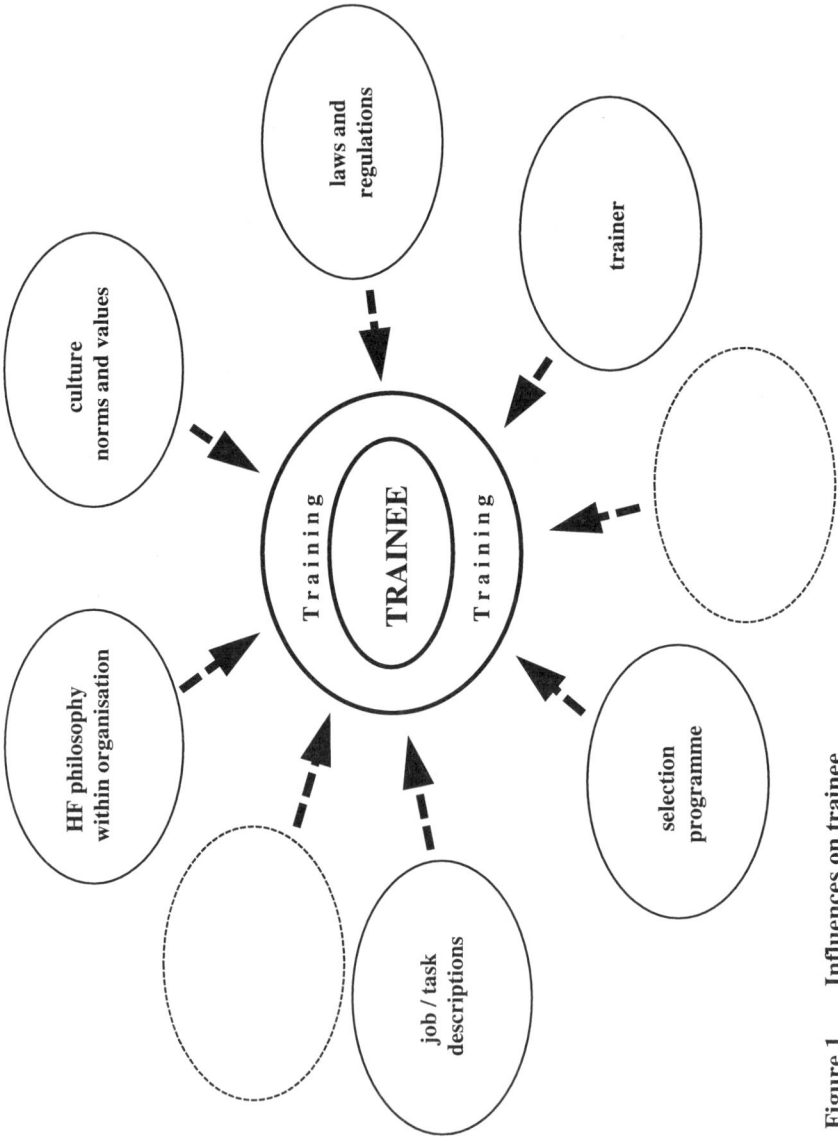

Figure 1   Influences on trainee

- Often it seems to be useful to involve mixed groups (e.g. cockpit crews, cabin crews, dispatch personel) whenever possible, since pilots do not operate in a world of their own.
- Finally, from the practitioner's point of view, HF-training has to be a dynamic, process-oriented training, not an once-in-a-life-time event. Hence it must become an integrated part of standard pilot training, with its behavioural components being accepted and stressed in the same way as the so called technical skills. Fortunately, at least the regulatory agencies have commited themselves toward this insight.

As a summary:
- Be creative, use more than one method in your training.
- Surprise your students, keep them involved and entertained;
- But never forget the underlying message.

18 Integration of human factors-training

Marieke C. Verhoef-de Groen
KLM Flight Crew Training Department, The Netherlands

Introduction

Airlines must start assessing Non-technical or Human Factors skills in the near future. But is it possible, and how should we do it? We are convinced that, before we are able to assess HF-performance, we have to make sure that our training in HF-skills is adequate and sufficient. And that the people who will coach our cockpit crew on HF-skills (and in the near future will assess them), have the right tools to do so.

So first we have to have a good picture of what integration of Human Factors training is and define the main difficulties and obstacles to attaining integration.

In this paper, I would like to give you an overview of the questions that have to be answered:

- Can Non-technical or HF-training be separated from flight technical training?
- Which are the obstacles in attaining integration and the possible solutions to overcome these 'roadblocks'.
- How should we accomplish integration of non-technical and technical skill training?

Can Non-technical or HF-training be separated from flight technical training?

If we take training seriously, it is important to regularly evaluate the training package and training approach. Out of this we will come to the conclusion, that all important training items - to ensure a good working cockpit crew - are covered, but still there is something missing. We have our skill training, LOFT training, Crew Management training, a training in Public Address techniques, etc., but they are all separate courses or subjects; there is no real relation between the flight technical and HF training. Subjects taught during, for instance, our Crew Resource Management Training, are - by many of us - not reinforced during simulator training.

An aircraft cannot be flown by 'black boxes' alone. Neither is it desirable to consider the HF-skills in isolation. A balanced approach is crucial. Therefore HF-training can not be separated from flight technical training. There is a need for a structurally integrated approach of technical training and HF- training. Practice shows that, as soon as one has finished a course, skills which are rarely or never used, deteriorate. Also a decline in the norm occurs for skills that have become routine. In a refresher training the participant's skills are brought back up to standard.

Traditionally technical skills have always been well-developed (Type Recurrent Training and Proficiency Checks). The HF-skill should be developed to the same level, but not given predominance. As a consequence the instruction of HF-skills within our airlines are not as effective (due to separation) as it could be.

Roadblocks in attaining integration and possible solutions to overcome these roadblocks

Integration of HF- training in the current 'daily' training (type qualification, type recurrent, proficiency check and route check) is subject to a number of 'roadblocks' (see the next two tables for observed and mentioned roadblocks.

Main roadblocks observed:	Options / activities to overcome:
no tool / system to effectively counsel HF-skills.	development of a tool / system to effectively counsel HF-skills; use of clear, objective and observable criteria (behaviour),
no support of management	- ask for the responsibility of management in this - prepare management and organization by means of informing and discussing implementation strategies, - pick an implementation date, so that it is visible to the whole organization / management when the the system will be implemented officially.
wrong expectations of HF-consumers	- prepare each crew member - clarify expectations - be honest about (your) possible limits - try out of the system and evaluate, take worries/doubts into consideration

Main roadblocks mentioned:	Options / activities to overcome:
just a minority is interested in HF	- involve the 'not interested ones', during the development of the system, training and assessment - highlight previous incidents which were dealt with successfully - demonstrate the cost benefit - using natural interest in behaviour - influence opinion leader
avoid to be a 'Non'-technical	- be proud of your profession
lack of time and money	- demonstrate efficiency

Main roadblocks mentioned:	Options / activities to overcome:
inappropriate training contents	- designing specialised integrated trainings for the needs of pilots and FE and make sure, that these trainings are 'ongoing'. - consider the use of modular interactive courses.
profession of trainer	- restructure all flight-, route- and ground instructor- and check pilot/FE trainings. - select instructors who 'fit' the job - prepare the instructors to use the system and make sure they are properly trained in instruction techniques as well as briefing-, observation-, debriefing-, and reporting techniques.
competence of the psychologist	- speak the language of aircrews - get trained/informed - become professional in aviation

How to accomplish integration of HF-training and technical skill training?

Before HF-training can be integrated into the existing training set-up, it is necessary to map out the present training process. In this way it will become clear which factors play a role and how they influence each other. It also makes clear where to start when integrating (see Figure 1).

Figure 1   Diagram of the training process

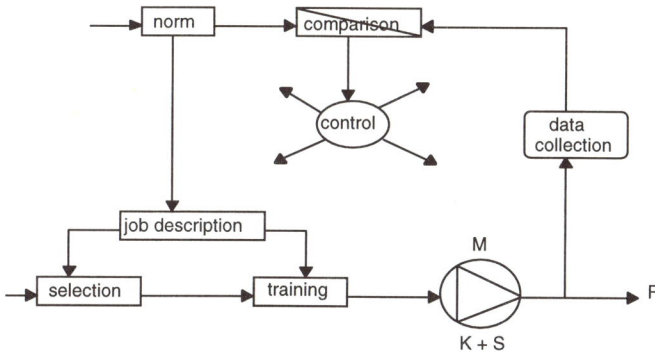

P = Performance
M = Motivation
K + S = Knowledge and Skills

The process diagram can be described as follows: The objective of the company, expressed in the quality expectation concerning the performance of the cockpit crew, determines the norm to which pilots and flight engineers must adhere. The objective also determines the expectations of the company, and therefore the job profiles which are applicable to the various crew members.

As a result of job profiles, selection criteria and contents of training programs are determined. On the basis of a person's skills and knowledge and his motivation a certain performance is achieved. A company wants to know how its employees perform.

By collecting data about the performance and by comparing this to the norm, the process can be monitored. This means counselling individuals, spotting trends in a division or in a corps so that selection and/or training can be adjusted, or if the norm changes (for instance due to changes in the objectives of the company), changing job profiles, selection criteria and / or training.

The job profile plays an important role in this process.

- It is important for the selection criteria.
- It determines what must be trained.
- It forms a frame of reference to determine if a person is performing as required, or to determine the quality of the training and selection process.
- It offers a frame of reference for the person in question. When someone's performance is being measured, that person has a right to know what is expected.

Conclusions

From the above we can conclude that if one wants to accomplish integration:

- non-technical training must already be introduced at 'ab initio' stage
- non-technical training cannot be a once-only activity, but must be integrated into the existing training set-up. Every time a refresher is given concerning technical skills, the non-technical skills must also be included .
- it must be made clear what we expect from pilots and flight engineers (see the importance of the job profile). All pilots and flight engineers need to attend basic and recurrent CRM courses.
- the instructors must have the necessary tools to effectively counsel non-technical aspects. This has consequences for the training of instructors.
- The responsibility of management in this and our acceptance is of essential importance for the success of the set-up.

19   HPL- and MCC-training as part of the airline transport pilot course

Karsten H. Severin
Lufthansa Flight Training GmbH, Pilot School, Germany

Introduction

In the old multi-crew cockpit tradition the captain was the master of the aeroplane, not necessarily the helmsman or pilot. Later, when he/she literally took over the controls of the plane, everybody else served as an assistant, guided by the captain's order.

Today's aeroplanes and pilots offer unequalled efficiency and safety. The reason for still having multiple crew members in the cockpit is the safety principle of redundancy. Contrary to single-pilot cockpit operation multi-pilot crews also need to optimise effective team work on the flight deck by following specified procedures. These procedures are usually developed under the influence of regulatory requirements and the company's own philosophy (Degani & Wiener, 1994). As an integral part of human factors-training they reflect the importance of team-orientation and team-performance as a safety factor in modern flight deck philosophy.

Multi-crew co-operation training

Multi-crew co-operation- versus other human factors-training programmes

Because of the many acronyms presently used for different kinds of human factors-training programmes, it is sometimes confusing to differentiate between them. While Human Factors (HF) includes the whole interdisciplinary scientific field of the complex human-machine-environment system and its components interaction, Human Performance and Limitations-training (HPL) as required by the Joint Aviation Requirements / Flight Crew Licensing (JAR-FCL) refers to human factors aspects, regarded as relevant for pilots by the Joint Aviation Authorities (JAA). The HPL part is divided into three parts: (1) Human Factors: Basic Concepts, (2) Basic Aviation Physiology and Health Maintenance and (3) Basic Aviation Psychology. (All further statements by the author regarding HPL do not refer to the physiological part because it is not skill or behavioural oriented but aims at theoretical knowledge transfer only.)

Crew Resource Management- or more recently Company Resource Management-training (CRM) emphasises the optimal '...use of all resources available to the flight crew, including equipment, technical/procedural skills, and the contributions of flight crew and others' (Taggart, 1994) by means of psychological knowledge.

Based on the CRM-philosophy, Multi-Crew Co-operation-training (MCC) primarily determines the task organisation and distribution on a flight deck by applying defined Standard Operating Procedures (SOPs). Since aeroplanes vary in their cockpit design and sometimes offer limited access to dials and switches, these company procedures are not unrelated to particular hardware requirements. MCC therefore occasionally may have to adapt to these particulars, thus reaching beyond the basic, more general oriented type of HF-training (Figure 1). However, the purpose of crew co-ordination procedures is to support effective team behaviour and ensure an uninterrupted human redundancy during critical phases of a flight.

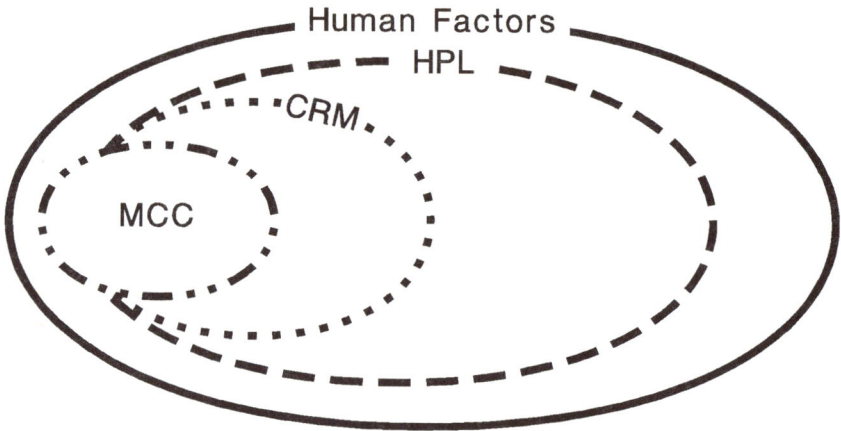

Figure 1   **Relationship between human factors-training programmes**

Objectives of MCC-training

As stated in JAR-FCL 1, AMC FCL 1.250(1), the aim of an MCC-Course is to train flight students or pilots to work professionally as part of a cockpit crew in order to safely operate multi-pilot aeroplanes. Here the use of checklists is strongly emphasised and their different background philosophies are understood (Degani & Wiener, 1993).

The objectives of MCC training shall be promoting optimum pilot behaviour in

- use of checklist
- communication
- division of tasks
- mutual supervision
- mutual support
- decision making

throughout all phases of flight under normal, abnormal and emergency conditions. It is not only to be viewed as a training with the goal of producing technically competent individuals, but as an effort towards team orientation among pilots, with a redundancy-by-teamwork philosophy. In order to accomplish this philosophy, trainees must have the opportunity to practice the necessary skills in a realistic crew setting. As with HPL- or CRM-courses trainees need to recognise their individual behavioural impact on overall crew functioning and the resolution of responsibilities for team leaders and members.

This training approach supports today's trend within the airline industry to have pilots share responsibility on the flight deck by e.g., conferring the right to 'force' an indisputable go-around manoeuvre during final approach upon the first officers[1]. While the ultimate command-responsibility remains with the Pilot In Command (PIC), the authority-gradient between captain and first officer has reduced in favour of an assumed redundancy superiority through team-responsibility due to equal professional competence.

HPL and MCC: What are the common interests? What are the differences?

The content of the MCC- and the HPL-training are defined by JAR-FCL, Section 2, Subpart F and Subpart J. There is an overlap in the objectives: all MCC-items can be found within the HPL-syllabus (Table 1).

---

[1] For example, Lufthansa Flight Operations Manual (DV FLI) points out, that 'A decision to initiate a go-around rests with the PIC as long as the aeroplane is higher than 1000 ft above GND in IMC or 500 ft above GND when runway in sight and clear of clouds. As soon as the aeroplane is lower than defined above a go-around has to be executed as soon as any active crew member calls out 'go-around' regardless of who is PF/PNF.' (DV FLI, p. 3.5.23-24, Rev. 178)

Table 1   Corresponding HPL- and MCC-contents
(MCC = Subpart F;HPL = Subpart J)

JAR - FCL 1, Subpart F	JAR - FCL 1, Subpart J	
(a) Interfaces • example of software, hardware, environment and liveware mismatched in practice.	040 010 100 040 010 101	**Human Factors in Aviation** Competence and limitations • SHEL model of human factors
(b) Leadership/"followership" and authority • managerial and supervisory skills • assertiveness • barriers • cultural influence • PF and PNF roles • professionalism • team responsibility	040 010 102 040 030 402 040 030 403 040 030 404	Becoming a competent pilot • the traditional approach towards "proficiency" • the human factors approach towards "professionalism" Co-ordination (multi-crew concepts) Co-operation • small group dynamics • leadership, management styles • duty and role Communication
(c) Personality, attitude and motivation • listening • conflict resolution • mediating • critique • team building	040 030 104 040 030 404 **040 030 500** 040 030 501 040 030 502 040 030 503	Response selection • learning principles and techniques • drives • motivation and performance Communication **Personality** Personality and attitudes • development • environmental influences Individual differences in personality • self-concepts Identification of hazardous attitudes
(d) Effective and clear communication during flight • listening • feedback • standard phraseologies • assertiveness • participation	040 030 404	Communication • communication model(s) • verbal and non-verbal communication • communication barriers • conflict management
(e) Crew co-ordination procedures • flight techniques and cockpit procedures • standard phraseologies • discipline	040 030 402 040 030 403 040 030 503	Co-ordination (multi-crew concepts) Co-operation Identification of hazardous attitudes

While HPL is a basic HF-training - seen to raise awareness for immanent human problems and interface deficiencies, evoking safety-minded attitudes, stressing the superiority of team-performance, and teaching adequate behavioural skills - subsequent CRM-training programmes serve as specifically tailored supplements in the domain of human performance and limitations (Table 2).

Presently JAR-OPS assigns for four types of training programmes to cockpit crews:

1) *CRM-recurrent* course, the repetition of basic and introduction of additional human factors topics,
2) *CRM-transition* course, if changing aircraft,
3) *CRM-transition* course, if changing operator,
4) *CRM-command* course, if being promoted to captain.

Table 2 **Objectives of human factors-training programmes**

	HPL-Training	**MCC-Training**	**CRM-Trainings**
Introduction of	human factors awareness	multi-crew co-ordination knowledge	in-depth human factors knowledge
Standardization of	basic human factors knowledge	multi-crew co-ordination behaviour	human factors skills/behaviour
Shaping of	basic human factors skills/behaviour	multi-crew co-ordination habits	human factors habits

The overall goal of all three human factor-training courses is the implementation and establishment of necessary behavioural habits on the flight deck. These habits are based on individual knowledge and skills and motivated by appropriate attitudes supported by the company's work philosophy. Therefore, the behavioural objective, as the final instructional goal, is the most challenging one. Knowledge is no guarantee for adequate behaviour, just as skills are no guarantee for good judgement.

Active participation

While JAR-FCL 1 Subpart F explicitly states the necessity for practice and feedback of MCC, Subpart J is less specific regarding HPL. JAR-FCL 1.465 Requirement (JAR-FCL 1, Section 1, Subpart J - Theoretical Knowledge Requirements and Procedures for the Conduct of Theoretical Knowledge Examinations for Professional Pilot Licences and Instrument Ratings; page 1-J-1) states: 'An applicant for a professional pilot licence or an instrument rating shall demonstrate a level of knowledge appropriate to the privileges of the licence ...' . Knowledge is one presupposition for adequate behaviour (Figure 2), and appropriate group behaviour is the basis of efficient team performance. Since an ab initio flight student is expected to demonstrate competence in technical and non-technical knowledge and skills on the flight deck of a multi-crew aeroplane directly after passing the Airline Transport Pilot Licence (ATPL), the psychological part of HPL needs to be supported by an adequate practical training like the routinely applied training of other necessary pilot skills, e.g., radio-telephony or pitch-and-power control. Lecturing about human behaviour without allowance for practice is simply ineffective or inappropriate, because it would contravene the matter of content and neglect the trainees needs for adequate individual feedback, so he or she can improve necessary skills and grow personally. This is the reason for seeing active group exercises as the cornerstone of every human factors-training, in order to judge if it really does optimise the individuals behaviour and consequently the team performance.

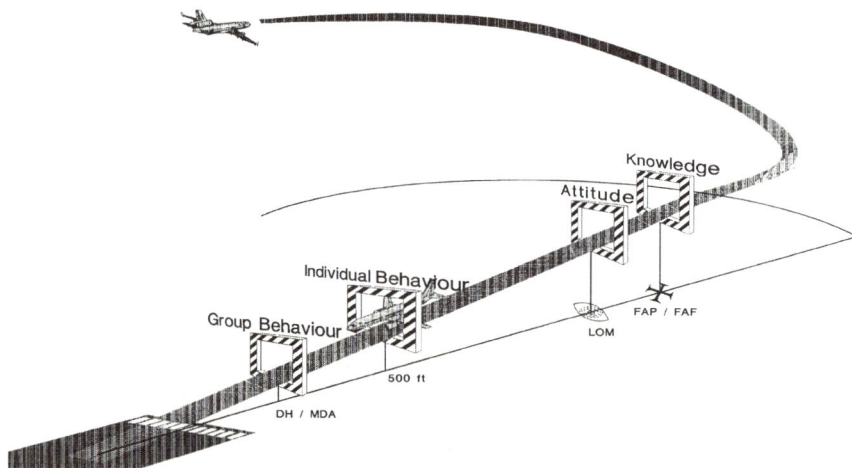

Figure 2   Gates to pass for team-oriented cockpit behaviour

Trainees need time to accomplish the appropriate behaviour, they require practice and feedback as well as permanent reinforcement to learn skills that will endure. This is why MCC-training, like any other Human Factors-training, should begin as early as possible within the ab initio programme. Multi-crew concepts and team responsibility as training content should begin immediately after the Private Pilot Licence (PPL)-check, when the newly qualified pilots need to gain more experience by allowing for PIC-time during 'team flights' in a crew setting. Later in the Instrument Flight Rule (IFR), a training phase in single- or multi-engine aeroplanes, the flight instructor may act as Pilot-Not-Flying (PNF) by routinely supporting the PF as assigned by the SOPs, thus supporting good MCC practice.

In simulator training two students should act as PF and PNF, also shaping/developing their MCC-skills and team-performance.

Conclusion / implications

Instructing Human Factors with the goal of optimised behaviour on the flight deck requires practical training. Training is referred to as active participation of the trainee by the means of exercises and simulations.

There are good reasons to have the introduction into MCC procedures incorporated into the HPL training part 'Basic Aviation Psychology', e.g.:

- As required by AMC FCL 1.250(1), 'Instructors for MCC training should be thoroughly familiar with human factors and crew resource management (CRM). They should be current with the latest development in human factors training and CRM techniques.' For this position an aviation psychologist/human factors specialist with a strong aviation and psychology background would fulfil these requirements without extensive additional training.
- All of the required theoretical knowledge for the MCC-course is part of the HPL syllabus. As an integrated part of an ATP ab initio course it can be efficiently taught at the appropriate time within the HPL framework, and continuously adapted to the trainees level of training experience. For CPL/IR holders it can be adequately modified and - if desired - integrated into a HF-recurrent course or CRM transition training.

Behaviour can be trained but initial training does not guarantee its future contingency. Only a pilots personal attitude and the operators offer of continuous HF-training programmes will succeed in maintaining the necessary and required standard to fit the demands of today's multi-crew flight decks.

20   The effects and effectiveness of human factors training

André Droog
Human Factors Department, KLM Flight Academy, The Netherlands

Introduction

Why organise and practice human factors training? Does it work? Effectiveness is the issue here. HF trainers and CRM facilitators ask themselves about the effectiveness of their training. In general, the aviation industry, in particular those who control the financial resources, will ask for evidence of results. 'Believers' may make positive statements about the effect of HF training on the safety of the aviation system, but what are the benefits and the costs? 'The vast majority of cockpit management training programs have been highly praised by individuals and organisations that have used them. But in these austere times, management and government authorities alike can legitimately demand 'proof' of the effectiveness of safety measures, including cockpit management training. The most convincing evidence would be a statistically significant reduction in catastrophic accident rates' (Alan Diehl, 1992).

If we want to learn about effectiveness, we must first know about effects. Although we aim at success, effects may be positive or adverse. *Effectiveness* means, that we evaluate effects against the goals or standards we strive for. Evaluation, in turn, implies *measurement*. When measurement in the mathematical or physical sense is not possible, we turn to *assessment*, which means 'to *estimate* the size or quality of...'.

Measuring effects of training

Helmreich, who has done a lot of research into the effectiveness of CRM training, concluded (1991) that: 'Crew members overwhelmingly *acknowledge the value* (italics by the author) of the training. Highly significant, favourable shifts in attitudes are found. The *observed behaviour of crews shows significant changes* in the direction of practising CRM concepts. When the *organisational climate* reinforces and requires the practice of CRM concepts, acceptance grows over time'. The quotation demonstrates, that different 'levels' of evaluating the effects of training can be distinguished.

Level 1: Reactions	the *subjective evaluation* of the training by the trainees
Level 2: Learning	*have the behavioural objectives of the training been reached?*
Level 3: Job behaviour	*'transfer of training'*, the level of learning manifest in the job situation
Level 4: Organisation	*changes in the behavioural norms of the organisation (e.g. safety culture)*
Level 5: Cost effectiveness	evaluation of the *cost effectiveness* and the *contribution to the overall goals of the organisation (e.g. profit, safety, continuity, motivation)*

The importance of feedback to the trainers and to the airline management on *all five levels* may be obvious:

- Level 1-evaluation is important with view to the acceptance of the training programme by the trainees.
- Level 2-evaluation supplies feedback about the efficiency of the programme, it *validates* the training programme (which is 'internal validation'; 'external validation' means: to ascertain by assessment whether the *right* training needs were identified and the *right* training objectives were chosen in relation to the criteria of effectiveness adopted by the organisation).
- Level 3-evaluation is the real proof of the pudding when it comes to the question of 'changed attitudes and behaviour' (Chapter 21 deals with the Level 2 and Level 3 issues).
- Level 4-evaluation deals with the safety culture of the organisation and
- Level 5-evaluation is the 'macro' level and most relevant to both the organisation and the aviation system as a whole. Hamblin (1975) once defined the evaluation of training as: 'the assessment of the total value of a training system, training course or programme in social as well as in financial terms'. Obviously this is a 'level 5' definition. The problem, of course, is to quantify the social value and to estimate the financial gains and losses.

Statistical (correlational) evidence on decreased accident rates as a result of the introduction of CRM programmes, for example with the U.S. Air Force Military Airlift Command, is summarised by Alan Diehl (1992).

It must be assumed that these decreases in accident rates saved the mentioned organisations a lot of money. On the other hand, no figures about the investments in training time and money are known, neither if other factors may have contributed to these improvements. However, the costs of having accidents are huge and not easily equalled by investments in training.

Improving conditions for HF training

Human factors training and the improvement of training are part of the improvement of flight safety, but they are certainly not the only factor. Better cockpit design, better maintenance, better management decisions, the supply of financial resources, and the reduction of latent errors in the organisation, they all contribute to safety and may even reduce the necessity of training.

However, when it comes to the improvement of human factors training programmes, and the likelihood of success of this training, those people responsible for implementing training probably will meet a number of obstacles. For example: no support from the management, shortage of financial resources, operational restrictions (training is time-consuming, pilots have to fly), no human factors or safety culture within the company, resistance to change, criticism of pilots and other groups, etc.

Which options have aviation psychologists or human factors specialists to overcome these obstacles? In order to convince airline management and get their support, it will be at least necessary to show that HF factors training has a pay-off, that it generates money by enhanced safety (which is equivalent to the prevention of loss of money) and enhanced reputation (which generates money). Clear and realistic goals for HF training must be set. Evaluation of HF training or CRM training vis-à-vis organisational goals is essential.

Table 1   Operational evaluations by Alan Diehl (1992)

Organisation/Subjects	Materials	Accident Rates
Bell Helicopters Inc. World-wide, Jetranger Pilots	Aeronautical Decision Making	36 percent decrease
Bell Helicopters Inc. U.S.-only Jetranger Pilots	ADM	48 percent decrease
Petroleum Helicopters Inc. Commercial Pilots	ADM & CRM	54 percent decrease
U.S. Navy All helicopters, Crew members	CRM	28 percent decrease
U.S. Navy A-6 Intruder, Crew members	CRM	81 percent decrease
U.S. Air Force Military Air Command Transports, Crew members	CRM	51 percent decrease

21 Evaluation of human factors performance

Marieke C. Verhoef-de Groen
KLM Flight Crew Training Department, The Netherlands
(With acknowledgements to Capt. Lucio Polo, Alitalia Human Factors Training for his article 'Assessment of CRM skills')

Introduction

Airlines must start assessing non-technical or HF skills from 1st April 1998. But is it possible and what do we loose or gain the moment we start to assess HF skills. What are the state of the art and the problems connected with evaluation of HF performance?

In this paper, I will present an overview of the questions which have to be answered:

- What is necessary for evaluation of behaviour?
- Conditions / requirements to be met for proper evaluation of HF performance.
- Is assessment of HF performance possible? What could be the disadvantages or consequences?
- Who should assess HF performance?

What is necessary for evaluation of behaviour?

The performance effectiveness of pilots and flight engineers is besides motivation, determined by their technical and non-technical / HF knowledge and skills. To gain proper insight in the level of their technical and HF performance, a method / model / or system should be developed which measures their performance, compares it with a norm and enables a feedback or appraisal. This method is an instrument which is meant to give feedback as objective as possible, with unambiguous conceptions. This in order to sustain a high level of performance or bring about a desirable behaviour change in order to improve the HF performance of cockpit crewmembers.

It is about making pilots and flight engineers aware of their HF behaviour. Once they are aware and it is evident that their HF behaviour is ineffective a specific training advice should be given. If behaviour was effective, then reinforcement of that behaviour is possible.

Conditions / requirements to be met for proper evaluation of human factor skills

Evaluation must be based upon observable effective behaviour. Why is that so important? Behaviour is principally situation dependent. Similar behaviour can in one situation be particularly effective. However in another situation the same behaviour could be rendered ineffective. Furthermore, it is about observable behaviour. The feedback is consequently about what actually happened, not on what could have happened or was likely to happen.

Is assessment of HF performance possible? What could be the disadvantages or consequences?

Although assessment of HF performance is (almost) a fact considering JAR-OPS, still there are many questions which need to be filled in the moment you start assessing. Questions like: What is the validity of a HF model? Is assessment of HF performance possible? What could be the consequences? Or: On what can a pilot or a crew be evaluated / assessed?

Models concerning the so called CRM skills have been developed observing and analysing good and bad performance of cockpit crews in LOFT in relation to flight safety. These ones brought forward also the importance of cabin crew behaviour and the integration and coordination of both components of a crew.

The relevance of these models is based on the hypothesis that if the performance / behaviour had been correct the accident or the mistake could have been avoided. This unfortunately cannot be proven on facts. Another source of information comes from those crew members who more or less anonymously, say that the day was saved by one or more of those behaviours or that the near miss was so close because relevant behaviour was missing. Furthermore, the model relevance can be detected in the positive attitude that crew members express during or after CRM training and the consequential increase of these behaviours in everyday operational life.

A person, already proficient in his job, will accept to modify his / her behaviour, already proven to be good in thousands of occasions, only if he / she becomes involved and foresees an extra value in doing according to a model. In harmony with this, a CRM training (of any kind) is and shall be proposed as a tool offered to pilots to improve their performance. Which one of the proposed tools they put in their tool-box (mental pilot case), which one they will retrieve and how they use it, must be left to their best judgement.

In CRM we insist on 'Judgement' implying evaluation / use of resources and decision making and say that this must be integrated with consistent autonomous behaviours and compliance to rules. None of them can substitute one or more of the other skills. So we must be coherent and accept that in any occasion the CRM behaviour is 'at crew discretion'. This includes any situation of assessment or evaluation.

On what can a crew be evaluated / assessed? The operational performance is the only one that can be assessed by methods that have a resemblance to an objectivity and can be acceptable to pilots. Obviously tracing the causes of a bad crew performance, even in a simulator, we have a good hance to find poor CRM skills. That does not mean that anybody is in a position to say to a person from 'one up standpoint': 'Your Communication, your Critique, or else, is rated 3, 2 or 5' or 'You two violated your aircraft minima and limitations because you did not look for mutual feedback or where not assertive enough' or 'Your check ride is 'Unsatisfactory' because your leadership was not tuned to the situation'.

Finding the possible CRM causes of a bad operational performance or a mistake, even in a simulator, must be done with the co-operation of the crew involved but that is not 'Evaluation'. That is similar to the same process that enabled the aeronautical applied psychology to find CRM models. It is even more powerful because the crew can tell their inner truth and learning is then tailored on personal needs.

But ... it requires the appropriate setting to have a chance of success! This situation can hardly be found during any evaluation unless profound evaluees, evaluators and authorities cultural changes take place. JAA cannot define rules taking this change as granted or a consequence of the rule in itself.

Who should evaluate / assess HF performance?

Who should evaluate / assess non-technical performance? Should it be a specialist in this field, a psychologist? The answer is no, such specialists lack the technical knowledge needed. Without that knowledge, situations are difficult to put into perspective: Which results in counselling? Which is less accurate. Instructors / facilitators do know about the technical aspects. With training in HF field, they will be best available persons for counselling pilots and flight engineers.

Conclusions

- EAAP should not recommend a rule on pilot CRM / HF skill assessment. Nevertheless 'very broad and flexible' behavioural markers / categories should be defined. Markers' purpose should be determined, by JAA, in a way that clearly states that: related skills have to be trained, they are required items in flight crew competence, markers do not constitute an evaluation grid.
- A key point in improving CRM / HF skills are instructors and check airmen. Accordingly they shall become familiar with facilitation skills and gradually (since the legislation starts) demonstrate competency in them. Such a training program should incorporate the following principles of learning: active participation, knowledge of results and practice. In addition, the training program should be designed to teach instructors / facilitators / check airmen, how to define effective / ineffective behaviour, how to observe, how to

minimise rating errors and how to perform a debriefing. Furthermore, the training should teach and habituate the instructors / check airmen to the 'to be evaluated' behaviour markers / categories. [1]

---

[1] Footnote of the editor: The NOTECHS working group is defining a set of broad NTS scales for administration in check events. It will result in a proposal to JAA for the formulation of the respective AMC. The NOTECHS work will be finished in October 1997. In the following program JAR-TEL the reliability / validity of the NTS assessment in check situations will be investigated by empirical research.

References

Argyris, C. (1973) *Intervention theory and method*. Addison-Wesley Publishing Company, Massachusetts

Argyris, C. (1988) Problems in producing usable knowledge for implementing liberating alternatives; in: *Decision Making*, David E. Bell, Howard Raiffa, Amos Tversky, Cambridge University Press

Boekaerts & Simons (1993) *Leren en instructie*, Dekker & vn de Vegt, Assen

Degani, A. & Wiener, E.L. (1993). Cockpit checklists: Concepts, design, and use. *Human Factors*, 35 (2), 345-359.

Degani, A. & Wiener, E.L. (1994). Philosophy, policies, procedures and practices: The four P's of flight deck operations. In N. Johnston, N. McDonald & R. Fuller (Eds.), *Aviation Psychology in Practice* (pp. 44-67). Aldershot: Avebury.

Droog, A. (1986) *De verkeersvlieger als manager*, Utrecht

Droog, A. (1990) Becoming a captain: personality development by non-technical training and education, ICAO Flight Safety and Human Factors Seminar, Leningrad, USSR, April 1990

JAA (1996). *JAR-FCL 1: Flight Crew Licensing Requirements (Aeroplane)*. Hoofddorp: Joint Aviation Authorities.

JAA (1995). *JAR-OPS 1: Flight Operations Requirements (Aeroplane)*. Hoofddorp: Joint Aviation Authorities.

Mintzberg, H. (1973) *The Nature of Managerial Work*, Harper and Row, New York

Stammers & Patrick (1975) *The Psychology of Training*, Methuen & Co Ltd, London

Taggart, W.R. (1994). Crew resource management: Achieving enhanced flight operations. In N. Johnston, N. McDonald & R. Fuller (Eds.), *Aviation Psychology in Practice* (pp. 309-339). Aldershot: Avebury.

Telfer, Ross A. (1993) *Aviation Instruction and Training*, Ashgate

Warren & Jahoda (1979) *Attitudes*, Penguin Books

Section 4

Psychological Counselling and Intervention

Course Manager:

Reiner Kemmler

22   Clinical psychology applications in military aviation

Wolfgang Roth
German Air Force, Institute of Aviation Medicine, Germany

In military aviation clinical psychology is applied in different fields in order to help air force personnel to cope with critical life situations. Systematic psychological approaches have been developed for the following fields:

- diagnostics and consultation
- stress prevention
- after-action stress debriefing
- air sickness prevention and therapy.

This chapter gives examples for these four fields. Most of the presented information refers to methods and experience of the division 'Aviation Psychology' at the Institute of Aviation Medicine of the German Air Force (GAF).

Clinical diagnostics and consultation

If a member of the GAF flight crew is developing performance or behaviour problems, he will be sent to clinical aviation psychology where a stepwise procedure starts:

1. Symptoms / flight status / statements
   statement of flight surgeon
   statement of superiors
   flight records
   medical records
   psychological records
2. Biography
3. Behaviour analysis
   through information from introductory session (exploration)
   through different test methods (redundant)
   personality tests

aptitude tests
4. Explanation of test results to the individual
5. Decision (to the individual and to the flight surgeon)
6. Counselling and recommendations
7. Selfmanagement – training
8. Therapy (e. g. behaviour therapy).

   Cases representing different problem areas will explain the work of clinical psychodiagnostics and consultation much better than an abstract text. Therefore, four exemplary cases are reported:

Case 1 (26-year old Jet-Pilot, 450 flight hours)

Flight surgeon statement

Multiple gastric maladies accompanied by diarrhoea, nausea and vomiting without any medical reason → psychological symptomatic was assumed.

Subject's statement

He could not have breakfast in the morning because of pressure on / in his stomach
*   it happened that he threw up between two flights
*   he threw up when he saw his name on the schedule
*   he was very nervous before his flights
*   never he felt such an inner resistance against flying as during the weapon operator training
*   up to this point he has had a lot of fun while flying, and he was a good pilot according to his records
*   but now certain manoeuvres like high-speed low-level flying with partially severe lateral position ('the whole side window was filled from ground') violate his need (desire) for safety
*   he also could not stand to be for better or for worse in bad weather on the wing of a comrade
*   this kind of dependence makes him insecure so he was partially not able to take required actions → in the course of this insecurity it happened once that he erroneous let the gear down instead of releasing the speed brakes
*   those errors made him think about quitting flying - today he is ready to give up jet flying
*   after he quit flying the symptoms disappeared completely, he is balanced and relaxed, his wife did realize a very positive development.

Selection statement (7 years ago)

- Personality: An active open officer candidate who deals critical with his environment; he is about to stabilize himself and is looking for ideals; the overall development point at a initiative and enthusiastic personality.
- Intellect: Average intelligence; more verbal abilities; he is able to think rational and logical; sometimes his argumentation is too emotional.
- Functional (basic flight abilities):
  - he carried out simple tasks automatically after a short period of training
  - in coping with multiple tasks he showed a flexible distribution of attention in the beginning
  - with increasing workload his concentration and his multiple task performance decreases
  - his reactions became unsure and there was a lack of anticipation with a tendency to a jerky and cramped (rigid) handling of the controls.
- Behaviour: In unaccustomed / unusual situations he needs practice and time to gain security and self-confidence (slow-starter)
- Remarks: Depending on the development of his personality he could make it through the flight training because of overall useful flight abilities.

Questions

1. Diagnosis:
How do you discriminate between fear of flying and airsickness?
How do you discriminate between fear of flying and burnout?
How do you discriminate between fear of flying and Post-Traumatic Stress Disorder (PTSD)?
How do you discriminate between fear of flying and psychosomatic disorder?
What kind of diagnostic measures would you apply?:
     a) personality tests
     b) performance tests
2. Counselling / intervention / therapy:
What kind of Intervention (counselling, treatment, therapy) would you recommend?
Should the pilot be allowed to fly while in therapy / treatment?
3. Prevention:
What conclusions would you consider as far as prevention is concerned?
In which phase of a flying career would you expect one or more of these symptoms / disorders?
When would you start to take preventive measures (basic-Training, line-Flying, transition phases, advanced level of flying, captaincy, ...)?

Results

Diagnosis and recommendation:
- it is a case of fear of flying which refers to special situations in flying a jet aircraft
- the reason is a high need for safety corresponding with a lack of risk-taking
- in the course of the training he did not show any anxiety of fear, because the training conditions in the USA did not violate his safety concerns
- fear / anxiety came forward under other conditions like the weapon system training in Europe
- sometimes he had psycho-vegetative symptoms in the USA too.

The attrition from flying was recommended because of fear of flying (FOF). No generalized anxiety had developed. Nevertheless, there is a high risk that the symptoms occur again under subjective emotional (adverse) conditions.

Case 2 (21-year old student pilot)

Flight surgeon statement

Severe signs of airsickness after 8 flight hours in basic flight training. Minor signs of anxiety.

Subject's statement

Almost no problems in student orientation flights (SOF), besides sometimes minor stomach irritation
- he overcame those irritation through proper nutrition and physical training
- in flight 8 he experienced severe airsickness after returning from the training area
- it was a very hot day
- it was very 'bumpy' in 3000 ft
- airsickness occurred in the landing phase.

History

- No motion sickness in childhood
- the day before there was an incident in the landing phase: IP took over because he (the student) came too close to another aircraft in the traffic pattern; he reacted too slow according to the IP
- IP was very angry in debriefing; he said something like 'safety risk'.

- up to this point he has had a lot of fun while flying, and he was a good student according to his records

IP-statement

- No problems so far, except the landing phase in flight # 7
- student felt a little tense after the incident flight
- he might have been a little harsh to the student, but the situation was a 'close call'
- airsickness occurred suddenly, without any signs
- overall a good student; showed good progress until flight #7

Selection statement (3 years ago)

1. Personality: A committed officer candidate with a positive outlook concerning his future; looking for ideals; very interested in flying.
2. Intellect: Highly intelligence; he is able to think rational and logical; his argumentation is very rational.
3. Functional (basis flight abilities): he carried out tasks automatically after a short period of training
   - in coping with multiple tasks he showed a flexible distribution of attention
   - with increasing workload his concentration lacks
   - sometimes there was a lack of anticipation; then his reaction were delayed.

Questions

1. Diagnosis:
Airsickness or fear of flying?
How do you discriminate between airsickness and fear of flying?
What is the cause of the airsickness/fear of flying?
What kind of diagnostic measures would you apply?:
      a) personality tests
      b) performance tests
2. Counselling / intervention / therapy:
What kind of Intervention (counselling, treatment, therapy) would you recommend?
3. Prevention:
What conclusions would you consider as far as prevention is concerned?
In which phase of a flying career would you expect one or more of these symptoms / disorders?
When would you start to take preventive measures?

Results

Diagnosis and recommendation:
- it is a case of a stress-induced airsickness in combination with a single event
- he did not experience a similar situation before in his career
- in the course of the training he did not show any anxiety or fear so far.

A re-ride and a close supervision were recommended. If airsickness continues a decision should be made about possible measures (e.g. Anti - Airsickness Training Program AATP).

Case 3 (46-year old helicopter pilot, more than 5000 flight hours)

Flight surgeon statement

Lack of performance. He suspects fear of flying.

His statement

Almost no problems so far in his flying career (2500 hours helicopter pilot)
- After several Iraq-missions he felt kind of burned out
- he did not get an expected promotion; other (younger) guys were preferred
- his physical fitness was very low lately
- sometimes he hates to do his job
- there were discussions about closing down the squadron
- in Iraq he always felt unsure because of the circumstances of the flying business there
- they were flying UN-inspectors over several months
- it was a psychological frustration and very stressful situation
- they were on duty 14-16 hours per day
- in more than one flight he had major safety problems
- the public pressure was high depending on the political situation
- sometimes they were threatened in the hotel
- they did not leave the hotel in their spare time because it was too dangerous
- there was at least one event in which he feared for his and his comrades life

Statement of his commander

- Engaged and experienced officer with good airmanship
- always willing to work overtime and to do several tasks
- seems a little bit 'overworked' lately
- no sign of fear of flying detected so far.

Questions

1. Diagnosis:
How do you discriminate between fear of flying and burnout?
How do you discriminate between fear of flying and psychosomatic disorder?
How do you discriminate between fear of flying and PTSD?
What kind of diagnostic measures would you apply?:
        a) personality tests
        b) performance tests
2. Counselling / intervention / therapy:
What kind of Intervention (counselling, treatment, therapy) would you recommend?
Should the pilot be allowed to fly while in therapy / treatment?
3. Prevention:
What conclusions would you consider as far as prevention is concerned?
In which phase of a flying career would you expect one or more of these symptoms / disorders?
When would you start to take preventive measures (basic-Training, line-Flying, transition phases, advanced level of flying, captaincy, ...)?

Results

Diagnosis and recommendation:
• Burnout through to loss of motivation; anxiety due to situations in Iraq.

     Psycho-physical training were suggested; no further Iraq-missions, not too many side-jobs.

Case 4 (28-year old Pilot, 1500 flight hours, former pilot in the East German Army)

Flight surgeon statement

Essential Hypertonia.

His statement

• Lots of sorrows during the time as 'the wall came down' (German reunification)
• at that time he did not know about his personal future
• he is someone who always was fighting for others, especially when he thought they (the system, the superiors) let someone down

- fighting for others was not always easy in the former East German Army; sometimes he did not have a chance to help others, otherwise he would have had a personal disadvantage
- he always had to suppress his emotions and aggressions and sometimes he felt kind of helpless; he sometimes adjusted himself to the system
- often he felt that he was caught in the system; finally he resigned
- for several months he was feeling better, he changed his nutrition, he did more sports and he lost some weight.

Statement of his commander

- He had no problems in flying so far
- engaged officer; good airmanship; good comrade
- interested in others.

Performance

- Slow starter, after adjustment one of the best in his age group.

Questions

1. Diagnosis:
How do you discriminate between psychosomatic disorder and burnout?
How do you discriminate between psychosomatic disorder loss of motivation?
How do you discriminate between psychosomatic disorder and fear of flying?
What kind of diagnostic measures would you apply?:
        a) personality tests
        b) performance tests
2. Counselling / intervention / therapy:
What kind of Intervention (counselling, treatment, therapy) would you recommend?
Should the pilot be allowed to fly while in therapy / treatment?
3. Prevention:
What conclusions would you consider as far as prevention is concerned?
In which phase of a flying career would you expect one or more of these symptoms / disorders?
When would you start to take preventive measures (basic-Training, line-Flying, transition phases, advanced level of flying, captaincy, ...)?

Results

Essential Hypertonia.

Diagnosis and recommendation:
- learned helplessness (Seligman) due to circumstances of system
- suppressed aggressivity
- psycho-physical training monitored by the flight surgeon
- if symptoms aggravate (which is expected) a behaviour therapy is indicated.

'Stand the heat! Coping with stress' – the German Air Force stress concept to out-of-area stress prevention in military flying

In the German Air Force, units are usually well prepared for UN-missions - if you look at the military training for specific missions. Medical services are of course also provided and the care for family members while the servicemen are away from their families becomes more and more a big issue. But what about the psychological preparation for those missions? 'We are going to go to war now. We are going to do what we are trained to do - but never thought we'd have to do. They could have given us a bit more notice! - I felt, all this is happening to someone else, but not to me'... this was said by John Peters, a Tornado-Pilot from a fighter squadron in England, as he learned that they were going to the Gulf-War.

In Iraq, after a political rage against the US and all western states, the mob threw stones against a German CH 53-helicopter which carried UN-inspectors. They threatened the crew and their passengers to kill them and they could save their lives only because they flew in a flash from the scene. They were very lucky.

In former Yugoslavia two French pilots were shot down and captured by Serbian civilians. Pilot and Weapon Systems Officer where about to be lynched by the mob. They were very lucky that the Serbian military police entered the scene and took them away - of course as hostages. By the way - one of the Serbian farmers who held the two at gun point, asked them to hold their hands up in German: he thought they would understand German better than English.

Such examples - and there are many more of them - raise the question: What do servicemen think about such situations? What goes on in their minds?

Flying has always been a demanding job and a source of stress. We know a lot about the stress that pilots and crews experience. Taking into account individual flying abilities and varying physical condition of the pilot, it was relatively easy to determine what would be stress in routine military flying activities.

But workload cannot be equal to stress. Stress which someone encounters is a combination of workload on the one hand and resistance on the other hand - and resistance is a combination of workload and individual abilities to cope with stress.

The stress resistance depends upon individual mental and physical strength. Thus the resistance to different workloads varies according to the individual pilot.

Whereas a pilot with a low resistance shows a declining performance under minor workload a pilot with medium or high resistance will be able to cope with high workloads.

With increasing workload our first pilot will be unable to perform whereas a pilot with a high resistance will be able to perform even in high workload conditions although his resistance may slightly decline.

The effects of varying workloads on the pilots with different resistance may lead to the following stress symptoms: There is a differentiation between temporary and continuous stress symptoms.

Temporary stress symptoms are:

- fatigue
- inability to concentrate his attention to his duties
- temporary mental disorientation
- slips of the tongue
- reduced resistance towards other stress factors.

Continuous stress symptoms are:

- vegetative disregulation
- stomach aches
- fear and anxiety
- disturbed behaviour
- inability to perform.

Such symptoms did already occur under normal flight resp. stress conditions. But what about UN-missions?

In his article 'Blue Helmet Nightmares' Harald Bräutigam writes: 'Recently at the Brussels airport excited Belgian soldiers stepped off the plane which brought them back from their UN-mission in Kigali, Africa'. Blind of rage and disappointment because of their experiences in Rwanda, they tore their blue barrets off their heads and burned them. Military surgeons and psychiatrists asked themselves: 'Is this a normal process to cope with their problems or do we have to treat those people?'

Experts call such extreme emotional reactions Post Traumatic Stress Disorders (PTSD) occurring among UN-servicemen relatively often.

Nowadays PTSD is well known, but for example during World War I such disorders were unknown and in World War II the occurrence of psychological problems were simply neglected. Soldiers experiencing those symptoms have been sorted out and punished, usually they got killed by martial law.

During the last 3 years a stress concept was developed for the German Air Force. In close connection with the units e.g. the transport squadrons, aviation psychology evaluated the experiences undergone by the crews in more than 2000 flights to Sarajewo, numerous Night-Drop-Missions over Bosnia and during all other flying activities.

The concept

The concept consists of four mayor parts:

- pre-mission training
- mission training
- post-mission training
- additional measures.

The mission training is going to be carried out by an assigned psychologist who is then part of the squadron. In the GAF there are no psychologists in the squadrons on a regular basis like the flight surgeons are. Those assigned psychologists do their duties somewhere e.g. at the German Air Force Institute of Aviation Medicine and in case of a UN-Mission they support their squadron in psychological matters like psychological mission training and counselling.

The post-mission training will be carried out as a post-mission debriefing and maybe additional measures. In this phase the treatment in cases of PTSD takes place. PTSD-treatment will be carried out at the Institute of Aviation Medicine or at the military hospitals. Additional measures are the psychological training of flight surgeons and the instruction of flying personnel in charge.

One may ask why a pre-mission training is done? Is it not better to let sleeping dogs lie? Do we not make people feel insecure by giving them too much information about their job? Should we not rather wait until psychological problems arise and see later how to treat them? ... and so on.

For an answer, this situation can be compared with a normal influenza or a cold. Taking preventive measures like sauna, etc. one will be less susceptible to get the flu. Similar things happen in case of a psychological 'infection'. If someone is psychologically well prepared for a mission one will be less likely to run into deep stress-problems.

In the section 'Clinical Psychology' of the German Air Force Institute of Aviation Medicine, about one hundred clinical-psychological examinations are carried through per year; the patients are sound pilots and flight crews most of whose psychological problems are normal and turned up during 'normal' flying activities. Time and again it was discovered that stress-induced diseases could have been avoided in many cases, if information had been provided in time, e.g. about the importance of psycho-physical fitness and about stress prevention. Additional findings stemming from the research of flight accident causes confirm this fact.

In the course of the psychological pre-mission training the following measures are to be taken:

Basic training (for all military flying personnel)

- information about stress and stressors
- relation between workload and stress
- information about what to expect in the mission
- information about adequate and inadequate coping strategies
- information about the importance of psycho-physical fitness

- information about relaxation methods and mental training
- relaxation training (e.g. Jacobson)
- mental training (e.g. visualization)
- psychological self-help and buddy aid.

Advanced Training (for military leaders)
- basic training, plus
- psychological conversation
- after-action-stress-debriefing

Perspectives

When fully put in practise this new stress concept in its modular structure will have the following benefits:
- military flying personnel will be able to recognize stress symptoms in themselves and in others and to provide psychological self-help and buddy aid.
- any crew member will able to cope better with threatening and/or traumatic situations and their consequences
- military leaders on any level will be capable to apply methods of psychological conversation and to carry out an after-action stress debriefing (AASD)
- for the first time psychological care and psychological training will be offered to the crews of the German Air Force as a whole
- flight safety will increase considerably, as flying crews will be better prepared for stressful situations, with its own benefits for daily flying activities

The after-action-stress-debriefing: 'You can come upon stress anytime'

As soon as one opens the newspaper or watches the news on television it's obvious that one can face a traumatic situation easily.

Military actions and missions mean a priori the possibility to run into extreme stressful situations (e.g. deadly accidents during military training, military actions, UN-missions, other humanitarian missions). Mainly the changing missions as far as military flying is concerned request for every crew member to be able to cope with threatening and / or traumatic situations. One can not take away the threat for pilots and crew members or neglect it. But one can, mainly through useful preventive measures (e.g. relaxation training, mental training) and post-action measures (e.g. after-action-stress-debriefing), ease up the coping process as far as stress situations are concerned.

Experience with extreme stress leaves traces as well in the individual as in the group. Lots of people suffer from physical, psychological and social stress symptoms after having had a traumatic experience. In some cases those stress symptoms lead to a long-term functional breakdown, which damages the physical health, the psychological well-being and the social relations. The group too can be under pressure after having had a traumatic experience resulting in reduced performance, low moral and less cohesion.

'First aid' as a remedy against traumatic stress

The after-action-stress-debriefing could be understood as emotional 'first aid' after a stressful situation. It offers an important psychological help for people which are otherwise healthy but suffer under extreme stress.

How does an after-action-debriefing after a stress-situation look like?

In the beginning of an after-action-debriefing after a stress-situation the afflicted persons retell their stress experience. Everyone describes his personal impression step-by-step according to the real timeline to make sure that all important aspects of the event can be identified and enlightened. This affords the group an opportunity to cope better with the traumatic incidence and the interconnected stress.

What is the purpose of an after-action-debriefing?

In a safe and comfortable environment the AASD offers an opportunity to share the stressful experience with others who had been in a similar situation.
The advantages are:
- explanation of misunderstandings and their consequences
- recognition and review of emotions and anxiety
- exchange of similar experiences and feelings
- reduction of the symptoms which could lead to long-term post-traumatic-stress-disorders (PTSD) and illness
- encouragement and support to self-help
- counselling about other support groups
- support of the recovery and mourning phase
- improvement of the communication within the group
- strengthening the group cohesion
- preparation of the group for new stressful situations

Who is leading (guiding) an after-action-debriefing?

After-action-debriefings are mostly carried out by psychologists and/or medical personnel with psychological qualification. By providing professional guidance it can also be done by formal and informal superiors of the group like flight-surgeon, priest, medics, head of a unit or other indoctrinated personnel.

Where and when does an after-action-debriefing take place?

An after-action-debriefing should take place as soon as possible after a stressful situation. One should pay attention that first of all primary needs (e.g. eating, drinking, need for sleep) come in first place.

The after-action-debriefing should take place at a safe and unendangered place which is known by the group.

During a mission a meeting place would be a good place for an after-action-debriefing. If the debriefing should take place within the barracks it would be better to meet in the unit instead of meeting in a clinic or a military hospital.

How does someone lead (guide) an after-action-debriefing?

The person who carries out the debriefing helps the group by providing a 'road-map' according to the real time-line as for as the important events are concerned. Along this time-line a step-by-step thinking and discussion process is been done concerning the 'who, what, when, where, and why' of the incident.

The facts are going to be proved by the group and the stress factors should be verified. Experiences and emotions should be exchanged. Different opinions should be tolerated unconditionally. Every witness is treated equal.

During the process of retelling the leader guides the conversation about thoughts, emotions and actions of the afflicted crew-members and helps them to develop the right feel for their own stress.

Everyone is encouraged to actively seek the conversation and so relax from the stress. The leader is looking for signs and symptoms of dysfunction and gives information about normal stress reactions. He also provides hints for the group members for self-help and for developing coping strategies.

Conclusion

Who takes part at on a sensible After-Action-Stress-Debriefing is able to gain distance towards the stressful and/or traumatic situation. He also will be able to do his job again efficiently very soon.

The after-action-stress-debriefing should be a 'first aid' for military groups who are strongly afflicted by a traumatic event.

Military leaders, flight surgeons as well as medics and the priest should be familiar with these measures.

Psychological training, airsickness prevention and airsickness therapy

Otto Lilienthal, who carried out his first flight in 1891 certainly would have had reported certain symptoms of airsickness if he had been asked. Those symptoms could have been pallor, cold sweat, nausea, loss of concentration, fatigue and vomiting. But how about Lilienthals successors? Is airsickness still a problem? The answer is yes, nobody is immune from becoming airsick. What can be done against it?

Almost precisely 15 years ago the GAF Aviation Psychology started developing procedures and experiments to eliminate airsickness. This was started in connection with the positive experiences that were made when the British Royal Air Force applied procedures of behaviour therapy to flying and also in connection with the well-known effectivity of psychological training methods in competitive sports which are used to improve learning capacity and efficiency, but also to reduce negative stress reactions. Airsickness - or in more general terms motion sickness, is a common problem among aviators.

The basic concept is to adjust and to stabilize pilots and navigators who had begun to suffer from airsickness in their toleration against unfamiliar vestibular motor stimuli and related or additional unfamiliar stress reactions of their own bodies.

The procedures applied were an individual behaviour analysis, relaxation training, mental training, physical fitness training, gyro-wheel training, spatial disorientation training and systematic desensitisation (in vitro and in vivo).

The qualification requirements were voluntariness, the exclusion of organic defects of the sensory systems, high flying motivation and the co-operation of the flying unit. To avoid the risk of helping the wrong person whose flying performance is limited we accepted only students whose flying performance was at least average. This prerequisite could not be determined by the test results alone, it was rather necessary to obtain a statement from the instructor pilot. For this reason only those persons were selected whose flying performance was judged at least average by their flying instructors in a written evaluation and for whom a good prognosis was established.

As far as flying motivation is concerned, it is evident that it had to be maintained at a high degree. However, it was found that it is an essential criterion of flying motivation whether it is accentuated intrinsically, that is by flying itself or the chances of success, or rather extrinsically, that is by external factors like pressure from superiors, reputation and career prospects of the persons. The latter seems to be less promising.

Too much motivation can also hamper the training process, since persons unintentionally manoeuvre themselves into a higher state of activation and tension when putting their extreme motivation into action and reduce the level of complex performance functions.

Since experience shows that general physical fitness and circulatory efficiency provide some, however non-specific, protection from stress, fitness training became a requirement for participating in the training program. Furthermore, a specific fitness training was to sharpen individual perception of stress reactions, build up self-confidence and create favourable conditions for the relaxation training, which we found to be much more efficient after preceding strain. The time required for learning was thus reduced and relaxation capability gained in quality.

The physical fitness training consists of a daily 30-minute endurance training (mainly running, swimming or cycling). After the athletic training a three-phase relaxation training is given, a combination of progressive muscular relaxation according to Jacobsen and autogenic training according to Schultz, which is carried out independently by each person with audio-tapes according to specific instructions.

The mental training used is a method known from industrial science and competitive sports. What is meant is a conscious, systematically repeated mental performance or an internal realization of a sensomotoric action without the performance of observable concrete movements.

In highly complex demand situations mental training serves to accelerate and stabilize sensomotoric learning processes and to enlarge the degree of freedom of action by storing behaviour programs in other (subcortical) regulatory levels and thus creating new capacity for grasping and dealing with information in unexpected situations or situations imposing stress. The efficiency of this training has in the meantime been proved especially in competitive sports, but also in flying.

Daily training of a maximum duration of 30 minutes on the basis of the training syllabus together with relaxation exercises is a highly effective preparation for the real situation. It makes the subsequent desensitisation measures easier and preserves the practical relation to flying.

During this phase the 'Rhoenrad'-training with increasing load is started. After habituation to the device exercises are requested comprising a higher rolling speed, additional changes of handles, one-handed rolling, additional movements of the head in the form of search tasks and finally rolling with closed eyes, forwards and backwards.

The final and most important phase is the desensitisation in the Spatial Disorientation Simulator (SDS). This is a closed cockpit which can be turned around its vertical and centrifugal axis and in which the test person moves his head to the right and to the left as well as upwards and downwards in the different sessions in which the cockpit is moved according to a preset order. The test person reports in set periods the state he is in which he rates on a 10-point scale ranging from normal to a strong feeling of nausea. Rotational speed is increased continuously up to 15 rpm.

Additional homework, like the already mentioned circulatory efficiency training, the mental training and the 'chair flying' supplement this phase.

However, an essential and critical part of the Anti-Airsickness Training Program (AATP) is desensitisation in vivo ('in the real situation'), during which the airsick student pilot must learn to apply the newly learned behaviour patterns and training tips in flight.

The above-mentioned eight missions in the SDS are important for preparing the pilot to enter an aeroplane again. During these missions the test person learns to rate his feelings when separate motion occurs (in this case without outside references) and to increase the individual threshold with regard to the occurrence of airsickness symptoms with increasing degree of difficulty.

All in all, this phase is the most important and sensitive phase, since it is part of the real situation in the aeroplane. The desensitisation phase is continued in three flights in the following manner: the first flight (00.30 hrs) is performed mainly by the flying instructor (straight and level), the second flight (01.00 h) is performed by the student pilot analogous to SOF-02 according to his standard and the third flight (01.30 h) is performed by both the student pilot and the flying instructor as a full screening flight.

Care will be taken that these flights which are critical for the course of the program will only be performed by instructor pilots who know the AATP basics and are good 'psychologists' themselves. Not until these three flights have been performed the AATP is considered to be completed, and only then a decision as to whether the student pilot may remain in the screening phase of basic flight training can be made. The final decision includes the consultation of the squadron commander, instructor pilot, flight surgeon and aviation psychologist.

Results

Figures of the past ten years prove that about 70% of the student pilots who took part in the AATP were able to continue the flight screening.

In conclusion it can be said that a specific selection of airsick student pilots was successfully trained and rehabilitated with the use of psychological behaviour methods and a systematic, step-by-step adaptation to kinetosis-causing stimuli conditions without any medication. The proposed procedure can most likely be improved by means of biofeedback methods and further development of motion simulation devices.

The AATP still shows considerable success even after things had gone wrong. But what about preventing things from going wrong? Here it comes to a matter of prevention which is in most medical and psychological questions a challenge to science and daily practice. This is especially true for one of the 'interfaces' of medicine and psychology, the wide field of psychosomatic medicine.

The question of how airsickness can be prevented or at least reduced within the scope of a preventive measure arose in the German Air Force after the number of student pilots who developed airsickness symptoms strongly increased in 1988.

At the same time less personnel were available for carrying out the AATP which requires a relatively large number of personnel and much time. This forced the Clinical Psychology and Screening branch to think about measures of preventing airsickness.

This was the hypothesis: A prevention program reduces the number of cases of airsickness in the subsequent flying training. This airsickness prevention program was introduced in January 1989.

At first it lasted an hour and consisted of the following:

- Introduction to the tasks of our division
- Information on the correlation between motion and airsickness, for instance, how do I act on my very first flight?
- Unsuitable or wrong mental attitudes
- Correlation between attitude and airsickness
- Correlation between wrong mental attitude and airsickness
- Information on visceral reactions
- Information on stress and coping
- Psychophysical training like relaxation training, mental training, sport within the scope of training.

The frequency of the occurrence of airsickness in a group of student pilots who did not participate in a preventional program (n=164) was compared with two other groups who had participated in such a program. The two latter groups differed from another in two other aspects: the place at which the flying part of the basic screening was performed and the duration of the prevention program.

The first of these two groups had performed the flying part and the airsickness prevention program in Fürstenfeldbruck, Germany (n=98), while the other group had performed its training in Goodyear, Arizona (n=88).

In April of 1990 the flying part of the screening was transferred from Fürstenfeldbruck to Goodyear. There the flight psychologist of the 3rd German Air Force Training Squadron was not given any time to conduct the Anti-Airsickness Training Program.

He was, however, permitted to extend the prevention program somewhat. This newly designed program now includes the subjects which were already prepared by the one-hour version in Fürstenfeldbruck as well as four additional hours in which the relaxation training and the mental training procedures were practised.

The frequency of the occurrence of airsickness was significantly lower after the airsickness prevention program was conducted before the flying part of the screening. 'Symptoms of airsickness' means light and severe forms of airsickness (the person was airsick once or twice or more than three times). 'Minor airsickness' means that the student pilot showed certain indications or symptoms of airsickness, but was nevertheless able to overcome these symptoms and to finish the flight without any intervention by the flying instructor. 'Major airsickness' means that the student pilot was airsick on one or two or on three or more flights and that he had to stop these flights.

If three flights were incomplete, one had to make a decision whether the student pilot was to be rejected or whether he could go on to the AATP.

Of the total of 164 student pilots for whom the airsickness prevention program was not conducted 20.7% had light to severe indications of airsickness, while only 9.2% of the 98 student pilots in Fürstenfeldbruck for whom the airsickness prevention program was conducted had symptoms of airsickness. This difference is statistically significant. The airsickness prevention program was most effective for student pilots who had severe symptoms of airsickness three times or more often.

After the flying part of the screening was transferred to Goodyear in Arizona, the frequency of occurrence of airsickness slightly increased in all areas. This may be due to the different conditions like heat and turbulences. But if one compares the respective figures with the figures of the group of student pilots who had not participated in any preventional program in Fürstenfeldbruck one will realize that the percentage is still significantly lower.

It would be going a bit too far to deduce from this experience that an airsickness prevention program is generally effective. For this reason the German Air Force made its airsickness prevention program palatable to the US-Navy.

Since there existed no figures on the frequency of occurrence of airsickness in the US-Navy, it was important to determine these figures. A questionnaire was introduced in 1990 / 1991 and distributed to 842 students and instructor pilots at the Naval Air Station Whithing Field.

It turned out that 402 (47.74%) of these 842 persons were airsick on one or more flights. After everyone had been excluded with more than 68 flying hours (N = 360), the rate of airsickness even increased slightly and exceeded the 50% limit (50.56%). Most of the student pilots became airsick on the first or second flight. The frequency of occurrence of airsickness decreased drastically on the subsequent flights.

After the one-hour version of the airsickness prevention program was introduced, the frequency of airsickness within the US Navy also decreased significantly. Only 30.85% of the group of student pilots who had participated in the prevention program (n = 94) became airsick. This resulted in a highly significant difference compared to the frequency of occurrence of 50.56% among the student pilots who had not participated in a prevention program.

It turned out that student pilots - with or without a prevention program - who were airsick on the first flight had a considerably higher rate of airsickness on the following flights than student pilots who were not airsick on the first flight. This fact itself indicates that it is absolutely necessary to prevent airsickness on the first flights. Thus, the aim of our prevention program is mainly to perform the first two flights properly.

Conclusion

Considering the figures of the German Air Force and the US Navy, it becomes clear that the airsickness prevention program

- had a strong influence on reducing the frequency of occurrence of airsickness and
- has reduced the necessity of an Anti-Airsickness Training Program that requires a lot of time and personnel.

23 Clinical-psychological diagnostics and consultation in commercial aviation

Reiner Kemmler
Lufthansa German Airlines, Germany

In civil aviation similarly as in military aviation (see Chapter 22) clinical psychology has to deal with individuals who develop behavioural disorders which are related to the job demands and may seriously diminish their performance at work and their personal well-being. So far as pilots are concerned in the future (1999 ff) the psychodiagnostics will be done according to JAR-FCL 3 'Psychological Evaluation' (see Chapter 10). For other occupational groups in aviation (e. g. flight attendants) modified diagnostics could be more applicable, but this depends on the given question. After the diagnosis is made six steps will follow:

1. Explanation of test results to the individual and Aeromedical Section (AMS).
2. Max. 3 to 4 counselling sessions about consequences on basis of self-competence and self-management.
3. Recommendations for psychological training and/or treatment.
4. Performance of training and treatment / transfer to experts.
   In case of treatment airline psychologists should transfer clients to external specialists.
5. Re-evaluation / quality control (feedback / reporting system)
6. Permanent focus on improvement of internal / external social and expert network

Three case studies may demonstrate clinical psychology applications in civil aviation:

Case 1 (35-year old Helicopter-Pilot , 2400 flight hours)

Flight surgeon statement

Increasing tendency of fear of flying after 1 accident with 1 fatality and 4 incidents within 5 months.
- Severe stress symptoms during flying.

Subject's statement

- Despite the series of events he wanted to continue flying
- he is observing himself as more and more in a state of tension during flying
- he is wondering himself about his coolness after having seen his colleague burning to death after the first emergency landing
- during flying he is becoming afraid of sudden eventualities, especially linked to a hammering noise and rotational movements of the heli, especially in the Bell UH - 1 D
- in-flight he is trying to be absorbed by side tasks not to be confronted with his thoughts
- he is denying any fear of flying
- he is convinced to be aware of all reactions of anxiety and being able to control them
- he thinks, his behaviour is related to a higher level of concentration to be prepared for unexpected flight situations
- he is very often totally exhausted after duty.

Psychological evaluation

- In his biography there is no indication for any experience of high stress or fear of challenging situations
- he likes flying due to the feeling of freedom
- he belongs to the best of his group (police squadron), he is holding a license for 4 different heli types, he is Instructor Pilot since 10 years
- he gets the most sensitive flights within his group
- there is a normal level of trait anxiety, but a high level of state anxiety in-flight
- his personality profile does not show any significant abnormalities
- there is a slight trend to loose self-confidence
- there is a significant trend to be not as dominant and assertive as before
- the proposal of the flight surgeon to undergo a psychological investigation is irritating him.

Questions

1. Diagnosis
How do you discriminate between fear of flying and PTSD?
How do you discriminate between fear of flying and burnout?
How do you discriminate between fear of flying and psychosomatic disorders?
What kind of tests would you apply?
       a) aptitude tests?
       b) personality tests ?
2. Counselling / intervention / therapy
What kind of measurement would you recommend?
Should he continue flying during treatment?
3.Prevention
What consequences would you consider with respect to preventive actions?

Results

Diagnosis and recommendation:
- Specific Phobia DSM-IV 300.29, ICD-10 F40.2
- he underwent a behaviour therapy (exposure therapy technique) successfully
- continuation of flying career.

Case 2 (30- year old Flight Attendant, 8 months in service)

Flight surgeon statement

Fear of flying due to a flight with bomb alert.
- Low level of stress coping behaviour or insufficient motivation for flying

Subject's statement

- She is afraid of each flight now
- she is always expecting bomb alarms or explosions
- she started to continue flying, but is going out of control the evening before the next flight
- she likes flying very much, there is no alternative in the future
- her reactions are not understandable for herself
- she is wondering, why she seems to be the only one of the whole flight crew who is reacting like that
- after the event she took one day off to recover
- all seemed to be normal, but when the passengers arrive at the A/C she is panicking

- during taxiing she hardly can control herself, she is trembling and shaking
- there are strong wishes to leave the plane before take-off
- during work on board there are no problems, but in the breaks panic reactions are starting
- she is experiencing some strange feelings concerning herself
- there is more and more distance to others and herself
- she never wants to come into such a situation (exploding into pieces)
- at home she starts vomiting when anticipating work situations (to serve passengers)
- she is permanently aroused, her heart is beating fast, she is loosing control about her body
- she is afraid of loosing her job if she gets sick after such a short time flying as an attendant
- the event has been 2 weeks ago
- it occurred 30 min before landing, a passenger detected a small strange package attached inside the aft toilet (small electric devices, cables and a battery, could be identified)
- all passengers were evacuated as far as possible from the place
- she and her colleagues reacted according to procedures
- during approach and landing she had to sit at her designated place in the aft section close to the toilet, strapped in the seat, unable to protect herself
- she was permanently expecting an explosion
- her thoughts went to her relatives, how they would be able to identify the small pieces of the rest of her body
- there was no real relief after landing, because they had interrogations from security and police for hours
- nobody took care of her state
- in the hotel she had some kind of break-down due to her mental and physical exhaustion.

Questions

1. Diagnosis
What kind of measures would you apply?
How do you discriminate between fear of flying and PTSD?
How do you discriminate between fear of flying and burn-out?
2. Counselling / intervention / treatment
What kind of intervention would you recommend?
Should she continue flying during intervention?
3. Prevention
What considerations do you have about prevention for this case?

Results

Diagnosis and recommendation:

- acute Post-Traumatic Stress-Disorder DSM-IV 309.81, ICD-10 F 43.1
- she underwent a behaviour therapy (exposure therapy technique) successfully
- she continued flying for several months, but experienced recurrent anxiety symptoms and finished finally flying as flight attendant after one year.

Case 3 (35-year old Flight Attendant, 13 years in service)

Flight surgeon statement

Vegetative state of exhaustion, fear of flying or burn-out

Subject's statement

- Flying was very exciting in the beginning (travelling into foreign countries, visiting friends, approaching different people and cultures)
- was supposed to become a teacher, but changed to flying
- first 5 years were fulfilling
- wanted part-time duty, but the management refused
- not fit for flying since 2 months
- severe hormonal dysregulation, a little better since grounding
- she considers herself as hyperactive, but nearly always exhausted, overloaded
- she feels guilty not being fit
- there is a general state of anxiety and emotional instability, weakness, tends to cry
- impatience, aggressive tendencies (if the passengers approach the A/C she wants to spit to them)
- she is avoiding close contacts to passengers and crew members, years before she liked and was rewarded for her attitude
- her mental performance (concentration, attention, organisation, flexibility) has decreased
- there are lots of complaints in different body system (inability to recover, sleeplessness, sexual problems, heart aches, head-ache, drowsiness, increase of body weight, digestive dysregulations, changing eating habits)
- reduced responsibility
- lack motivation, not only related to work
- intolerant and repulsive attitude towards the management (rostering, social care, time pressure, minimum free time)
- unable to prepare her flight equipment before going to work
- several break downs at dispatch

- especially avoiding long-range flights
- does not leave the hotel room during layover
- 'staying at home is much nicer than to be in the Caribbean'
- no need or interest in active help, psychological investigation or treatment (fulfils only the request of the flight surgeon)
- does not want a special health recovery program
- she simply wants to quit.

Psychological Evaluation

- Normal level of trait anxiety
- high level of state anxiety (flying duty)
- significant trend to be undercontrolled, tendency for acting out,
- positive self-image
- positive social capacity (open-minded, empathic behaviour).

Questions

1.Diagnosis
How to discriminate between fear of flying and PTSD?
How to discriminate between fear of flying and burn-out?
How to discriminate between fear of flying and psychosomatic disorders?
What kind of tests would you apply?
2.Counseling / intervention / treatment
What kind of intervention would you recommend?
Should she continue flying during intervention?
What is the prognosis for this syndrome?
3.Prevention
What consequences would you consider with respect to prevention?

Results

Diagnosis and recommendation:
- Generalised Anxiety Disorder DSM-IV 300.02, ICD-10 41.1
- she refused psychotherapeutic help
- she finished her flying career as flight attendant and started a totally different training.

24 Neuroses, psychoses and drug addiction in aviation personnel: A clinical experience

Antonio Tundo*
Fulvia Marchetti*
* Centro per la Ricerca in Psicopatologia, Italy

During our activity as clinical psychiatrists we have treated 19 patients who were pilots or flight attendants on international flights.

The population consisted of 13 (68%) patients suffering from Mood Disorders, 2 (11%) from Alcohol Abuse, 2 (11%) from Obsessive Compulsive Disorder, 1 (5%) from Panic Disorders, and 1 (5%) from Social Phobia. Among the 13 patients with Mood Disorders 4 (31%) presented a further diagnosis of alcohol and / or substance abuse too (cannabis or cocaine).

It is known that the Mood Disorders are a complex psychopathological condition divided into: Unipolar Recurrent Depression, characterised by recurrent depressive episodes, Bipolar I Disorder, consisting of depressive and manic episodes, and Bipolar II Disorder, characterised by depressive and hypomanic episodes (Goodwin 1990). In the presented cases 5 patients out of 12 were Unipolars, 1 out of 12 Bipolars I and 7 out of 12 Bipolars II.

A comparison between these data and some other data from literature reviews has not been possible. In fact, Medline research about the period 1986-1996 does not report any papers about the incidence of psychiatric disorders among pilots and flight attendants on international flights. To my knowledge, during this decade only 3 papers have been published about alcoholism in airline aviators, its treatment and the risks connected with it. (Wich 1992, Flynn et al. 1993, Holdener 1993).

However, with our data, some considerations are possible. First of all the anxiety disorders, better known in the past as 'neurotic disorders', do not seem to be very frequent among pilots and flight attendants on international flights. These subjects seem to be more at risk for Mood Disorders, in particular for Bipolar II Disorders. Moreover, according to others authors, the alcohol or substance abuse seem to be not rare. This abuse seems to be often connected with a Mood Disorder. At this point we could analyse the main clinical characteristics of the Mood Disorders, the possible therapies and the form of prevention. As described above the Mood Disorders are characterised by the recurrence of depressive episodes (unipolar recurrent depression) or the recurrence of depressive and manic or hypomanic episodes (Bipolar Disorders).

The essential feature of depression is the low mood: patients are sad, tearful and look despondent. Another characteristic of depression is the incapacity to take an interest and derive pleasure. With this loss of interests, or anhedonia, there is a reduction of function in many areas. For example, loss of energy and concentration. There is a pessimism about the future and feelings of guilty may be present. Many patients with depression have concomitant feeling of anxiety. They may experience physical symptoms like tension, restlessness or agitation, or the anxiety may take the form of unjustified worrying. In its more severe forms, the depression may be accompanied by delusions or hallucinations whose content is consistent with the typical depressive themes of personal inadequacy, guilt, disease, death or deserved punishments. Appetite, sexuality and sleep can change, usually they are reduced, but occasionally they may be increased.

In mania the mood is abnormally elevated. The patient is over cheerful or euphoric and expansive, often there is an excitement with an excessive sense of power and self-confidence. Pressure of speech makes it difficult to interrupt. Behaviours can be very labile, and switch rapidly from elation to irritability and hostility. Aggressive outbursts or physical violence are common. Patients often experience an unusual sense of well-being and increased energy. An excess of energy leads to overactivity, restlessness and often patients do a lot of plans. Cognition and perception are greatly impaired. The subjective experience of the patient is that he feels particularly well and has clear ideas, rapid associations and strong memory. In reality the patient lacks the ability to maintain attention and is very distractible. Judgement is decreased and there is a loss of social inhibition. Even in mania delusions and hallucinations may be present and their content is consistent with the typical manic themes: for example power, identity, special relationship to a deity or a famous person. Sometimes there are persecutory delusions and ideas of being controlled. Cardinal signs of mania are the decreased desire or need for sleeping, the inattention to nutrition and the sexual excesses.

The hypomania is a degree less than mania. Patients have a persistent mild elevation of mood with increased energy and activity, there is a marked feeling of physical well-being and a mental efficiency. The need for sleep is decreased. The difference between hypomania and mania is based on the severity of the symptoms. Episodes are not severe enough to cause a marked impairment in social or occupational functioning. Hypomanic patients do not need hospitalisation and there are no psychotic features. The hypomanic experience is often pleasant and the patient may be unaware of it or can tend to deny it.

An appropriate therapy of Mood Disorders aims to enable the patient to achieve and maintain complete remission of symptoms. The treatment can be considered in three phases.

Phase I - Treatment of acute episode

Patients with florid depressive symptoms are treated with antidepressant drugs like tricyclics, selective serotonine reuptake inhibitors, while in the so called atypical depression they are treated with monoamine oxidase inhibitors.

Patients with florid manic symptoms are treated with antimanic agents like lithium, valproate, carbamazepine. These drugs are often associated and in combination with antipsychotic agents and benzodiazepines. In the hypomanic episodes antimanic agents are usually sufficient.

Phase II - Prophylactic treatment to reduce the risk of further episodes

Patients with unipolar recurrent depression can receive as prophylactic treatment the same antidepressant used during the acute episode. It would be better to use the new antidepressants, for example the selective serotonine reuptake inhibitors. In fact they do not influence the capacity of concentration, the attention, the quickness of reflex, moreover they provoke less side effects. Patients with bipolar disorders can receive as prophylactic treatment lithium, valproate and carbamazepine often associated.

Phase III - Psychotherapeutic treatment of psychosocial effects of mood disorders

1. In addition to drug treatment some patients can benefit from a specific psychotherapeutic treatment, maintenance psychotherapy, psycho-analysis, cognitive or behavioural therapy. The goals of the psychological approach are:
2. patients can receive a great help in facing the problems connected with Mood Disorders, in particular alcohol abuse.
3. they can learn to identify precipitants or early manifestations of acute episodes and thanks to this fact the right treatment can be promptly initiated.
4. they can overcome the emotional problems and the sense of inadequacy caused by the recurrent manic-depressive episodes such as the sensation of a sense of insanity, the loss of the self-esteem, the fear of being not well considered because of their illness, the difficulty with normal social behaviour and especially with the working career.

But why pilots and flight attendants on international flights would be at risk for Mood Disorders, in particular for Bipolar II Form?

Nowadays depression and mania are conceptualised as the clinical manifestations of a dysfunction of the limbic-diencephalic areas of the brain (Akiskal 1995). Various factors, either biological or psychological, converge in producing this dysfunction: heredity, gender and early loss. Usually the limbic-diencephalic disregulation produces the temperamental characteristics of the subject, i.e. the subject's usual energy level and mood (Koukopoulos 1983). Mood disorders can occur when a predisposed patient is exposed to specific physical or psychic stress.

It is very important to underline that physical or psychic stress do not generally seem to cause ex novo episodes but mobilises them in those people with a personal and a family history of Mood Disorders.

Pilots and flight attendants on international flights are frequently exposed to some physical stressors which today seem to be one of the cause that triggers a mood disorder (Wehr 1986, Koukopoulos 1990).

Among these stressors the most important are: flying over different times zones may have precipitating effects, the change of the sleep-wake rhythm, an irregular and/or reduced sleep, the frequent changes of climatic conditions (for example temperature, humidity, the light wave-length).

These factors may trigger a mood disorder for the first time in predisposed people in whom the disease would have remained latent and without clinical manifestations if these factors had not occurred.

The data presented in this paper must be considered as preliminary data. In fact some aspects could create the following bias:

1. The number of examined cases is limited.
2. The patients were examined in a private Centre specialised in Anxiety and Mood Disorders.
3. In the literature there are no other possible data to compare.

If in the future the clinical experience will confirm these data it could be useful to take some aspects into account:

- patients suffering from alcoholism should be examined in order to search for a possible concomitant mood disorder; in this case a specific treatment should be established
- during selections for pilots or flight attendants on international flights, psychologists should draw the attention to the risk factors for Mood Disorders. In particular the predisposing heredity and the affective temperament should be very carefully investigated.
- the subjects at risk should follow some simple rules which can help them to avoid the onset of a mood disorder. Among these rules there are the abstention of the consumption of substances like alcohol, caffeine; and a regular sleep.
- when the very first symptoms of an episode appear the right treatment and, if necessary, a prophylactic treatment, should be established.

References

Akiskal, H.S. (1995) Mood Disorders: introduction and overview. In: Kaplan HI, Sadock BJ (Eds): *Comprehensive textbook of psychiatry/IV*. Baltimora, Williams and Wilkins, 1067-1079

Flynn, C (1993) Sturges M, Swarsen R, Kohn G: Alcoholism and treatment in airline aviation: one company's results. *Aviation, Space, and Environmental Medicine* 64 (4): 314-318

Goodwin, F.K. (1990) Jamison KR: *Manic-depressive illness*. New York, Oxford University Press

Holdener, F. (1993) Alcohol and civilian aviation. *Addiction* 88 (7): 953-958

Koukopoulos, A., Caliari, B., Tundo, A. et al (1983) Rapid cyclers, temperament, and antidepressants. *Compr Psychiatry* 24: 249-258

Koukopoulos A, Tundo A (1990) Floris GF et al: Changes in life habits that may influence the course of affective disorders. In Stefanis CN, Rabavilas AD, Soldatos CR (Eds): *Psychiatry: a world perspective*. International Congress Series 990. Amsterdam: Elsevier, 478-483

Wehr, T.A. (1986) Jacobsen FM, Sack DA et al: Phototherapy of seasonal affective disorder: time of day and suppression of melatonin are not critical for antidepressant effect. *Arch Gen Psychiatry* 43: 870-875

Wich, R. (1992) Alcohol and pilot performance decrements. *Alcohol, Drugs and Driving*: 8 (3-4): 207-215

Section 5

Human Factors Accident Investigation and Prevention

Course Manager:
Robert Lee

Section Editor:
Brent Hayward

25   Introduction and overview

Brent Hayward
Asia Pacific Resource Management, Australia

Introduction

The final section of this book deals with the phase of aviation which all too frequently forms the last chapter of the lives of those involved in aircraft accidents. This section will focus on the human factors of aircraft accident investigation from the perspective of aviation psychology, and will also detail strategies for accident prevention.

What follows is based on the final training course of the 22nd Conference of the European Association for Aviation Psychology, held at Sabaudia, Italy, in September 1996. The course on *Human Factors in Accident Investigation and Prevention* was led by Dr Rob Lee of the Australian Bureau of Air Safety Investigation (BASI). He was assisted in development and delivery of the training course by Alan Hobbs of BASI, Kristina Pollack of the Swedish Air Force, and Brent Hayward of Asia Pacific Resource Management.

Those who attended the course were provided with a number of documents which are considered as essential reading for those involved in aircraft accident or incident investigation. These included copies of Annex 13 to the Convention on International Civil Aviation: 'Aircraft Accident and Incident Investigation', a suite of ICAO Human Factors Digests, and two exemplary accident investigation reports. While these documents cannot be reproduced within this publication, they are readily available from their publishers and are referenced at Appendix A to this section.[1]

The course was focused on presentation of information on current subject matter and investigation techniques, followed by sessions featuring the practical application of these techniques to selected case studies. Due to the applied nature of this training, it is impossible to reproduce the content of the course in its

---

[1] An abridged summary of the BASI report on an accident to Monarch Airlines, originally published in the *ICAO Journal* (International Civil Aviation Organization,1995) is reprinted at Appendix C.

entirety within the pages of this book. What follows is the authors' attempt to provide a solid background to the issues covered within the training course, together with further information pertinent to the subject. Rather than focus on the 'nuts and bolts' of aircraft accident investigation procedures,[2] it is our intention to provide the reader with an understanding of current thinking in relation to the philosophy of aircraft accident investigation. As such, it is emphasised that this section should be read in conjunction with the documents listed at Appendix A. The curriculum for the course is detailed at Appendix B.

A central thesis of the training course was the recognition that many aircraft and other industrial mishaps are now investigated with a view to comprehensively examining the systemic factors which may have contributed to the occurrence and to the context within which they take place. The aviation psychology and human factors community has contributed significantly to the development of systemic accident investigation methods, in addition to techniques aimed at the prevention of accidents. These include the development and management of appropriately targeted selection methods, an ever-evolving understanding of the complex relationship between humans and machines, the skilled application of solution-oriented counselling and intervention techniques, and the implementation of comprehensive, operationally relevant human factors training programs. These factors can have a direct impact on the primary goals of organisational safety and efficiency, and are covered in some depth in preceding sections of this book.

Also of increasing importance are the various cultures (national, organisational, vocational) within which the world's aviation professionals carry out their daily operational duties, and the fit between those cultures and proposed safety solutions (eg., Crew Resource Management training). This section will overview current trends in air safety investigation, discuss methods available to organisations to enhance their operational safety performance, and will also examine the broader notions of culture and aviation safety.

Overview

The reader's attention is drawn back 20 years to 1977, the year of an event which endures today as he world's worst aviation disaster: the collision on the runway at Tenerife between two B747 'jumbo' jets, resulting in the tragic loss of 583 lives. Ironically, the accident occurred at the commencement of an era which may well be looked back upon as a watershed development period for aviation psychology and human factors. It followed just 17 months after the landmark 20th Technical Conference of IATA (International Air Transport Association, 1975) in Istanbul, which was dedicated to human factors for the first time, and concluded by

---

[2] For the interested reader these procedures are detailed in publications such as ICAO's Human Factors Digest No 7 (International Civil Aviation Organization, 1993), and Annex 13 to the Chicago Convention on International Civil Aviation (International Civil Aviation Organization, 1994).

predicting the onset of such a disaster if the application of human factors to aviation continued to be neglected. The accident at Tenerife also occurred little more than a year before the now infamous crash of a DC-8 due to fuel exhaustion at Portland, Oregon in 1978, after which the NTSB report discussed the impact of factors such as crew coordination, management, and teamwork (National Transportation Safety Board, 1979).

Amongst other events, these two accidents can be seen as precipitating the initial aviation industry responses to the vexed problem of 'crew caused' accidents. In Europe, this took the form of KLM's *Human Factors Awareness Course* (KHUFAC; see Hawkins, 1987), while in the United States, United Airlines' *Command, Leadership, Resource Management* training course (C/L/R) paved the way for what is now known globally as CRM training. In essence, the targets of these courses were the same; they set out to address the issues identified in the 1970's as the major causes of flight crew involved accidents: breakdowns in crew communication, teamwork, leadership, followership, and judgement. In summary: poor management of available resources. These initiatives (as with most advances related to air safety, born of necessity rather than pure invention) were rapidly followed by similar developments in Australia (TAA/Australian Airlines' *Aircrew Team Management* training program: ATM; see Margerison, McCann & Davies, 1987) and elsewhere.

At the time of these accidents, it would have been difficult to foresee the extent to which we now view many aircraft and other industrial mishaps as 'organisational accidents'. While much is still to be achieved, it is encouraging to see the depth to which some investigations now delve when attempting to get to the bottom of accident causality. Elements of the aviation industry have been leaders in the move towards a more enlightened consideration of the precursors to accidents and the contexts in which they occur. The Australian Bureau of Air Safety Investigation (BASI) is one such element, and BASI's reports on the 1993 Monarch Airlines Piper Chieftain accident at Young in New South Wales (Bureau of Air Safety Investigation, 1994) and the landing of a B747 at Sydney Airport with its nose-wheel retracted in October 1994 (Bureau of Air Safety Investigation, 1996), are palpable examples of the growing trend towards the systemic investigation and reporting of aircraft incidents and accidents.[3]

Aviation and Australia are not alone in the search for deeper roots to accident causality. Amongst others, reports on the sinking of the *Herald of Free Enterprise* channel ferry (Sheen, 1987), the King's Cross Underground railway station fire (Fennell, 1988), the Clapham Junction railway accident (Hidden, 1989), and the March 1989 crash of an F28 at Dryden in Canada (Helmreich, 1992; Moshansky, 1992; Maurino, Reason, Johnston & Lee, 1995) provide testament to this comparatively recent trend. They also add weight to the argument for a change in traditional yet rudimentary thinking regarding operator error,

---

[3] BASI's approach to aviation occurrence investigation exemplifies many of the points made within this chapter, and is outlined in detail in the following chapters authored by Lee and Hobbs.

previously exemplified within aviation by widespread inappropriate use of the term 'pilot error'. As observed by Lee (1996), if accident investigators continue to concentrate only on traditional 'sharp end' factors, then the investigation agency itself becomes part of the safety problem.

Understanding human error

Technological systems... are designed, built, operated and maintained by human beings. It is hardly surprising, therefore, that people make the largest contribution - for good or ill - to the 'safety health' of such systems (Reason, 1994b).

A growing interest in developing our understanding of the antecedents of human error has precipitated an evolution towards a more thorough understanding of industrial mishaps. In particular, the work of Professor James Reason and his colleagues at the University of Manchester (Reason, 1990, 1991a, 1991b, 1994a, 1994b, 1995, 1997) has been responsible for widespread improvement in the understanding of the causes and consequences of human error. Reason's modelling of organisational accidents, as detailed in Figure 1, builds on the work of Rasmussen (1983, 1987) and others, and is increasingly recognised within the aviation community as a means for understanding and investigating organisational anomalies. The Reason model and its use in accident investigation and prevention will be discussed in detail in the chapters which follow.

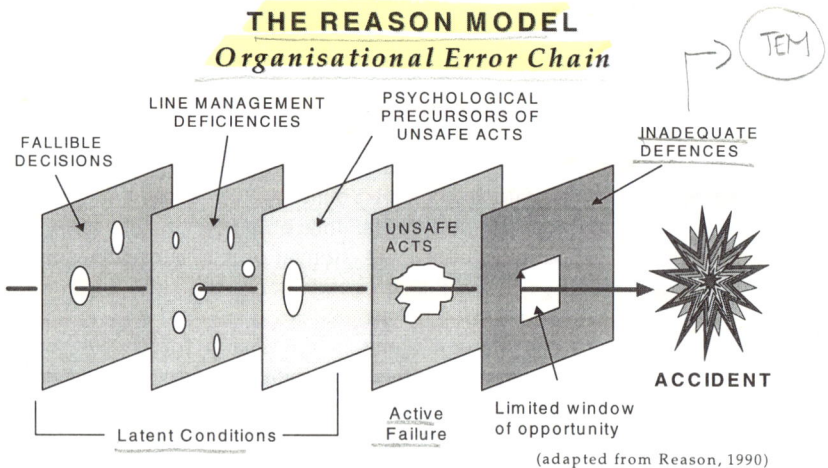

THE REASON MODEL
Organisational Error Chain

Figure 1   The Reason model
(Adapted from Reason, 1990)

Helmreich (1993a) employed Reason's notions of latent organisational pathogens, together with the model of flight crew performance proposed by Helmreich and Foushee (1993) in a systemic analysis of the January 1990 Avianca

B707 fuel exhaustion accident at Cove Neck, New York. As depicted in Figure 2, the Helmreich and Foushee model seeks to identify the *input factors* that each crew member brings with them to the flight deck, the *process factors* which reflect the interpersonal and technical enactment of group tasks, and the *outcome factors* which define the multiple dimensions of results - positive or negative - for the tasks undertaken.

Flightcrew Performance Model
(adapted from Helmreich & Foushee, 1993)

Safety
Efficiency

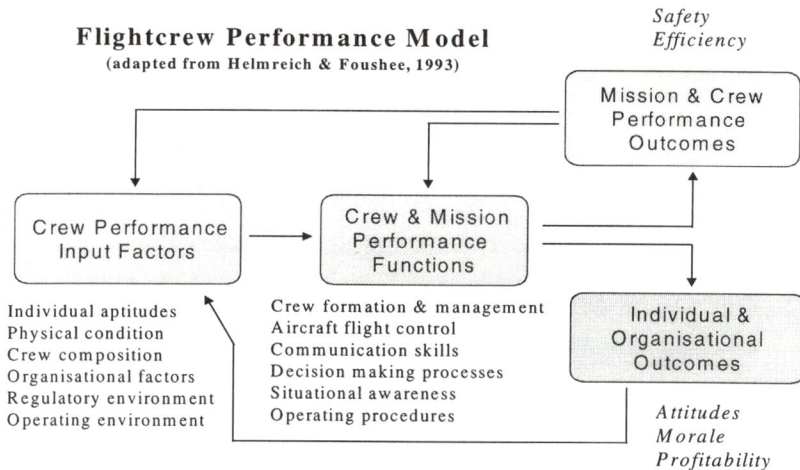

Mission & Crew Performance Outcomes

Crew Performance Input Factors

Crew & Mission Performance Functions

Individual & Organisational Outcomes

Individual aptitudes
Physical condition
Crew composition
Organisational factors
Regulatory environment
Operating environment

Crew formation & management
Aircraft flight control
Communication skills
Decision making processes
Situational awareness
Operating procedures

Attitudes
Morale
Profitability

Figure 2   Model of flight crew performance
(Adapted from Helmreich & Foushee, 1993)

Input factors may include national, organisational and vocational cultures and norms, organisational resources and practices including selection, training, standard operating procedures, logistics support, and maintenance, environmental factors including weather, operating equipment, and ATC, group composition, structure and norms, and individual factors such as personality, abilities, knowledge, motivation, and emotional state, etc. The feedback loops depicted in the model are critical to its potential to shed light on the system-wide factors which influence individual and group performance in the workplace. Process factors (crew and mission performance functions) influence not only task outcomes but will also impact on inputs to subsequent performance, and intermediate and final outcomes influence both present and future processes and inputs.

The approaches of both Reason and Helmreich are further explored and synthesised by Zotov (1996) in his thought-provoking proposal of an improved format for the investigation and reporting of the human factors of aircraft accidents. While his modelling is too extensive for reproduction here, his paper is recommended to readers interested in the exploration of lateral paths for mishap investigation.

Pariès (1996) also contributes substantially to the development of our thinking on aircraft accident investigation with his discussion of an evolutionary shift of the aviation safety paradigm towards systemic causality and proactivity. He points out that a major step towards a better understanding of human error was the analogy to biological principles of health and illness drawn by Reason (1990) through the metaphor of resident pathogens, triggering factors and system defences. He theorises that the next step in this evolutionary process might be to capitalise on the physiological concepts of biological autonomy and organisation.

Johnston (1991) was an early contributor to the discussion regarding the examination of 'organisational factors' in human factors accident investigation, and one of his more recent papers provides an entertaining overview of the shift toward systemic accountability for safety lapses in his broader consideration of philosophies for risk management in flight operations (1996). He employs the following hypothetical example of an incident and its subsequent investigation (originally used in Johnston, 1991) to illustrate how different approaches to investigation can impact upon the opportunities for risk management which are subsequently identified (1996, pp 8-10):

The circumstances:
- A twin-engined transport aircraft lands fast and deep, having completed an approach to landing with an unanticipated tailwind. Late application of braking, combined with an unidentified area of poor braking action near the end of the runway, leads to an over-run of a few feet.

The findings of Investigation 1:
- At 15 miles from touchdown the aircraft was 50 kts in excess of the approach speed mandated by the company Operations Manual.
- The inexperienced co-pilot did not give call-outs in accordance with Standard Operating Procedures (SOPs). He also failed to explicitly draw the Captain's attention to excessive height and speed at the Outer and Middle Markers, as required by company policy.
- The Captain exercised poor judgement in continuing the approach and failed to apply maximum braking immediately following touchdown.

The recommendations of Investigation 1:
- The crew failed to adhere to SOPs. Pilots should be formally reminded of the need to always follow SOPs and to operate in accordance with the provisions of the company Operations Manual.

While variants of this investigative scenario will be familiar to many readers, it is also the case that this style of investigation yields little in terms of proactive strategies for organisational risk management. Johnston now asks us to consider an alternative course of events, in which attention is paid by the investigators to the intentions, knowledge and understandings of the crew. These are set within the context of the operating practices and culture within the airline, as well as the knowledge, beliefs, attitudes and information which informed the crews' operational judgements and actions:

The findings of Investigation 2:

- It was established that the vast majority of pilots in the airline exceeded the mandated speed at 12 miles from touchdown. This speed was felt to be appropriate when the aircraft was first introduced ten years earlier; it was not updated when line practice showed it to be too conservative. High intermediate approach speed was normal in this airline; it was not a material factor on this occasion.

- The Captain anticipated a tailwind on the approach but under-estimated its strength. The inexperienced co-pilot never appreciated the existence of the tailwind, nor did he understand the general relationship between surface and approach sector winds.

- The Captain realised at a very late stage that his estimation of the tailwind was in error. Concentration on regaining an approach profile and an 'acceptable' touchdown point took all his attention and he never thought of the go-around option. He later felt that an input from the co-pilot might have drawn this to his active attention. The Captain's estimation of an 'acceptable' touchdown point was felt by the investigators to reflect a misplaced understanding of the aircraft's normal performance capabilities.

- The co-pilot testified that he eventually realised that the aircraft was going to be high and fast throughout the approach. However he made no calls to this effect since, in practice, the standard callouts were not used by the vast majority of pilots; he believed that most pilots found them to be excessively wordy and impracticable. Given that fact, he felt that it would be considered unnecessarily abrasive to start 'stating the obvious' to the Captain. After all, he expected there to be no problem on this occasion and, in addition, he 'would have to work with this Captain for many more years'.

- Neither pilot had ever experienced maximum braking in the actual aircraft and, reverting to normal operational practice, the brakes were not applied immediately after touchdown. The Captain said that this was just a reversion to normal practice and that he 'did not mean to do so'. Even when he belatedly attempted to apply maximum braking, he failed to achieve this objective.

It will be noted that the second hypothesised investigation did not accept existing organisational functioning as a *standing state* beyond consideration or challenge (Einhorn & Hogarth, 1986). It is clear, for instance, that various training and administrative recommendations follow, and that specifically targeted training would be appropriate for both crew members. Equally, however, it also raises important questions about the kind of training and line operation normal to this operator. This incident might, in fact, be telling the management more about their airline than about the capabilities of the individual pilots. And, by so doing, it is potentially providing them with valuable information relevant to future accident prevention. It will be clear that the goals of accident prevention and risk management can only be successfully achieved if the appropriate organisational lessons are formally drawn and that suitable administrative action is initiated. Otherwise the lessons which can be learned may not be learned, and opportunities for risk management will be lost.

Johnston goes on to discuss the importance of drawing the appropriate conclusions from accident investigations:

This example illustrates why it is critically important to distinguish between those causal factors which reflect individual deficiencies and those which reflect 'system' deficiencies. The prevention of similar incidents in the future implies going beyond criticism of individual crew members (however merited this might in fact be). The preferred model of causation will not emphasise the culpability of those immediately involved in the precipitating events at the expense of considering wider systemic factors. Nor should it seek to treat accidents and incidents as narrow events, as distinct from the outcome of organisational production processes.

Coming up next...

This would appear to be a suitable point from which to progress to a discussion of the processes by which exemplary accident investigations are conducted. The next chapters provide an insight into the models for investigation currently applied in Australia, Canada and Sweden. While the training course at Sabaudia focussed primarily on Australian and Swedish methods, the integrated approach of the Canadian Transportation Safety Board, which has many parallels to the methods applied by BASI, is also outlined below.

The following three chapters describe current practices in air safety investigation from the Australian, Canadian and Swedish perspectives.

26   The Australian bureau of air safety investigation

Robert Lee
Bureau of Air Safety Investigation, Australia

Introduction

Over many years the aviation industry, often as a result of bitter experience, has developed elaborate systems and procedures to maintain and ensure the safety of operations.   Many of the changes have resulted from the comprehensive investigation of aircraft accidents and incidents. As a result, aviation has long been, and continues to be, the leader in the field of transportation safety, and many of the lessons learned and methods developed in aviation have been applied in areas ranging from marine, road and rail transport, to medicine.

This chapter will outline one important area critical to aviation safety - air safety investigation - as it is practiced by the Australian Bureau of Air Safety Investigation, or BASI, as it is more generally known.   Secondly, new 'safety health' concepts being applied to improve the safety of world aviation will be described.

The Bureau of Air Safety Investigation

The Bureau of Air Safety Investigation is the agency of   the Australian Government which is responsible for the investigation of accidents and incidents occurring to civil aircraft in Australia and its territories.   BASI operates in accordance with Annex 13 of the Chicago Convention (International Civil Aviation Organization, 1994).   This annex sets out the international standards and recommended practices for the investigation of accidents and serious incidents. Australia has incorporated the provisions of this Annex into our domestic Air Navigation Regulations.

The objective of the Bureau is to promote safe aviation by disseminating information and safety recommendations based on the investigation of selected accidents and incidents, and on the results of research.   In accordance with Annex

13 it is not the purpose of BASI's investigations to apportion blame or liability. The Bureau exists purely for the purpose of air safety.

Australia is fortunate in that, unlike some other countries, most of the key elements of the air safety investigation function are within the one organisation - BASI has only minimal reliance on other agencies. It is the legal recipient of air safety incident reports (both mandatory and confidential), it investigates accidents and incidents, it conducts analysis and research, it develops proactive accident prevention programs, it maintains Australia's computerised aviation accident and incident data base, and it publishes its own reports. Each year the Bureau receives an average of 5,000 incident and 270 accident reports.

The results of BASI investigations are presented in terms of 'findings' and 'significant factors'. The Bureau does not utilise the term 'cause', and nor does it, as some other countries do, identify any one factor as the most important in a particular occurrence. In the Bureau's experience, to nominate any one factor - for example, as a single 'most probable cause' - results in most attention being concentrated on that factor alone, when the majority of air safety occurrences are the result of a complex interaction of many factors. Every one of these should be addressed for purposes of accident prevention, otherwise the effectiveness of the investigation process can be greatly reduced.

Like its overseas equivalents, BASI has no power to implement its recommendations. However, approximately ninety percent are accepted, normally by the regulatory authority - the Civil Aviation Safety Authority (CASA). If CASA chooses not to accept a BASI recommendation it must state its reasons for not doing so and these are published by the Bureau.

In recent years, the Bureau has adopted a policy of selective investigation, similar to many of our equivalent organisations in other countries. The traditional approach in Australia had been to investigate everything, no matter how minor. However, many categories of air safety occurrence are repetitive in nature, such as ground loops involving aircraft with tailwheel undercarriages, and no new prevention knowledge is gained by continuing to investigate such events. However, the law requires that all accidents and incidents must be reported. Because BASI receives all these reports, it retains the ability to monitor trends, and can initiate an investigation into safety issues raised - for example, by a number of relatively minor occurrences. While these events individually would not warrant full investigation, considered as a group they may be indicative of broader systemic safety deficiencies - a topic which will be addressed later in this chapter.

In practice the Bureau does not distinguish operationally between accidents and incidents - they are all 'safety occurrences'. The objective of selective investigation is to concentrate the Bureau's resources on indepth investigations which offer the greatest potential to enhance air safety. BASI has developed and refined various criteria to decide which events will be looked at most closely - one of these is a primary emphasis on the safety of fare-paying passengers in any category of operation - high capacity regular public transport (RPT), low capacity

RPT and charter, and other commercial operations involving fare paying passengers.

In addition, in part enabled by the redeployment of resources as a result of the selective investigation policy, BASI is placing a much stronger emphasis on applied systems safety studies. This is aimed at identifying and rectifying underlying factors within the aviation system which can impact upon safety at the 'sharp end' - that is, in the cockpit, cabin, control tower, maintenance workshop, or on the ramp. This systemic safety aspect of the Bureau's operations will be discussed in detail later in this chapter.

BASI is a relatively small organisation, with a total of 75 employees. The Bureau has a Central Office in Canberra, Australia's national capital, with field offices located in Melbourne, Sydney, Brisbane and Perth. The field offices each have a small number of staff, the investigators located in them being either pilots or licensed aircraft maintenance engineers (LAME's), or sometimes both.

Central Office contains all the Bureau's technical specialist facilities, including flight data recorder readout, computer graphics, engineering and audio laboratories, radar recording, and computing. Members of all categories of investigator are located in Central Office. There is a single employment category of 'air safety investigator', within which there are six different categories - operations (pilots), air traffic services (ATS), human performance, engineer, maintenance (LAME) and technical officer (eg., avionics, communications).

Contemporary aviation safety is no longer primarily the province of pilots and engineers alone - it is now a multidisciplinary endeavour, often requiring input from many diverse fields. Aviation is going through a process of rapid change in its operational, technical, commercial, economic, regulatory, and political dimensions. Developments in each of these dimensions can impact directly or indirectly on air safety. As an organisation the Bureau must therefore maintain a current awareness of these changes so that all staff fully understand the context within which they carry out their tasks, and the Bureau possesses or has access to the appropriate specialist expertise.

BASI employs a team approach to investigations. An investigation of a serious ATS incident, for example, could be carried out by a team made up of investigators in the categories of air traffic services, operations (pilot), and human performance. All these specialists work together as an integrated group to apply their different fields of professional expertise to the identification of the significant factors in the occurrence.

The Bureau's overriding concern is with maximising the safety of aviation as a transportation system. BASI shares this primary concern with all elements of the Australian and international aviation communities, and cooperates closely with them towards that safety goal, while maintaining complete objectivity and independence in its operations. BASI is also an adviser to the Safety Committee of the International Air Transport Association (IATA) and the Flight Operations and Safety Working Group of the Association of Asia Pacific Airlines. The latter is especially important because the Asia Pacific is the world's fastest growing region of aviation.

Because the Bureau is completely independent of the regulatory authority, CASA, it is able to operate its own Confidential Aviation Incident Reporting (CAIR) system in-house. Since its establishment in 1988, the scope of CAIR has been expanded to cover not only flight crews, but also air traffic services personnel, maintenance and ground handling staff and cabin crew. Each of these groups is provided with a special purpose form contained within the CAIR reporting package. The purpose of the extension of the CAIR program was to obtain the full air safety picture, not just that from the perspective of one particular professional group. For example, cabin crew are uniquely placed to provide certain kinds of critical information on passenger safety and emergency procedures affecting survival which may not be available from any other source. The CAIR program has been most successful and has the support of the aviation industry.

In addition to occurrence investigation and research reports, the Bureau publishes quarterly its own high quality safety magazine, *Asia Pacific AIR SAFETY*. With the exception of the year 1987, BASI and its predecessors have been producing an air safety magazine continuously since July 1953, a period of 43 years. Circulated to over 65,000 readers throughout the industry in Australia and overseas, *Asia Pacific AIR SAFETY* is a key element in the Bureau's strategy of communication with the aviation community in the region. It disseminates information on BASI operations, raises safety issues, educates the aviation community, and provides an essential feedback element of the CAIR program, as well as including a CAIR reporting package in each issue.

BASI is a highly computerised organisation. As well as our central computing facilities, every staff member has a powerful PC, and the system is networked throughout Australia. BASI has an integrated system to provide information support for all of it's operations - from investigation, research and analysis, occurrence reporting, financial and project management, production of reports, to office automation. The main component of the system is called OASIS - Occurrence Analysis and Safety Information System - and is in a continuous process of evolutionary development to provide even greater capability for safety analysis of the aviation system, and to adapt to changes in that system.

Accident investigation and prevention: the BASI perspective

In its first form the Bureau was established as the 'Accident Investigation and Analysis Branch' of the Department of Civil Aviation in 1952. Perhaps the single most important change in the Bureau's recent operations is the shift from a primarily reactive organisation, investigating accidents and incidents after they occur, to an organisation which is also proactive and equally concerned operationally with the prevention of air safety occurrences. The Bureau now dedicates considerable resources to the identification of deficiencies in the aviation system which have the potential, given the right combination of events and circumstances, to become significant factors in accidents or incidents. Similarly, this is true of the Bureau's accident and incident investigations. As well as finding out what went wrong at the 'sharp end' - in the cockpit, control tower, cabin or maintenance area - BASI aims to identify any underlying factors in the aviation system which may have contributed to the occurrence.

For example, if passengers are killed or injured because of problems of evacuation following a survivable accident, it is essential to determine what actually went wrong in the cabin, and to ascertain the immediate reasons why the cabin crew were unable to ensure the survivability of all occupants. But of even greater importance is the identification of any latent organisational factors which may have contributed to the failure of the cabin crew to achieve a successful evacuation - factors such as poor communication, inadequate supervision, or inappropriate training. Experience has shown that if such underlying systemic factors are not detected in investigations, and therefore remain unchanged, sooner or later the same kinds of failures will occur again. The Bureau's Systems Safety Branch is dedicated to the critical task of identifying these underlying latent deficiencies in the aviation system, both before and after accidents or incidents.

From the proactive perspective, BASI promotes active communication with the industry at all levels - for example, it is an important role of BASI investigators to act as 'intelligence gatherers', as well as conveying information to the industry on the Bureau and its operations. This provides an early warning system to enable BASI to become aware of safety issues as they develop, so that we may recommend remedial action without waiting for an accident to occur. The CAIR program described earlier also plays a key role in the achievement of this objective.

A central factor driving the adoption of a new conceptual approach to aviation safety by the world's aviation community is that although the world airline accident *rate* is very low, it has effectively plateaued. This means that if the accident rate does not change, and increases in air traffic occur as projected, then early in the next century the *number* of airline accidents will increase to a level which will be completely unacceptable to the industry and the travelling public - approximately one hull-loss every fortnight. Such a situation would also be financially unsustainable to the industry.

In many other categories of aviation, accident rates have also remained comparatively steady for many years, with little statistically significant change in either direction. It is therefore imperative that if the industry is to break away from this steady state, and achieve substantial improvement in what is already an excellent safety record, it cannot afford simply to recycle its present well established safety philosophies and procedures. It must do more to achieve significant change to the 'status quo'. By adopting new systems safety ideas and practical proactive approaches to air safety, BASI aims to enhance the safety of aviation operations in all areas.

The Reason model of systems safety

The work of Professor James Reason of the University of Manchester and his colleagues is fundamental to the Bureau and the international aviation community's contemporary safety philosophy. Reason and his team have developed a conceptual and theoretical approach to the safety of large, complex sociotechnical systems, of which aviation is an excellent example. As part of the development of his model, Reason analysed major accidents in aviation, shipping, rail, nuclear power, aerospace and so on. All of these case studies represented catastrophic failures of such systems.

Comprehensive details of Reason's work can be found in his first book on human error (Reason, 1990) and in a new book on '*Managing the Risks of Organisational Accidents*' (Reason, 1997). Descriptions of the model as specifically related to the aviation context can be found in Reason (1991a, 1991b). The concepts are further developed and applied to aviation case studies in another recent book which attempts to extend the boundaries of thought on contemporary aviation human factors (Maurino, Reason, Johnston, & Lee, 1995). In his following chapter (5.3.1), Hobbs provides some practical guidance on application of the Reason model for investigation of the human factors of aviation occurrences.

The Reason model has been translated into successful operational corporate safety programs by Shell (TRIPOD), British Rail (PRISM) British Airways Engineering (MESH), and most recently, Singapore Airlines. Most importantly, significant changes to ICAO Annex 13 which came into effect in late 1994 mean that it is now an international requirement that organisational and management information be formally addressed in aircraft accident and incident reports. This information should be provided for any organisation which influences the operation of the aircraft. Significantly, ICAO has recommended that the Reason model be used for this purpose.

Major BASI investigations such as the Monarch Airlines report (Bureau of Air Safety Investigation, 1994) and the B747 VH-INH report (Bureau of Air Safety Investigation, 1996) are structured in accordance with the Reason model. Both have had substantial impacts in redressing deficiencies in the aviation system in both the corporate and regulatory areas. As an example of the way in which BASI utilises the model in investigation, an abridged summary of BASI's Monarch report, originally published in the ICAO Journal (International Civil Aviation Organization, 1995) is reprinted at Appendix C to this section of the book.

The Reason model, as depicted in the preceding chapter, has many dimensions, and space permits only a brief outline of some of the concepts. Reason stresses the fundamental need always to adopt a total systems approach to safety. While this in itself is certainly not new, it is the manner in which Reason addresses and analyses the system that is of special interest. Reason (1991a) describes two kinds of failures in complex systems - 'active' and 'latent':

- *Active failures:* are defined as those errors or violations having an immediate adverse effect. These are generally associated with the activities of 'front line' operators: control room personnel, ships' crew, train drivers, signalmen, pilots, air traffic controllers, cabin crews etc.
- *Latent failures:* these are decisions or actions, the damaging consequences of which may lie dormant for a long time, only becoming evident when they combine with local triggering factors (such as, active failures, technical faults, atypical environmental conditions, and so on) to breach the system's defences. Their defining feature is that they were present within the system well before the onset of a recognisable accident sequence. They are most likely to be generated by people whose activities are removed in both time and space from the direct human-machine interface: designers, high-level decision makers, regulators, line managers.

Active failures have long been the 'traditional' concern of air safety specialists, - the focus has been on the behaviour of people at the 'sharp end', that is, those personnel most directly involved at the time of the occurrence - flying the aircraft, controlling air traffic, evacuating passengers, or carrying out maintenance.

In considering the nature of active failures, Reason (1990) developed the Generic Error Modelling System (GEMS), which incorporates Rasmussen's (1983, 1987) pioneering work on the classification of errors into skill-based, rule-based and knowledge-based categories. In aviation, the knowledge-based category is the primary target of crew resource management and pilot judgement training courses.

Reason (1991b) explains some fundamental ideas of his systems approach as follows: Like many other high-hazard, low risk systems, modern aircraft have acquired such a high degree of technical and procedural protection that they are largely proof against single failures, either human or mechanical. They are much more like to fall prey to an 'organisational' accident. That is, a situation in which *latent failures*, arising mainly in the managerial and organisational spheres, combine adversely with local triggering events (weather, location etc.) and with the *active failures* of individuals at the 'sharp end' (errors and procedural violations).

Reason argues that all large sociotechnical systems contain a core group of generic *general failure types* (GFT's), examples being: incompatible goals; organisational deficiencies; inadequate communications; poor planning; inadequate control and monitoring; design failures; inadequate defences; poor procedures; poor training; inadequate regulations.

Active failures can be regarded not only as separate entities in themselves, but also as 'tokens' of one or more GFT's. To illustrate, a company may experience a number of air safety incidents, each one being quite different on the surface, and apparently unrelated to the others. However, careful systemic investigation and analysis may reveal that all these incidents are tokens of an underlying GFT in the company, such as poor training.

Identification of the functional relationship between these 'types' and 'tokens' is a critical objective of the proactive corporate safety programs referred to earlier. These proactive safety programs involve the regular input of information from staff, both workers and managers. The programs identify and continuously monitor the GFT profile for the organisation, which thereby enables management and staff to develop and focus remedial action upon those specific organisational deficiencies which are of greatest concern. The programs also identify local latent failures in the workplace.

Reason (1991b) identifies a number of stages in the development of a system failure, such as an accident. This schematic model depicted in Figure 1 below also shows the information feedback loops involved.

To be specific: referring to Figure 1, an example of a fallible policy decision made by corporate management might be to maximise the profitability of an airline regardless of any other considerations. This decision then places great pressure on the company's line managers to translate this policy into effect. A consequence is the development in the workplace of a psychological climate in which staff under pressure, and perhaps in fear of losing their jobs, constantly try to cut corners to save money, and thereby commit unsafe acts - both unintended errors and deliberate violations - such as inadequate maintenance work, substandard emergency procedures training, and so on. When the defences of the system fail - for example, the final inspection of maintenance work by supervisors is not properly carried out, - a 'window of opportunity' for a system failure such as an accident or incident may result, given the right set of circumstances.

Referring again to Figure 1, the traditional approach of air safety investigation agencies has been to move around the outer of the feedback loops (loop 1). However, it is obvious that on this basis an incident or accident has to actually occur before the information necessary for the prevention of similar occurrences in future could be obtained. In the wide body era, the industry cannot afford to continue in this vein - that is, to wait for the loss of aircraft or the occurrence of serious incidents to identify significant system deficiencies, or latent failures, which were already present and which could, and should, have been addressed before these events.

The real challenge for future air safety investigation is to penetrate more effectively the 'inner loops' of the Reason model diagram - to detect and to rectify the fallible decisions by corporate managers, the line management deficiencies, the psychological precursors of unsafe acts - sometimes referred to as the 'organisational climate' - and the unsafe acts themselves, together with any deficiencies in the defences of the system, before a catastrophic system failure results. As noted earlier, within Australia *Asia Pacific AIR SAFETY* provides the continuous feedback to CAIR reporters which is essential to the success of any confidential reporting system. With the invaluable assistance of CAIR, together with its industry awareness program and research, the Bureau is increasingly able to interrogate the inner feedback loops of Figure 1. Thus we are gaining access to critical safety information without having to wait for accidents and incidents to occur.

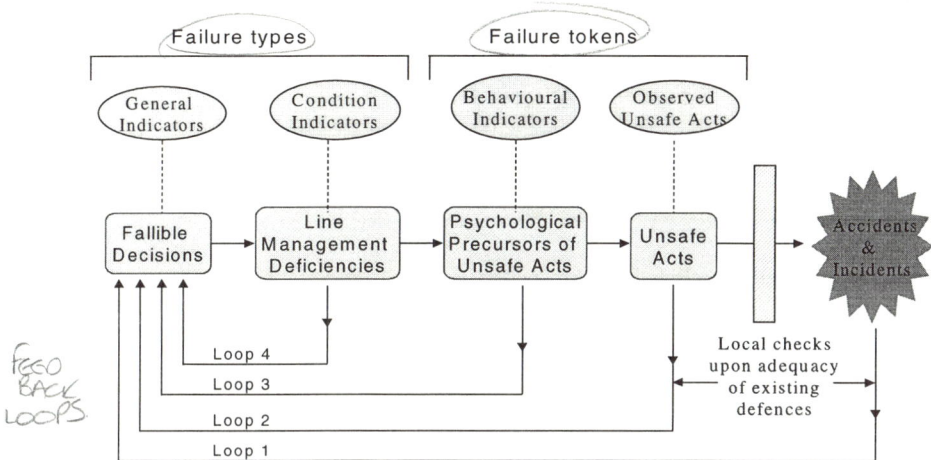

Figure 1   Stages in the development of a system failure   *(Schematic model)*
(Adapted from Reason, 1991b)

A good example of a significant conceptual change incorporated in the systems safety approach is the way in which BASI now regards an accident. In contrast to the traditional view, Reason argues that accidents should not be considered as isolated, infrequent one-off events, but instead should be regarded as the consequences of particular sets of circumstances in which active and latent factors, sometimes acting in combination with external environmental factors, facilitate a failure of the system.

'Normal' errors made by humans in the system, which, as Reason emphasises, are occurring all the time, may not be always detected by the system's defences and thereby become significant factors in an accident. The point is that such errors are characteristic of human performance; they do not occur only in accident or incident situations. As a result, accident and incident data alone are not valid indicators of the degree of errors made by people in the system, and therefore do not provide a true index of system safety. In other words, if an operator has had no accidents over a given period, this does *not* mean that performance by the company's personnel has been error free during this time. For management to conclude that it has can create an extremely dangerous state of affairs for the company. For instance, management might decide that because the company is not actually having accidents, the safety department can be eliminated to save some money.

In Reason's terms, the proactive corporate systems safety programs described earlier measure organisational 'health' rather than organisational 'illness', and, among other things, aim to detect latent failures, or 'resident pathogens' and to remedy these, in this way reducing the system's overall vulnerability to failure. The already successful operational applications of the Reason model by several large corporations have provided a firm foundation upon which to work, even though the BASI perspective is somewhat different because of the Bureau's role as a government air safety investigation agency.

SIAM - a new accident prevention tool

Traditional means of collecting and recording air safety occurrence information, particularly of high volume/low detail air safety incidents (referred to by BASI as Category 5 occurrences), severely limit the degree to which this information can be effectively used for systemic analysis. The international aviation community has recognised that such analysis is essential to accident prevention and safety enhancement.

Even the most advanced aviation accident and incident data bases currently available are primarily 'ad hoc' in nature. They are not structured on the basis of an integrated model of systems safety. The hundreds of descriptive and explanatory factors typically contained in such systems, together with their modifiers, tend to do little more than model the spoken language, rather than offer any real insights into system safety.

In the light of these considerations, BASI has substantially modified its existing Occurrence Analysis and Safety Information System (OASIS). The Bureau has developed and introduced SIAM - the Systemic Incident Analysis Model. SIAM is a new component of OASIS, and is a fully integrated system based upon the theoretically sound and practically proven systems safety approach developed by James Reason and recommended by ICAO.

As well as collecting the normal factual information regarding air safety occurrences, SIAM takes a completely new approach by adding information and value to each report specifically from a systems safety perspective. SIAM provides new safety information in terms of real, potential and apparent outcomes; what defences in the aviation system failed to allow each occurrence to happen; what were the latent and active failures in the system; and, where appropriate, what were the recovery measures that prevented an incident becoming an accident.

The SIAM model has been designed for capturing basic statistical information on systems safety from the high volume, low detail occurrences. In the Australian system, this is the only category of occurrence which has sufficient numbers to make in depth statistical analysis possible and productive. Australia has had a comprehensive mandatory aviation incident reporting system since the 1950's and the Bureau receives around four to five thousand reports each year. All of these are entered into the OASIS database. Most of these reports are what BASI terms 'Category 5', or relatively minor occurrences.

Until recently OASIS, like many similar systems focused on *events* only. In contrast, the primary emphasis of SIAM is upon *outcomes*, as well as events. An outcome is the primary reason why a safety body such as BASI would be interested in an air safety occurrence. Ultimately, this means aircraft crashing into the ground or colliding with each other, or breaking up in flight - although the model allows more detail than this.

A significant innovation in the SIAM system is that the outcome attached to an occurrence is not necessarily what *actually* happened, but also what *could potentially* have happened, or *appeared* to have happened. In very basic terms, the fact that a serious outcome could have happened, but did not, is the difference between an incident and an accident, and the assumption is that a recovery measure was successful in controlling the potential consequences.

Occasionally, an outcome only *appears* to have happened - in other words there is a false alarm. These typically arise either from a breakdown in a warning or monitoring system (that is, failing safe), or from the threshold sensitivity of some warning systems. These are integrated into SIAM and the failures modelled as either technical breakdowns or latent failures respectively.

Defences are in place in the aviation system to prevent negative outcomes. Examples include such engineered safety features as engine monitoring systems and navigation equipment, and procedural defences such as flight rules and maps and charts. At the very least, it ought to be possible to determine that a given defence failed in some way in even a minor occurrence, although this may occasionally require a limited degree of further investigation of a Cat 5 occurrence than has occurred in the past.

When available, the type of defence failure can also be specified. This falls into essentially three categories: technical breakdown, latent failure and active failure. Technical breakdowns are obvious. A latent failure of a defence is when a general, pre-existing weakness of the defence is responsible. An active failure is when an otherwise perfectly good defence is somehow bypassed or defeated by the action of a person or persons - for example, a mistake, error or violation.

Recovery measures are very much like defences, differing only by the point in an occurrence at which they operate. The aviation system is such that the failure of a single defence alone rarely results in an outcome, rather two or three defences typically have to fail in sequence. In this way, the system can be described as defended in depth. In effect, recovery measures are a special class of defence in that by the time they are needed, the system has already become unsafe - in other words, they often represent the last level of protection.

As an example, take the outcome of 'mid air collision'. Such an event might become likely if the defence of 'navigation' fails, and a loss of separation occurs. This only becomes a *collision* if the pilot fails to recover the situation, aided by such recovery measures as TCAS or a warning by air traffic control. In SIAM it is intended that occurrences are tagged with the recovery measure which 'saved the day'.   By this method, clear indications can be obtained of what particular elements of the aviation system are being most relied upon to maintain the safe operation of the total system, and which areas are most vulnerable.

Many incidents do not become accidents through pure good fortune.   For example, violations of controlled airspace happen quite frequently.   In SIAM these are recorded as a potential collision with another aircraft.   Generally, there is no other aircraft present in exactly the same portion of airspace at exactly the same time, and the more serious outcome of 'mid air collision' is averted simply by chance or good fortune - the latter category being incorporated into SIAM.

SIAM was extensively trialed by a small number of line investigators within the Bureau.   This was followed by a comprehensive staff training program, prior to its operational introduction throughout BASI in October 1996.   As noted previously, SIAM has been designed with the maximum potential for evolutionary development as operational experience with it accumulates.

SIAM generates a weekly statistical summary, and as had been hoped when SIAM was envisaged, this information clearly identifies areas of the aviation system on which attention needs to be focussed. A most interesting feature of the early SIAM data is that, while human factors are identified as significant contributors to the majority of air safety occurrences, it is also the case that in by far the greatest number of cases it is also humans who *prevent* incidents from becoming accidents. In other words, while active failures by people are involved in the majority of accidents and incidents, it is also the humans in the system who play the primary role in accident prevention, that is in keeping the system safe. This provides a perspective on the aviation system rather different to the more traditional view, which has tended to emphasise the negative aspects of human performance.

The use of a 'potential outcome' category in SIAM indicates the seriousness of various categories of occurrence, should the aviation system fail or be degraded in some way.   If the provisions in the system which prevent these potential occurrences becoming real are absent or deficient, then the aviation industry will clearly be in very serious difficulty. Similarly, the category of 'good fortune' shows that on 110 occasions during the first 10 weeks following the introduction of SIAM this is all that saved the day - a sobering finding. Again, this is a systems insight which has not been previously available in this kind of statistical form.

Although still in its initial development stages, SIAM offers a major advance on previous systems because it incorporates a proven model of systems safety, and provides new kinds of data on air safety occurrences. Already SIAM is proving its worth in adding value to the high volume, low detail occurrence reports, and represents a major advance in accident prevention.   BASI believes SIAM shows great promise and is actively continuing its development.

Accident prevention strategies: the Boeing approach

Complementing the Reason approach is important work being carried out by the Boeing Commercial Airplane Group (Russell, 1994). Boeing has reanalysed 232 major airline accidents occurring between 1981 and 1992. The objective was to determine how many opportunities existed for intervention to stop the accident before it occurred. Boeing has identified a number of 'intervention strategies' and found that there are often several of these for each accident - in one example up to 20. In other words, there were always a number of opportunities to prevent the accident. Of real concern is the fact that non adherence to procedures by the flying pilot and other operational procedural considerations consistently emerge as the most significant factors.

The critical question now is to determine what are the factors within the world aviation system which consistently deliver this picture year after year. Boeing researchers and James Reason have been discussing this problem, and the combination of the two approaches offers great safety enhancement potential.

Conclusion

New legislation passed through the Australian Parliament in late 1995 gave BASI additional powers to investigate safety deficiencies in the aviation system without the need for such investigations to be triggered by an accident or incident. This was a major step forward in accident prevention, and substantially increased the Bureau's pro-active safety capabilities.

In the dawning era of the 800 passenger airliner, the loss of just one of these aircraft, let alone a mid air collision between two of them in crowded airspace over a major city, would constitute a disaster of unthinkable proportions. A final sobering point to consider is that such a large airliner can also easily be brought down through collision with a light aircraft. Consequently, because many categories of aircraft operation share parts of the same airspace, the aviation system as a whole needs to operate safely.

Fortunately, the aviation community is well endowed with dedicated professionals in all areas who are dedicated to meeting the safety challenges that lie ahead. Their outstanding record of achievements to date indicates that they will be successful in the future.

Author's note

Sections of this chapter have been previously published in 'Human Factors in Cabin Safety: A Systems Approach', contained in the Proceedings of the Tenth International Aircraft Cabin Safety Symposium, Feb 8-11, 1993 Costa Mesa California, sponsored by the Southern California Safety Institute. The chapter in its earliest form was first presented at the conference of the Chartered Institute of Transport - 'Transport Safety... at what cost?', Brisbane, August 1993. The present chapter is a substantial revision and update of the original.

27   The transportation safety board of Canada

James Nottrodt*
Maury Hill *
Elizabeth McCullough*
* Transportation Safety Board of Canada

An integrated approach to investigating for human factors

Introduction

As an accident investigation agency, the Transportation Safety Board (TSB) of Canada has as its principal objective the advancement of safety in the marine, rail, commodity pipeline, and air modes of transportation. This is accomplished primarily by investigating accidents and incidents, and examining the causal factors leading to these occurrences in order to identify systemic safety deficiencies. Where appropriate, safety actions are generated to prevent the recurrence of such events. It is readily apparent that to conduct effective investigations, the investigative approach of the TSB should ensure that multicausality is considered and an emphasis is placed on the human element's involvement in the occurrences. To facilitate these requirements, an integrated process for occurrence investigation was developed by the TSB's Human Performance Division for use by investigators and safety analysts. The process combines a number of models, drawn from the human performance literature, which involve descriptions of work system elements, work organisations, and human error and behaviour. The purpose of this paper is to review the rationale behind the development of the process, provide a brief description of this integrated process and, finally, discuss its utility at the TSB in support of recent aviation occurrence investigations.

The rationale

Accidents and incidents, such as transportation occurrences, are rarely the result of a single cause. Rather, they occur as a result of the combination of failures or deficiencies in organisational policy and procedures, human actions and equipment (Cox & Tait, 1991). This complexity necessitates that both the proximate and underlying causes, as well as their interrelationships, be considered in investigations. Unfortunately, most accident investigations tend to stop when a proximate cause is found (Reason, 1991c).

A review of the literature specific to transportation occurrence investigations revealed that *human factors* have been recognised as primary causal agents in the majority of transportation accidents and incidents (eg., Wilde & Stinson, 1980; McCullough & Hill, 1993; O'Hare, *et al.*, 1994). This should not be too surprising, since: i) all facets of technological systems involve the human element to some extent in terms of its design, construction, operation, management, maintenance and regulation (Reason, 1995); and, ii) the *human factors* category has often been a convenient place for cause-related circumstances of occurrences which could not be attributed to a failure of the equipment, facility, service or other component of the system (Fawcett, 1986).

To compliment our research into multicausality, and the role of human factors in accident causation, a detailed analysis of the needs of our investigators was conducted by the TSB (Hill, 1993). This analysis indicated that there was a clear recognition of the need to investigate systematically for human factors in the course of an accident investigation, and a desire for a unitary tool to guide them through that activity. To that end, an integrated process for occurrence investigation was developed for use by TSB investigators and analysts. The models which provide the foundation for the process involve descriptions of work system elements, work organisations, and human error and behaviour.

The integrated process

The occurence investigation is an integrated process consisting of seven major steps. Although the distinctions between adjoining steps may at times appear arbitrary, the sequence order for the process is purposeful in that the preceding steps set the groundwork for those later in the sequence. An important feature is the 'reverse-loop' pathway which promotes iterative assessments as the occurrence facts are reconstructed. The following provides a brief description of the process steps.

Step 1 - Collect occurrence data

The first step in any investigative process must be the collection of work-related information regarding the personnel, tasks, equipment, and environmental conditions involved in the occurrence. A systematic approach is crucial to ensure that multicausality is considered and that the logistical requirements of collecting, organising and maintaining an occurrence-related database are met. This necessitates that the investigator recognise from the outset that transportation workplaces, such as aircraft cockpits or air traffic control centres, are parts of larger 'work systems', with each work system consisting of varied and interrelated elements, i.e., human, task, equipment, and environment elements. The SHEL model, originally developed by Edwards (1972) and later modified by Hawkins (1987), was selected as a tool to organise the TSB investigators' workplace data collections because it compels the user to consider these important work system elements and their interrelationships, and then focuses on how these factors can influence human performance.

Step 2 – Determine occurrence sequence

As the investigator moves to addressing questions of 'how and why', there is a need to link the events and circumstances identified in the first step of the process by determining an occurrence sequence. As depicted elsewhere in this text, Reason's (1990) model of accident causation provides a framework that can be used by investigators as a guide in developing an occurrence sequence. This further organisation of the data may also add to an understanding of how the work system influenced human performance. The occurrence sequence is developed by arranging the information regarding occurrence events and circumstances around one of five production elements that are themselves basically aligned in a temporal context. By establishing the sequential ordering of the cause-related data (using Reason's concepts of *active* versus *latent* factors), the proximate and underlying causes, and their interrelationships, can be defined.

In practice, these first two steps of the process may not be mutually exclusive. As investigators begin the data collection, it is only natural to attempt to place the information into the context of an occurrence sequence. To facilitate this concurrent activity, the SHEL and Reason's models can be combined into a more robust hybrid tool where the data collected using the multiple components of the adapted SHEL model can be organised into a framework surrounding an occurrence sequence template, based upon the Reason model. In this way, each occurrence can be described by a unique blueprint of events and circumstances which constitute the occurrence's causal factors.

Steps 3, 4 & 5 - Identify unsafe acts/decisions and conditions and failure modes

At this point in the process, the analysis portion of the investigation assumes a reductionist nature. When an unsafe act, decision or condition is identified, the focus shifts to examining why that particular causal factor existed (or perhaps still exists) within the given work system. Further investigation or analysis may reveal another layer of hazardous events or circumstances (as defined by other unsafe acts, decisions or conditions) antecedent to the causal factor that was initially identified.

To discern why specific unsafe conditions existed for a particular occurrence or series of occurrences, TSB investigators and analysts have used a variety of valid techniques (eg., engineering tests, computer simulations and environmental assessments). However, similar techniques to probe why unsafe

246 Aviation Psychology: A Science and a Profession

acts or decisions occurred were not as readily available until recently. Reason's (1990) generic error-modelling system (GEMS), which employs Rasmussen's (1987) performance or behaviour based on decision-making, was added to the process to afford this function. Simply, GEMS provides a method to link an unsafe act or decision identified at Step 3 to an underlying causal factor which is the product of Step 6. This is accomplished by first identifying what was erroneous about the action or decision (i.e., error type identification in Step 4) and then placing the erroneous action or decision into a behavioural context (i.e., identification of a failure mode at Step 5). GEMS has proved to be particularly useful when exploring hypothetical reconstructions of the occurrence factual information.

Step 6 - Identify behavioural antecedents

As accident investigations tend to stop when a proximate cause is found, it was necessary to ensure that a step dedicated to the identification of the underlying causes, was embedded in the process. In Step 5, the focus of the analysis, as noted above, is on the identification of failure modes which characterise erroneous decision-making. To uncover the underlying reasons behind an unsafe action or decision, it is important to consider if there were any factors in the work system that may have facilitated the expression of a given mode of failure and hence the original unsafe act or decision. These factors have been termed behavioural antecedents and can be found by examining the work system information collected and organised in earlier steps, which emphasises the iterative nature of this investigative process. Such factors may include other unsafe actions and decisions, and/or conditions intrinsic (eg., physical, physiological, psychological and psychosocial) or extrinsic (eg., environmental, task, managerial and organisational) to the individual or group involved in the decision-making.

Step 7 - Identify potential safety problems

The identification of potential safety problems is based extensively on what factors emerged as behavioural antecedents. Where appropriate, hazards identified either directly as unsafe conditions at Step 3 or indirectly through unsafe acts and decisions using Steps 3 to 6 are used to define potential safety problems. These potential safety problems are further analysed to determine if systemic safety deficiencies exist and to propose recommendations for safety actions.

Concluding remarks

The TSB is exploring modifications to all of its modal databases that would optimise both the capture and analysis of data collections which employ the integrated process. Currently, the database for the Marine Investigations Branch (i.e., MARSIS) has a module embedded in its structure that mimics the format of the process; one important preliminary finding has been that the module and its required database inputs act to reinforce the use of this investigative process by TSB staff.

The integrated process has been used successfully in multimodal applications in well over 200 occurrence investigations by both TSB human performance and line investigators. It has been particularly useful in ensuring the required data were collected, sorting out the merits of competing hypothetical occurrence reconstructions, validating the link between antecedents and behaviour, identifying organisational and managerial influences on operator performance, and ensuring proposed safety actions have the required degree of specificity and accuracy.

Authors' note

An earlier version of this chapter was presented as a paper to the Ninth International Symposium on Aviation Psychology, Columbus Ohio, April 27 - May 1, 1997. The present chapter is a substantial revision and update of the original.

28 The Swedish board of accident investigation

Kristina Pollack

Swedish Air Force, Flight Safety Department, Aviation Psychology, Sweden

Introduction

Historically, flight safety was mainly a technical concern. The problem was for obvious reasons concentrated on constructing a machine with the capability to stay in the air in a safe way. The approach to aviation was naturally scientific and the human in the system was from an early stage playing a secondary role. This has gone on during the decades.

There are the concept of airworthiness is one example in which the role of the human in the system is underestimated. The regulations to certify the machine for flying are strict. But who is responsible for the airworthiness of the human being? The answer to that question is not easy.

There are still many examples of how the human plays a secondary role in the aviation system, such as in the way money is distributed for research in the human factors area in aviation, the way the qualifications and limitations of the human being are taken into consideration in aviation, the way the structures of the aviation organisations and human factors committees are built up, and the way the human factors issues are taken care of in the accident investigation boards in some parts of the world. The list can go on.

Human factors has as many definitions as predecessors and the definitions have varied with its development through the years. The concept of 'human factors' originated from a technical world, and became (and still is for many people - especially those with a technical background) synonymous with the concept of ergonomics.

For years we have been living with the concept of 'pilot error' as an accident cause, because in the past the investigations were mainly technical. In those cases where no technical cause to the accident was found, the conclusion was drawn that the cause of the accident must be a human error problem. There was no special interest or expertise available to analyse why this 'error' had occurred. No special safety actions could therefore be taken, except to suspend the pilot(s) involved. This action was taken to show the 'world' that the performance of these pilots was not acceptable or to palliate their action with comments like 'we are all humans with some limitations'.

When different kinds of professions with different types of expertise became involved in the aviation business, especially in accident investigation, the concept of human factors broadened. Today, we can agree that the definition of the concept of human factors is at least as complex as the most advanced technology of the day.

When the system users - the pilots - became part of the accident investigation team, their qualifications as human factors investigators were limited due to a general lack of professional psychological knowledge of the human being, and of the methodology they could apply. Their strength was their operational experience. The syndrome to 'keep it in the family' or the risk to be uncomfortable in the system could also influence the investigation result.

In the late 1970's the accident investigation boards began to open their doors to bring complementary competence into the investigation teams. Individuals with professional knowledge of the human were brought into the boards, and brought with them special methodology to collect information and data as well as to analyse the findings. The aim was now to find out what was behind the behaviour / performance previously referred to as an 'error'. When the boards developed a more multi-disciplinary approach to finding the root causes of accidents, to find out 'why it happened', the investigation boards or teams now had enlarged possibilities to recommend relevant flight safety actions.

However, when human factors experts were introduced to accident investigation teams or boards, there was an obvious lack of insight into their role and the contribution they could make to the investigation. The human factors experts and investigators were not recognised as a self-evident part of the team, such as taking part in the hearings, etc. Frequently the human factors data was presented as a separate part of the investigation and the facts and human factors analysis were not integrated into the final conclusions.

Today it is obvious for many of us: Accident investigation work is team work. To come as close as possible to the root causes of accidents we must use different kinds of competence, different kinds of methodology, different ways to reach the facts, and different minds to analyse them. For example, we should never let a non-technical person investigate the technical part or a non-pilot the operations part of the investigation.

With this in mind, it is obvious today that we need a psychological / cognitive scientific trained person for the human factors part of the investigation. The differences in the professional backgrounds, technical, operational, as well as the professional knowledge of the human being, are the key elements in the investigation as well as in flight safety work. The difference in the professional backgrounds gives the team strength in the dialogue in order to reach the most probable causes of the accident and the best solutions for safety actions.

Today, with the highly automated technical aircraft systems, it should be even more clear that we must bring cognitive scientific competence into all levels in the aviation business in order to understand the consequences of the system and to get a better adaptation of the technique to the qualifications and limitations of the human. Ambitions to work in this direction differ, due to political, cultural and economic interests.

The Swedish model

In Sweden we have an independent government authority established to investigate all serious accidents. This authority investigates both civil and military aviation accidents. The Swedish Board of Accident Investigation is a small organisation with just a handful of people employed as chief investigators. The structure of the organisation is built upon the idea to bring in experts for every single accident to form a board. Most of them are trained in the investigation field. The regulations say that the chairman investigation must be one of the lawyers who work for the Board.

In 1982 I was asked to be one of the experts for the investigation boards. As an aviation psychologist, my contribution would be in the human factors area. At that time the human factor investigator was quite 'new' in the field and I am sure that many former investigators asked themselves, 'what can she add to our competence?' A woman? A psychologist? Not even a pilot? Since 1982 I have been a member of close to 100 accident investigation boards, both civilian and military. The understanding of the importance and the influence of the human factors area has grown in Sweden as well as internationally during the last decade. The human factors input has been more and more visible in our Swedish accident investigation reports. The MD-80 accident at Gottrora, Sweden in 1991 is a good example.

Methodology

Investigation tasks

The task of the human factors accident investigator is to investigate:
- What basic abilities/capacity and personality antecedents did the involved individuals have to succeed in the task they were asked to perform?
- What conditions were given for the involved individuals to succeed in the task they were asked to perform?

Consequently the human factors investigator has to investigate the *central level*, the *local level*, and the *individual level* in the aviation organisation. Questions to be asked will include: What conditions were given concerning:

DESIGN/CONSTRUCTION
out of human factors aspects

CENTRAL LEVEL
CIVIL AVIATION AUTHORITY
Rules, regulations, standards
Supervision standard

AVIATION COMPANY
Goals
Organisational culture
Policy and Standards
concerning:
Personnel
Training
Operation
Flight Safety

LOCAL LEVEL
Goals, standards
and policy realised
on the operational management floor

INDIVIDUAL LEVEL
Did the operational personnel fulfil
the organisation's requirements and standards
at the time of the accident?

Investigation phases

1. Collection of data by the complete investigation team: 'what happened?'
2. Individual collection of data by the different professional groups involved in the investigation team.
3. Regular presentation of findings to the complete investigation team followed by a team discussion and a dialogue of ways to continue the investigation. The decision is made by the chairman of the team.
4. Further collection of information and data on the professional group basis.
5. Presentation of findings to the investigation team members and a dialogue and group discussion to analyse 'why it could have happened?'
6. The chairman and the chief investigator write together a draft report.
7. The draft report is presented for the members of the investigation team and the draft is probed by all members. Every member has to debate with the investigation team their statements and suggestions of changes for the final report.

8. The discussion to analyse the causes of the accident is a process which concludes with an agreement among the team members.
9. The final accident report is published. The report is an official act for all Swedish citizens.

Requirements concerning human factors investigation

- The human factors investigator has to be a full member of the investigation team.
- The human factors investigator must be present from the very beginning of the investigation to be able to gather immediate and complete information, together with the rest of the team.
- The human factors investigator must have a mandate to collect the additional and relevant information from individuals in the organisation. The units' requirements must however be respected.

Basic considerations concerning the human factors investigation

- The sole objective of the investigation is to work for improvements to safety actions and safety implementations.
- The human being must be respected in all aspects in spite of ambitions to reach the 'truth'.
- The human factors investigation must lead to an analysis of complex root causes.
- The analysis must be contextual based on cognitive / psychological sciences.
- When the chain of causes are non-linear, the analysis must be qualitatively based on a great quantity of facts. This means an understanding of the context.
- The human factors analysis must be considered together with the operational and technical analysis - not in isolation.
- The final result of the investigation must be an analysis of the whole, and not an analysis of the different parts individually.

Criterion of the human factors investigator / expert

- The human factors investigator is the tool to collect, analyse and implement the human factors aspects into the investigation result.
- The result of the investigation is a consequence of the quality of the tool the investigator.

The human factors investigator must:

- Have professional education and training in cognitive / psychological sciences, with an applied emphasis.
- Have a good knowledge of the demands and the requirements in the world of aviation.
- Be well oriented within aviation organisations and in their operational conditions and issues.
- Have the abilities, personal qualities and personality to:
  - ➤ communicate in an understanding and trustful way;
  - ➤ identify, interpret and see the crystallisation of the importance in the whole;
  - ➤ be honest;
  - ➤ be humble, but be able to fight for their statements and opinions;
  - ➤ be a flexible team player.

The investigation of the human factors contribution to safety

In the Swedish Air Force the human factors causes of accidents have been as frequent as in the rest of the military and civil aviation worlds. To emphasise the importance of the human factors area, a group, consisting of members with varied professional backgrounds and expertise, as is the case with an accident investigation board, was established within the Flight Safety Department in Air Force Staff. The task of the group was to analyse the human factors related accidents over a period of ten years, to observe the trends, and to recommend safety actions.

The trend was obvious. The main recommendation for flight safety was to increase the training and education program in the human factors issues for all levels in the organisation.

I have realised through my experience in aviation, that there is an unconscious 'illusion of knowledge' spread among us. Our way of thinking has deep traces and our model of 'reality' is limited. Consequently we are not aware of what can go wrong, because we can not see the risks. What implementation the 'new' technique should have on education and training programs, is one example where we have not understood the consequences fully.The concept of 'situational awareness' is frequently used as a measure of quality for those who work in the cockpit. The concept is, however, not less important for the rest of the individuals involved in the aviation business. We all need situational awareness, which means to have control of the consequences of our actions. Basically it is a question of knowledge. To get it, we need to communicate and co-operate.

As in accident investigations, there is a need for various kinds of expertise - operational, technical and cognitive/psychological. The development of the best techniques and the human beings' qualifications must be seen as one concept and we have to work together to achieve that concept.

The competence in the aviation business has to be broadened. This is the main basic underlying human factors recommendation for enhancing flight safety in the future.

29 Investigation of human and organisational factors

Alan Hobbs
Bureau of Air Safety Investigation, Australia

General

It could be said that in complex technological systems such as aviation, accidents do not happen to individuals, but to entire organisations. There has long been an acknowledgment that system breakdowns or safety occurrences[1] typically reflect not only individual human failings, but also systemic or organisational problems. In recent years there has been a growing awareness that organisational and systemic issues as well as the more traditional human factors, must be considered in an occurrence investigation.

The Reason model of system safety provides a widely understood and accepted framework within which to conduct a systemic investigation (see Figure 1). While the model is not the only systemic approach to accident analysis, it is rapidly attaining the status of industry standard and its adoption can be recommended for this reason alone. The model has been used to analyse a diverse range of safety occurrences including aviation accidents and incidents, chemical plant mishaps, fires, shipping and rail accidents, and medical misadventure. According to the model, accidents rarely result solely from the actions of system operators. Rather, most accidents are due to a combination of failures originating at all levels of the organisation and from factors outside the organisation.

Reason distinguishes between active failures and latent failures. Active failures are the errors or violations committed by operators, such as pilots or air traffic controllers. Latent failures on the other hand, are the conditions which influence the way operators perform their assigned tasks, or which influence the ability of the system to cope with unexpected behaviour or circumstances. Latent failures can include component failures, such as structural failures or system malfunctions. Latent failures can be present in the system long before the breakdown or accident occurs.

---

[1] Throughout this chapter the term *occurrence* may refer to either an accident or an incident.

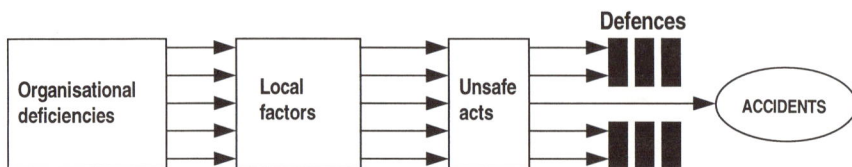

Figure 1   Simplified schematic of the Reason model
(Adapted from Reason, 1990)

Latent failures which relate to the immediate environment in which an active failure occurred are known as local factors. This category of factors includes workplace morale, operator fatigue and local procedures. Those latent failures which relate to the wider organisation or aviation system are referred to as organisational deficiencies or systemic factors. For the purposes of this chapter, the terms 'systemic factor' and 'organisational deficiency' are considered to be interchangeable.

In a typical accident or system breakdown, local factors set the conditions for an operator to perform an unsafe act. This act then has consequences which are not identified or controlled by the defences or 'safety net' built into the system. The local factors and inadequate defences may, in turn be symptoms of wider systemic issues, such as poor communication or inadequate procedures.[2]

Human factors investigations

From the previous discussion, it can be seen that human factors may take the form of local factors or systemic factors. Many issues which have traditionally concerned human factors specialists, such as noise, fatigue, lighting and interpersonal communication fit neatly into the category of local factors. Systemic factors, on the other hand include the management or organisational issues which have long been of concern to organisational theorists.

Purpose of investigating human factors

While it may seem paradoxical, it can be argued that human factors are only of interest insofar as they point us towards system deficiencies. Identifying that a pilot made an error because she was fatigued or that a mechanic left a panel unsecured because he was distracted, may help to explain one accident or incident, but contributes little to improving safety unless a general deficiency can be identified which has the potential to affect the safety of operations in the future.

---

[2] For a more comprehensive review of the Reason model, refer to ICAO Human Factors Digest No 7 (International Civil Aviation Organization, 1993).

Putting this another way, if all the information in investigation reports was expressed in the *past tense*, little would be contributed towards the safety of *future* operations. Only when some of the findings of the investigation deal with currently active situations, expressed usually in the *present* tense, does the investigator make a direct contribution to accident prevention. As a general rule, accident factors which can only be expressed in the past tense tend to be local factors, whereas factors which can be expressed in the present tense tend to be systemic and possess the potential to become the raw materials for future accidents.

Local vs systemic factors

It can be difficult to make a distinction between local and systemic human factors. If the crew of the accident flight made an error because they were not trained to the appropriate level of skill, is lack of training a local factor or a systemic deficiency? In such a case, it would be sensible to consider the lack of skill as a local factor, and the inadequacies in the training system which led to this situation as a system deficiency. In analysing an occurrence, it is generally useful to draw an arbitrary line dividing local and systemic factors. So for example, when considering the performance of air traffic controllers, factors which exist within the control room might be considered to be local, while factors which exist beyond the door of the control centre might be considered to be systemic. Alternatively, the grammatical heuristic described above could be applied, so that factors are described as either problems that *happened* (generally local) or problems that are still *happening* (generally systemic). Ultimately, it doesn't really matter what label is applied to a factor, as long as continuing deficiencies are identified.

Establishing a sequence of events

One of the first objectives of a human factors investigation should be to identify the sequence of operational events in time order. The event sequence may be compiled from diverse sources such as cockpit voice recordings, witness reports and interviews with operational personnel. A typical occurrence will involve more than one event and several of these are likely to be active failures committed by operational personnel.

To be logically consistent, each active failure should be expressed in a subject-verb-object sequence, identifying the person who was involved, the action or omission which they committed and the task or object which this involved. For example: maintenance engineer (subject) did not secure (verb) access cover (object).

Once a sequence of events has been established, each active failure can be considered as a separate 'mini-occurrence', with its own local and organisation factors, including failed or absent defences.

Two stage test of factors, existence and influence

In attributing factors to explain human actions, it is helpful to apply a two stage test of validity. This test can be applied to local and systemic factors alike. First, the investigator should be satisfied that the factor was present at the time of the active failure. This could involve questions such as: Am I satisfied that the cockpit lighting was dim? Was the person suffering from fatigue? It may only be possible to answer such questions with less than complete certainty.

Second, if the investigator is satisfied that the factor was probably present, it must then be established that the factor influenced events on the day. This could involve questions such as: I am satisfied that the pilot was fatigued, but did this contribute to his error? Only when the investigator is satisfied on the balance of probability, that a factor existed at the time of the event and influenced the outcome of the event, should that factor be considered to have been a contributing factor in the occurrence.

Investigation of systemic factors

On a large investigation, separate investigators may be assigned to consider the local human factors and the wider systemic human factors which contributed to an occurrence. The following sections relate to the investigation of systemic contributions to an occurrence.

Relation to other groups

The organisational factors investigator has responsibilities which will overlap with those of other groups in the investigation team. It is important that the organisational investigator maintains a broad awareness of the progress of each group as group leaders may not always recognise the wider systemic or organisational implications of the information they collect.

Potential problems in a systemic investigation

As occurrence factors become increasingly remote from the immediate time and place of the occurrence, the potential subjectivity of the investigation increases, as do the opportunities for disagreement between those with a stake in the investigation. This is not however, justification for avoiding controversial organisational and systemic issues.

Before commencing work, the organisational investigator must bear in mind that all organisations have weaknesses. Finding such weaknesses during an occurrence investigation does not necessarily help to explain events. It should also be borne in mind that several organisations may be implicated in an occurrence, each with their own level of involvement. The organisational factors relating to each of these organisations should be considered separately.

In most cultures, there is a strong tendency to search for culpable individuals after an accident and a corresponding reluctance to consider the role of institutions such as companies or government organisations. The organisational investigator must resist such pressures, yet still consider how an effective organisational investigation can be conducted consistent with the national culture.

Methodology: general

Since each organisational investigation is unique, it is not desirable to prescribe in detail how each investigation should be conducted. The method section below describes how the Reason model can be applied to an occurrence investigation. This model provides a useful checklist to ensure that issues are explored and can assist in writing up findings in a form that is consistent with publications such as ICAO Circular 247-AN/148.

The Reason model is not the only possible method or framework which can be used in a systemic investigation. Other methods such as Management Oversight and Risk Tree (MORT) may be useful and the organisational investigator should not feel compelled to limit the investigation to issues covered by one particular model.

The application of the Reason Model to identify systemic factors

The organisational investigator may partly rely on other groups to identify active failures, local factors and failed or absent defences. As this information becomes available, the organisational investigator will be in a position to consider the underlying organisational and systemic factors which enabled the situation to develop.

In the event of a large accident, there may be daily briefings which will enable the organisational investigator to become aware of the progress of other groups. It may be appropriate however, for the organisational investigator to arrange for a member of each group to act as a contact and report information which may have a bearing on organisational issues. In the early stages of the investigation, the organisational investigator may need to attend key interviews conducted by other groups such as ATC or operations. This will ensure that potential organisational issues are not neglected during the interview. As the investigation progresses there may be a need to conduct interviews specifically directed at organisational issues.

In addition to relying on information from sources such as interviews, and documents, the organisational investigator may choose to collect information via additional means such as structured survey interviews or questionnaires.

Potential organisational weaknesses may become apparent as the investigation progresses. Yet these organisational weaknesses may have had no role in the development of the accident. If no evidence subsequently emerges to link these weaknesses with the active failures, local factors and defences of the accident scenario, the organisational investigator should not list these weaknesses among the occurrence factors. It may be appropriate to deal with such findings in an addendum to the report.

In general, it is recommended that the organisational investigator starts by listing the active failures and local factors related to the occurrence and then works outwards to identify the relevant organisational and systemic conditions. Investigators are cautioned against starting at perceived organisational weaknesses and then attempting to link these with the occurrence circumstances.

At the completion of the process, each organisational factor must be linked with at least one active failure, one local factor or one defence. Organisational factors which cannot be so linked fall into the category of uninvolved organisational weaknesses discussed above. It is important to find supporting evidence of each suggested organisational failure, preferably by looking outside the immediate circumstances of the accident. The identification of organisational factors is described below.

Potential systemic issues

In the following section, potential areas of concern are linked to possible questions which could guide an organisational investigator. These areas are by no means the only potential topics to be considered as part of an organisational investigation.

Corporate goals

Most organisations operate with goals which conflict from time to time, such as on-time performance and fuel saving. While goal conflicts are a normal aspect of many systems, the manner in which the organisation recognises the conflict and trades goals off with one another may be significant to the occurrence. The following questions may be useful when considering corporate goals:

- Does the organisation have a formal statement of goals?
- What are the performance expectations of owners (whether shareholders or government)

Organisational structure

The ability of the organisation to react to present events and plan for future situations is likely to be influenced by the structure of the organisation. Organisation charts or internal directories can help an investigator to become familiar with the formal structure and systems of the organisation. Potential questions include:

- Do problems stem from the structure of the organisation?
- Are management responsibilities clearly defined?
- What actions by managers and other staff are rewarded?
- What actions are punished?

Communications

A primary concern of management is to ensure that there is an appropriate exchange of information between individuals in the organisation. A small organisation can often rely on informal communication methods, however larger organisations or those which are geographically distributed will need formal communication channels, to feed information from management outwards, to inform management of operational issues and to enable lessons learnt in one branch of the organisation to be shared with other branches. Some questions to ask are:

- Would the occurrence have been less likely if internal communications were better?
- Do field stations communicate with headquarters?
- Is upper management aware of operational realities.
- Are there adequate systems in place to inform management of key indicators?

Planning

Successful organisations recognise that the environment in which they operate is rarely stable and prepare for foreseeable events. Many organisational difficulties such as shortages of staff or equipment may reflect underlying inadequacies in planning. It may be appropriate to consider the following issues:

- Does the organisation operate in a short-term environment?
- Does the organisation have difficulty anticipating events?

Design of systems and components

Design issues are included as systemic factors because the design of systems and components is normally an activity remote from day to day system operation. Some systems may not have been 'designed' at all, but may have developed over time. Systems which are complex to the extent that their workings are not understood by operators (opaque systems) can be particularly problematic. The following questions may be relevant:

- Did the designers receive feedback on the adequacy of the design?
- Were there opportunities to modify the design?
- Do operators understand fully the systems they use?
- If complex technical systems are involved, is there a single person who has a general understanding of system operation?

Corporate memory

The expertise of experienced staff can be one of the organisation's most valuable assets.

Organisations, like people can suffer from amnesia or can find themselves on a steep learning curve. The following questions may help to explore these issues:

- Has there been a recent loss of experienced staff?
- Have there been recent mergers or takeovers?
- Does the organisation have a well maintained corporate memory?
- Are there events remembered in the 'folklore' of the organisation which still influence the functioning of the organisation today?
- Has the organisation recently entered this particular field of business?

Procedures

Formal rules and procedures may be irrelevant, out of date or may fail to reflect operational realities. It may be appropriate to ask such questions as:

- Is there a conflict between informal norms and formal procedures?
- Would the organisation fail to function if procedures were strictly adhered to?
- Do local orders/instructions conflict with organisational orders / instructions.
- Are procedures accessible and useable?

Resources

Few organisations have the luxury of unlimited resources, however, an organisation which is financially unviable may operate with an unacceptable level of risk. It may be important to ask whether the organisation has the resources to recruit and train staff, maintain equipment and operate responsibly.

Regulation

There are many possible regulatory regimes, ranging from laissez-faire self regulation to strict government control. Nevertheless, regulations and regulatory authorities have a pervasive influence on aviation organisations. It may be important to know the following:

- How frequently do regulators visit the organisation?
- Are the regulators capable of administering the regulations?
- Do the regulators have available a range of measures (such as sanctions) to encourage compliance?

Corporate culture

Corporate culture is an extensive field of study in its own right, and it is not possible to do justice here to the full range of issues which could be considered.[3] In the context of this chapter, the following issues should be considered:

---

[3] Organisational and safety cultures are discussed in some detail by Hayward in the following chapter on Safety and Culture (5.4).

- Does the organisation condone risk taking?
- Is safety an important goal of the organisation?
- Does the organisation have a history of correcting problems?
- Does the organisation have a history of ignoring or covering up problems?

Safety management

The following questions may help to identify issues related to the company
- Does the organisation have a safety or quality assurance program?
- Is there a safety department? If so, to whom does it report?
- Has the organisation recently been the subject of an outside audit?
- Has there been a formal hazard analysis of the operation?
- Does the organisation have a risk management policy?

Final considerations

To be truly effective, investigations must consider the role of systemic factors, yet the investigation of such factors is likely to be heavily reliant on subjective judgement.

One of the most important subjective considerations in an investigation is knowing when to stop. Occurrence factors may be found far removed in time and distance from the occurrence itself and it may be difficult to know how widely the systemic investigation should extend. Such a decision will be influenced by the legal framework within which the investigating authority operates. A useful rule is that when the organisational investigator begins to arrive at circumstances which are beyond the control of managers, the investigation has exceeded reasonable bounds.

30 Witness interviewing techniques in aircraft accident investigation

Brent Hayward
Asia Pacific Resource Management, Australia

Introduction

The gathering and evaluation of accurate and unbiased evidence is essential to the successful conduct of any aircraft accident investigation. It is well established however, both by experimental and anecdotal evidence, that human beings are notoriously unreliable as observers, particularly when asked to recall the detail of significant events.

A major potential for error occurs at the 'playback' stage, when the recorded memory of an event is being accessed through interview. While most of us feel we can interview competently, and gathering evidence sounds simple, facilitating unbiased testimony is a surprisingly difficult and consistently underestimated task. Contrary to popular belief, getting witnesses to say what we want to hear is not representative of efficient interviewing technique. Even subtle, unintended variations in questioning technique or terminology can dramatically influence the content of recall.

Relevant to this, yet historically an aspect of some neglect, is the training of prospective witness interviewers: flight safety officers, board of inquiry members and accident investigators, in the techniques of eliciting accurate and unbiased testimony from witnesses.

The objective of this paper is to outline techniques which may prove useful to a prospective witness interviewers in coping effectively with evidence gathering in interview situations.

Limitations to the accuracy of witness recall

Figure 1 depicts some of the factors which have the potential to influence the accuracy of eyewitness recall and testimony, from the time of exposure to the event, the stimulus, until the time of describing, or relating the event, the output. These limiting variables are discussed below.

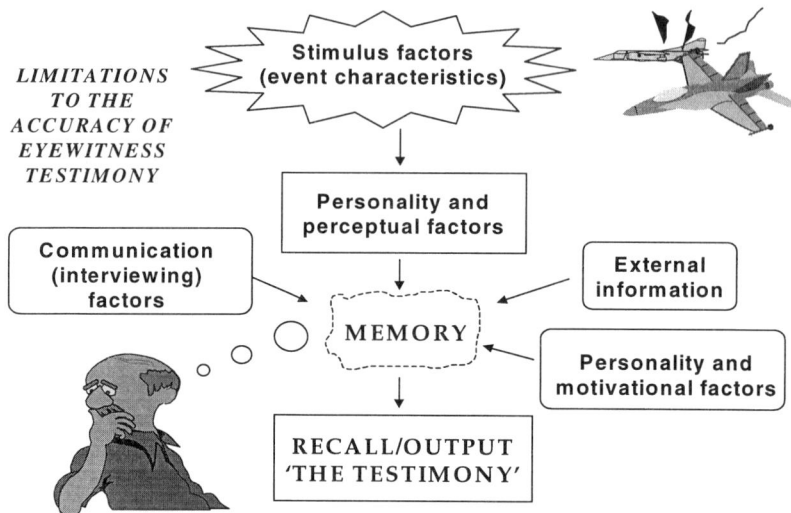

Figure 1   Limitations to the accuracy of witness recall

Stimulus characteristics

Naturally, various features associated with the event (stimulus qualities) will immediately limit the quality of the keenest observer's perception. The *clarity* of the event, for example whether it occurred by day or by night, or in a chaotic or comparatively serene environment; its *proximity* to the observer; its *complexity* as an event; its *duration* for the witness; and finally the *familiarity* of the event to the observer, will constitute critical limiting factors to total recall. In general, civilian eyewitnesses to military accidents have limited general knowledge of military aircraft or flying operations. Similarly, non-aviation personnel may be quite unfamiliar with the characteristics of aircraft or aviation in general. Consideration should be given to these event characteristics, especially when weighing the relative value and reliability of individual witnesses.

Human perceptual and personality factors

Human perception is rarely an accurate reflection of reality. Preconceptions, expectations, needs, cultural values and biases can all influence our perceptual interpretation of an event. Again there is much experimental evidence to support this thesis. Drawing an example from popular culture, 50,000 people at a football game may witness exactly the same event, yet half will agree with the umpire's interpretation, and the other half will disagree, often with considerable vehemence.

Psychologists have in the past performed extensive research on the manner in which mental 'set' or expectancy on the part of the witness can influence perceptions of events. In a classic study of the phenomenon, Professor Allport of Harvard University had subjects briefly examine a drawing of several people in a subway train carriage, including a black man and a white man confronting each other, the white man holding a razor in his hand. Fifty percent of the subjects later reported that the razor was in the hand of the black man.

These individual interpretations of reality occur largely unconsciously. Another process which operates unconsciously to filter or distort the accurate perception of reality involves psychological defence mechanisms. Defence mechanisms are protections built into personality, designed to prevent frightening or threatening perceptions from reaching consciousness. They can be thought of as acting like shock-absorbers for the mind. They are activated unconsciously at the onset of a potentially harmful or disturbing stimulus, and can distort its interpretation in a way which makes it less-threatening and easier for the human ego to deal with. The result is that people faced with stressful, dangerous and in particular life-threatening events, are likely to be prevented from recalling such events accurately. In the extreme, post-traumatic amnesia may result from intolerable exposure to threat, erasing all conscious memory of the experience. Witnesses to an unusual, shocking or violent event may unknowingly experience similar defensive interference to perception.

Even after an event is recorded in memory with some degree of accuracy, it is subject to distortion. Apart from the normal process of *memory decay* over time, witnesses continue to process information from the world between an event and their retelling of it to an official investigator. Most commonly, the event becomes the major focus of their attention in this intervening period. As such, their story is retold, to friends, relatives, and possibly to the press. Caught up in the accident milieu, a witnesses' personal memories are likely to become fused with others' versions of the event, and their own recollections may well suffer *contamination* from these external sources.

Another common behavioural tendency is for people to claim – in an attention seeking manner – that they were present when a significant event took place, when they were not there at all. In an experiment in this area a journalist once fabricated a story about a naked woman stuck to a newly painted toilet seat in a small American town, and circulated it on newspaper wire services. He later visited the town and interviewed several citizens who claimed to have witnessed and even to have taken part in freeing the woman in this fictitious event. Several instances of similar behaviour have been apparent following major aircraft accidents.

Interviewer induced bias

A major source of inaccuracy in extracting eyewitness testimony occurs during the testimony interview. The biases, expectations, prior knowledge, or simply the ineptitude of the interviewer can dramatically influence a witnesses' recall of an event.   Following discussion of some preliminary principles in eyewitness interviewing, these 'interviewer input factors' will be addressed in this paper.

Initial interviewing considerations

Timeliness

It is paramount that interviews are conducted *as soon as is practicable* following the occurrence of the event under investigation.   Post-event information (eg., through media coverage, or from others who saw or claim that they saw the accident) can supplement and in some cases supplant a previously acquired memory of circumstances and can seriously contaminate the individual's recall of what he or she actually saw.

Location

Flexibility in approaching the interview is an important determinant of success. Don't be afraid to move your interview location out into the scrub in search of valuable information.   An eyewitness' recall will be much improved if he or she can be interviewed at the exact place from which they viewed the accident.   In this situation however, do your best to avoid travelling to the interview site with the witness, as they will invariably start describing what was seen while in transit to the site.   This will limit the power of *in situ* recall.   The benefits of environmental cues, which can act as a powerful aid to memory, will be lost.

Rapport

Encourage the witness to relax and cooperate. Make appropriate introductions. Smile when you meet, and avoid being too businesslike or authoritative (first impressions *are* important).   Explain the purpose of the interview, and how you are going to proceed.   Ask permission to take notes and to make an audio tape recording of the interview (both are desirable) and explain why you're going to do so (to aid your poor memory).
Endeavour to establish an informal, even casual rapport with the witness. Help them to relax - they may well feel nervous or intimidated.   Witnessing the event may have been a traumatic experience for them.   Talk about the weather; the land; their work or family; etc.   Then ease into the interview.

Status

Minimise any overt status differences between yourself and the witness.   Dress appropriately.   De-emphasise differences in rank or status.   Don't appear officious or 'expert'. Again, be flexible and judge each situation on its merits. On occasion it may be appropriate for you to wear a flying suit, jungle greens or casual civilian clothing; *not* a suit and tie or military uniform. Civilians can be apprehensive about talking to 'government men'.

Language

Promote maximum communication by using language that the witness can understand and relate to. Avoid using military or aviation jargon, acronyms, or technical terminology with which the witness may be unfamiliar.

Emotional state

A witness may well be experiencing upset or distress over the accident, and although well enough to be interviewed, may not be especially alert, responsive or calm. Be sensitive to the individual's emotional condition, and structure the pace of the interview accordingly. Traumatic stress is also likely to have the effect of reducing the overall quality of testimony.

Questioning techniques

Unstructured free recall

The structure under which information is elicited is important. Beginning the interview with a period of 'unstructured free recall', where the witnesses' cognitive set is widest, will provide greatest overall accuracy. As there are no specific questions, the imperative to respond is low. In most cases, witnesses will not be confronted with a situation for which they have no response, and are unlikely to make any statement if unsure. Direct or closed questioning can afford more detail, but, as will be explained below, may inhibit accuracy. The most efficient interviewing technique involves a marriage of these approaches, always commencing the main part of the interview with periods of unstructured free recall.

One simple approach is to ask the witness to begin at a point relevant to the accident and explain, in their own time and words, what was observed. It is *essential* that this initial recounting of events proceeds uninterrupted. In most cases this initial statement will be brief, incomplete and unclear. It is then up to the interviewer to elicit additional information and/or clarify points already raised by the witness. This must be accomplished without altering or biasing the information offered. So, complement the witness on their initial description, and ask them to start again, from an appropriate point, providing a little more detail as they go. This approach can be repeated several times before moving on to ask some more specific but still open-ended questions.

Open-ended questions

Open-ended questions are designed to produce broad-ranging, non-specific responses. As described above they are used to open up discussion in the form of unstructured recall. As follow-up questions, they encourage further general or broad responses based around the interviewee's frame of reference. With open-ended questions, the witnesses' cognitive set is wide, there is less likelihood of them being confronted with a question about which no response can be made, and it is less likely that witnesses will volunteer information about which they are unsure.

The open-ended probing technique is 'non directive' in that it invites further content based on a previous response, but without defining the bounds or direction of the new content. A useful way to approach this phase of testimony is, after complementing the witness on the quality of his evidence, to begin by saying: 'I'm a bit uncertain about what happened after…, can you begin there and go over things again for me please', or 'can you tell me some more about…'. The extra detail revealed in these second or third accounts of events is sometimes quite staggering. Direct questioning can then be employed to fill in any remaining gaps in the testimony (eg. 'what colour?', 'what size?', 'which direction?').

- Some further examples of open-ended questions are:
- Tell me again what happened after …?
- Can you describe what you saw next?
- Can you tell me what the aircraft was doing then?
- How did he seem when you last saw him?
- What can you tell me about his behaviour around that time?

Encouraging responses

Encouraging responses include any verbal and non-verbal means by which the listener encourages the other person to continue talking. They are used to facilitate active listening; to indicate 'tracking' (following and understanding); to encourage further talking; to indicate support or empathy; and as a means of minimising the possibility of influencing the direction of conversation. Examples of encouraging behaviours include:

- Head nods, eye contact
- Facial expressions
- Body language, attentiveness
- Voice tone, level
- Minimal speech: 'uh-huh'; silence
- Brief repetition of words

Use these responses to give positive feedback as the witness is recounting what happened, demonstrating you are attentive and still following. When they have completed their initial description of events, compliment the witness on their recall of the situation before going on. This can raise confidence and reduce anxiety and thus promote better continued response. However, care must be taken to avoid providing too much positive feedback if the information being provided is beginning to confirm your hypotheses about what took place. Remain emotionally neutral.

Remember that good listening is an essential feature of good interviewing. It has been said that we have two ears and one mouth and that we should put them to use in those proportions: however, that would be too much talking for an accident investigator! Good investigators are perceptive, diplomatic, empathic, and above all, good listeners. There are only three reasons for the witness interviewer to be talking: to put the witness at ease and set the scene for the interview; to ask pertinent clarifying questions; and finally to summarise points and provide positive feedback and encouragement.

Paraphrasing

Paraphrasing involves re-stating what has already been said in summarised form. Paraphrasing is used to clarify or synthesise a possibly disjointed statement, and to confirm your perception, ie., to ensure that the message received was the message being sent. Paraphrasing has the additional benefit of demonstrating active listening, and a concern to hear your witness accurately. Some examples of paraphrasing pertinent to witness interviewing are:

- So the aircraft banked sharply, turned to the left, and then the nose appeared to drop suddenly?
- You're saying he was pretty upset about failing the check, and became quite moody for a few days?
- You said there was a flash first, then a loud noise?

Closed questions

Closed questions are those which require only a single word or brief answer. They are used to seek specific detail, and probe for qualification to a statement, or to confirm specific information. They encourage precision in memory by requesting factual information. Using a sequence of closed questions enables a complex response to be broken down into it's component parts or details.

Closed questions constitute much of our day to day conversation, and are thus easy to ask. Remember however, that they restrict the witnesses' freedom and range of response, and are thus inappropriate in generating the free recall component of an interview. They should *never* be used at the beginning of an interview. As is frequently demonstrated in cinematic depictions of courtroom scenes, closed questions carry an implicit imperative to respond to a question even if the witness is unsure about the issue under scrutiny.

Examples of closed questions are:
- Where exactly were you standing?

- What would you estimate the speed of the aircraft was?
- Can you point to where you first saw the aircraft?
- How long did you take to get to the site?
- At what time was that?

Leading questions

Leading questions anticipate the response.   In the context of eyewitness interviewing, they have the specific purposes of checking perception / understanding; testing reaction to a proposal; or establishing agreement or disagreement about a particular statement.   If required, they can confront the respondent's recall, even to the extent of appearing to question an unlikely or improbable recollection. Some examples of leading questions are:

- You're certain there were flames coming from the engine?
- You seem to be saying he had a history of showing off his flying skills?
- Did you really see it hit the water, or is that what other people have described?

Questions which lead to an anticipated answer have the obvious danger that they will lead to a particular, but not necessarily correct answer. This form of interviewer bias is very common and has the potential to seriously contaminate the eyewitness testimony. Interviewers should avoid asking leading questions even if it is thought that the answer to a question is obvious, and that time could be saved by avoiding lengthy deliberation by the respondent. 'Was he happy and alert when you strapped him in?' may provide the expected response, but could miss out in terms of accuracy compared with 'can you describe the demeanour of the pilot while you were strapping him in?'.

Even subtle and unintended references can influence a witness to respond in a particular way. Questions like 'how big?' or 'how small?' (compared to the more neutral 'what size?'), or 'how fast/slow?' (compared to 'what speed?') set a response frame of reference, which has been shown experimentally to alter recall.

Professor Elizabeth Loftus of the University of Washington is an expert on witness testimony, and has demonstrated that altering the semantic value of the wording in questions can cause witnesses to distort their reports. One experiment involved asking witnesses questions about a filmed car accident they had been shown. When witnesses were asked a question using the word 'smashed' as opposed to 'bumped' they gave significantly higher estimates of the speed involved in the collision and were more likely to report having observed broken glass at the scene – even though there was no broken glass present. Guard against the use of emotive terminology in your questioning of witnesses.

Care should also be taken to avoid corruption of the individual's recall during or even after initial interviewing. Any details introduced or disclosed by the interviewer may be included in or influence later testimony by the witness. Resist the temptation to demonstrate to the witness how much you already know about the accident. Play naive. Just as 'pub conversations', or media interviews can allow others' recollections to be confused with existing ones, the accident investigator should take care not to make reference to important details not already raised by the witness. Questions like 'Was there any smoke coming out?', or worse, 'what colour was the smoke?', before 'smoke' has been mentioned by the witness, encourage confirmation on a detail about which the witness may have no information at all. A neutral, open-ended alternative would be of the form: 'Did you notice anything else about the aircraft?'

Conclusion

To summarise, good eyewitness interviewing involves applying the same skills necessary for a well-conducted job selection interview, counselling interview, or performance appraisal interview. It is important to establish rapport and make the respondent comfortable with the interview situation. A greater quantity and quality of information will be obtained by a careful blend of open-ended questions, accompanied by encouraging responses, and followed up appropriately with 'closed' or even leading questions towards the end of the interview.

Many possible sources of error and bias in eyewitness testimony can be controlled by the interviewer. Professional interviewing which minimises interference with the most accurate recollections of the witness will be of greatest value to the goal of a successful accident investigation.

Author's note

This chapter is based on a document originally prepared by Brent Hayward for use in the training of RAAF aircraft accident investigators. Some revisions for an intermediate version of the document were contributed by Andrew Lowe.

31   Safety and culture

Brent Hayward
Asia Pacific Resource Management, Australia

Notions of culture

Underpinning much of the work on human error are notions regarding the influence of culture on individual and group behaviour. In spite of the belief of some observers that it is possible to create 'culture free' work environments, there is little doubt that there are a variety of cultures within which aviation professionals carry out their daily duties which impact significantly on the operations of the world's airlines. While national culture was the first of these to come under scrutiny, there is now a growing recognition amongst researchers and practitioners that a range of sub-cultures exist (eg., organisational, vocational, occupational, safety) which also impact directly upon our professional and interpersonal behaviours in the work place. While a solution to creating a culture-free work environment has been proposed - '...fill it with Australians' - (Hamilton, 1992), in practice even this does not work and it is evident that we are all, to some extent, culturally-bound in terms of our behaviours and attitudes.

National culture

The seminal research of Hofstede (1980, 1991) laid the foundation for the considerable body of work which has since examined the role of national culture in relation to flight crew behaviour and safety on the flight deck (eg., Ooi, 1991, 1992; Johnston, 1993; Maurino, 1994; Merritt, 1993, 1996). Hofstede isolated four dimensions on which national cultures can be classified. Two of these dimensions are particularly relevant to the way teams function within aviation. One defines the nature of relations between subordinates and superiors (*Power Distance*), and the second (*Collectivism vs Individualism*) reflects group interdependence versus independence. Anglo-Western influenced cultures tend to be high in individualism, and moderate to low in power distance. Many Asian and Latin-based cultures are collectivist, and high in power distance. As observed by Smith and Bond (1993), Hofstede's original work avoided the 'ecological fallacy' that others have frequently implied from his findings; eg., that because Australia scores higher on his dimension of *Individualism* than Indonesia, then a particular Australian must be more independent or individualist than a particular Indonesian. Hofstede's mean scores represent the average of the scores of those who responded to the questionnaire.

The work of Ashleigh Merritt (1993, 1996) explores cross-cultural similarities and differences with respect to attitudes toward flight management and the link to safe operations. Using the NASA/UT Flight Management Attitudes Questionnaire, Helmreich and Merritt (1996) were able to identify some attitudinal characteristics which appeared to be 'universally' applicable to airline pilots, and some in which large differences were displayed between the various cultures which made up their sample, as illustrated in Table 1.

Table 1   FMAQ Pilot 'universals', and items showing significant cross-cultural differences in 19 organisations
(Adapted from Helmreich & Merritt, 1996)

Flight Management Attitudes Questionnaire Items - COMMUNICATION, COORDINATION, COMMAND & STRESS	% Agreement across 19 Orgs.
Universals	
Good communication and crew coordination are as important as technical proficiency for the safety of flight.	85-100%
The captain's responsibilities include coordination between cockpit and cabin crews.	85-100%
The pre-flight briefing is important for safety and for effective crew management	85-100%
The pilot flying the aircraft should verbalise plans…and be sure the information is understood and acknowledged.	85-100%
I like my job.	85-100%
Significant cultural differences	
Crew members should not question the decisions or actions of the captain except when they threaten the safety of the flight.	15-93%
If I perceive a problem with the flight, I will speak up, regardless of who might be affected.	36-98%
Personal problems can adversely affect my performance.	38-78%
I am more likely to make judgment errors in an emergency.	17-70%

In her doctoral study, which attempted to replicate Hofstede's original work with IBM employees within the airline community almost three decades later,

Merritt (1996) met with considerable success.[1] Her results indicate that aspects of airline pilot work such as communication and teamwork were acknowledged as universally important by those who took part in the study. Attitudes toward stress reflected a strong (but seriously mistaken) pilot attitudinal norm that the true professional is invulnerable to environmental stressors.[2] This result has implications for the effectiveness of CRM training, and will be discussed in that context below.

The strongest cross-cultural differences found by Merritt were in the areas of command (Hofstede's dimension of *Power Distance*) and flexibility with rules and routines (*Uncertainty Avoidance*). Pilots from 'Anglo' countries (USA, Australia, New Zealand, Ireland, and British-born pilots based in Hong Kong) held very similar views, while amongst the non-Anglo countries, the more hierarchical command styles were differentiated by the relative importance allocated to rank (Brazil), rules (Taiwan), and relationships (Philippines). The unequivocal finding of the study was that national culture is a powerful influence on work performance, and that pilot training and international aviation regulations should reflect an awareness of this.

Much of the work on culture focuses on the seemingly apparent and generalisable differences between mainstream eastern and western cultural values. However, this is a very blunt tool with which to examine cultural differences. If we look at geographically small and contiguous regions of Europe, for example, we can observe rather significant differences in the thinking, attitudes and behaviours of the people (eg. the English vs the French). As reported by Johnston (1993, p. 369): 'an American medical journalist resident in Europe consulted various physicians about a recurrent medical condition. She found that opinion varied between the American, French, British and German doctors she consulted. She found a diversity in clinical practice which was determined more by national characteristics than by medico-scientific logic. Her research confirmed that cultural factors were a notable influence on interpretation of the medical literature'. Even though the differences may be more subtle, similar observations can certainly be made regarding the cultures contained within Asia (eg., Japan vs China, Malaysia vs Thailand), in spite of the fact that 'westerners' commonly refer to an 'Asian' culture or way of thinking, and the Middle East (eg., Israel vs Syria). It is noteworthy that an area as geographically contiguous as Papua New Guinea is reported to contain people from cultures speaking no less than 717 (45%) of the world's almost 1,600 languages (Lightbody & Wheeler, 1985).

---

[1] Hofstede's original work involved the mapping of several dimensions of national culture based on data gathered from IBM employees in 66 countries in the late 1960's and early 1970's. Merritt's study was based on data from more than 8,000 male commercial airline pilots, employed by 22 airlines, in 15 countries.

[2] For the interested reader an extreme example of this - manifested by feelings of invincibility and disproportionately high risk-taking - can be found in Kern's (1995) fascinating case study of a USAF B52 accident at Fairchild AFB.

It seems that the formation of national culture may be comparable to the complexity of the determinants of individual personality. While the nature vs nurture debate has been one of ebb and flow over the years, it is most likely that an individual's personality results from a complex interaction of numerous genetic and environmental factors. So too it must be with national culture, which is influenced by genetics, ritual, religion, colonisation, major historical events, immigration, cultural blending, and physical environment factors such as terrain and climate.

Cultures within cultures

Building on this point, it is of course possible to discern cultural differences within a culture which, at least from an external point of view, may appear to be relatively homogeneous. The work of Semin and Rubini (1990) illustrates this point rather neatly. They employed a somewhat novel approach to examine the cultural differences between northern and southern Italians, comparing the types of verbal insults used by the two groups. Their hypothesis, that subjects from 'more interdependent' Sicily would report a larger proportion of *relational* insults than those from 'more independent' Bologna and Trieste was upheld, as can be observed from a selection of the less-graphic insult-types presented in Table 2.

Table 2   A selection of culturally-rooted insults

Individualist insults (distinctive to northern Italy)	Collectivist insults (distinctive to southern Italy)
You are stupid.	*I wish a cancer on you and all your relatives.*
You are a cretin.	*Your sister is a cow.*
Swear-words referring to religious fixtures.	*You are queer and so is your father.*
Swear-words referring to sexual nouns.	*You are a communist.*
	Various insults relating to incest.

Vocational and work-group cultures

It is also true that certain cultural norms can be associated with those who work in various industries and occupations. As with most vocations, aviation attracts a wide range of personalities from a variety of socio-economic and ethnic backgrounds, yet there are certain cultural norms that are generally shared. Within the aviation industry, there exist a range of sub-cultures which can be labelled as occupational or work group cultures. Examples include the occupations of pilot, flight attendant, maintenance engineer, ramp, air traffic control, etc. While these aviation professions commonly share various vocational norms, there are also significant differences between their sub-cultures. For instance, pilots and flight attendants work together as members of the same flight crew, but there are many differences between them in terms of stereotypical characteristics. The cockpit/cabin crew interface research conducted by Chute and her co-workers at NASA Ames (Chute, Wiener, Dunbar, & Hoang, 1996) analysed the nature of the jobs to reveal some generalised differences in the demographics and roles of the two work groups, and their origins, as depicted in Table 3.

Table 3   Relative crew differences by dimension
(Adapted from Chute, Wiener, Dunbar, & Hoang, 1996)

Dimension	Cockpit	Cabin
Gender	mostly Male	mostly Female
Age	mostly 30-60	mostly 20-40
Workspace	Confined	Spacious
Physical Activity	Stationary	Active
Noise Level	relatively Quiet	relatively Noisy
Terminal Workload	High	Low
Cruise Workload	Low	High
Cognitive Orientation	Technical	Social

As anyone who has worked within a large organisation with employees based in several different geographical locations will recognise, there may be powerful differences which exist within the one occupational group, between various locations. Airline ramp employees at a large airport base may be very different in terms of their sub-cultural attitudinal and behavioural norms from those at a regional airport, even though they work in the same industry, for the same carrier, in the same job category.

Organisational culture

While national, vocational and work group cultures have an undeniable influence on individual and group behaviour at work, organisational culture has the potential to have a very significant direct impact on the safety performance of organisations. It is organisational culture which ultimately shapes workers' perceptions of safety, the relative importance placed on safety, and members' activities regarding safety (Merritt & Helmreich, 1996a). Numerous authors have provided rigorous discussion on the importance of an appropriate organisational safety culture and the role that human factors expertise can play in establishing and maintaining appropriate cultural norms (see Hudson, 1997; Johnston, 1991, 1996; Lauber, 1994a, 1994b; Lee, 1994; Maurino, 1994; Merritt & Helmreich, 1996a; Pidgeon & O'Leary, 1994; Reason, 1994a, 1997).

The work of Westrum (1993, 1995) provides considerable insight into what we can learn about an organisation from the styles of management it employs. He begins from the premise that 'aviation organisations require information flow as much as aircraft require fuel' (1995, p. 75), and moves on to examine three distinct patterns of coping with information used by aviation organisations: *pathological, bureaucratic,* and *generative*:

The first pattern (pathological) is typical of highly conflicted organisations, where information is treated as a political weapon. The second pattern is familiar from the textbook description of redtape, etc. Organisations that are bureaucratic are good at handling routine situations, but are bad at dealing with change and emergencies. The Generative pattern is typical of 'high reliability' organisations and highly creative ones. In these organisations, personnel assume that they have a licence both to think and to communicate.

Table 4 illustrates the patterns of information flow typical to these three styles of organisation. It may be instructive to take a moment to reflect on the behaviour of your own organisation. When feedback is provided to management detailing operational problems, or better, also suggesting a novel solution to these problems, how does the organisation respond? In a generative organisation the bearers of such tidings are encouraged and in fact may be trained to behave in this manner. In bureaucratic organisations, messengers may be listened to, if red tape does not prevent their arrival, but new solutions are rarely investigated or implemented. In pathological organisations, where denial is commonplace, such messengers are 'shot'... Which pattern best fits your organisation?

Table 4   Basic organisation communication styles
(adapted from Westrum, 1995)

Pathological	Bureaucratic	Generative
Information is personal power	Information is routine	Information is seen as a key resource
Responsibility is shirked	Responsibility is compartmented	Responsibility is shared
Messengers are shot	Messengers are listened to (if they arrive)	Messengers are trained
Bridging is discouraged	Bridging is tolerated	Bridging is rewarded
Failure is punished or covered up	Organisation is just and fair	Failure leads to inquiry/learning
New ideas are actively crushed	New ideas present problems	New ideas are welcomed

It is not suggested that there is a single organisational culture or corporate style for all organisations to aspire to. Just as many different personality types can make good airline pilots, cabin crew, or air traffic controllers, successful organisations within the same industry can be characterised by radically different cultures and operational styles. This becomes apparent when two independently successful companies are brought together by an organisational merger. By way of

illustration, when the Japanese banking powerhouses Dai-Ichi and Nippon Kangyo
were merged to form the leviathan Dai-Ichi Kangyo, a team of managers from both
sides were assigned the task of developing a 200-word glossary explaining what
each bank meant when using exactly the same words (Fisher, 1994). As employees
from the two companies began working together they searched their dictionaries
like tourists in a foreign land, asking for directions to the nearest toilet (bathroom;
restroom)... Not without its parallels is the early 1990's merger of two large
Australian airlines, both owned by the same government shareholder, each with
admirable service and safety records, but with vastly different organisational
cultures and corporate styles.

Safety culture and CRM

John Lauber (1994) has written and spoken at length about the importance of
nurturing an appropriate 'safety culture' within aviation organisations. A
company's safety culture is inextricably linked with, but can be distinguished from
its organisational culture.   Again, if asked to we can probably all think of
organisations, not just airlines, we know which we perceive as examples of good
and bad safety cultures. This will depend on factors such as the way in which the
organisation handles the often conflicting goals of safety and profitability, the
trade-offs between the two, and the level of demonstrated commitment to safety. It
also depends heavily on perceptions of the organisational communication styles as
detailed by Westrum and noted in Table 4 above. For example, if an employee is
concerned about the safety of a certain practice or procedure, are channels open for
that concern to be communicated to management. If so, how will management
respond? Is the flight safety department proactive or reactive? Are messengers
shot?

Hudson (1997) has built upon Westrum's classification of organisational
communication styles in his delineation of the development cycle of safety
cultures. As depicted in Figure 1, he contends that safety cultures can be
distinguished along a continuum commencing from *pathological* (caring less about
safety than about not being caught), through *calculative* (recognising that safety
needs to be taken seriously, but calculating risks and analysing cost-benefit ratios;
blindly following all the 'necessary' steps - safety is still an 'add-on'), to
generative (safe behaviour is fully integrated into everything the organisation
does). Hudson argues that safety performance will improve as the culture matures,
but there can only start to be talk of a real 'safety culture' once the calculative
stage of development has been passed (1997, p. 6).

Also imperative to the establishment of an appropriate safety culture is the
recognition that human error is unavoidable and that it is the responsibility of a
mature organisation to effectively manage that error. Reason (1994b) sets out a
framework to be followed to institute a program of comprehensive error
management, and expands on that in his most recent work to provide us with a
practical guide to error management tools and methods (Reason, 1997). Helmreich

and Merritt develop this argument to propose that organisational acceptance of human error (*not* violations) as ubiquitous and inevitable is a step to be taken by the next generation of CRM training (1996, p. 145): Using this approach, ...the goals of CRM become a new 'troika' - *reducing the likelihood of error, trapping errors before they have an operational effect, and mitigating the consequences of errors when they do occur.* To make this shift requires that organisations formally recognise human fallibility and adopt non-punitive policies regarding everyday error. In essence, this requires normalisation of error within organisations, and acknowledgment of its ubiquity - but not complacent acceptance of its consequences. This places CRM in the context of the system and makes the superordinate goal one of addressing system issues that can foster or reduce error.

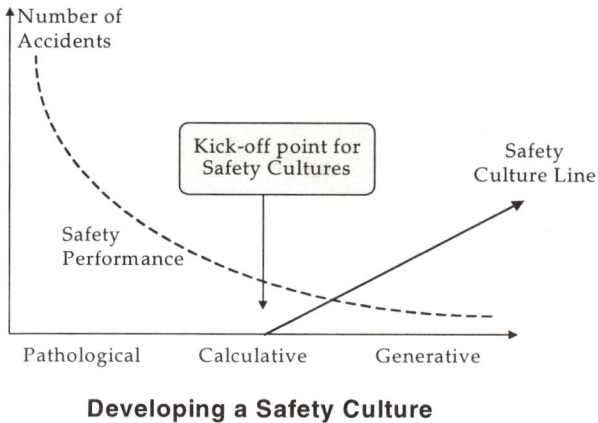

Developing a Safety Culture

Figure 1   **Stages in the development of a safety culture**
                  (Adapted from Hudson, 1997)

Specific behavioural techniques intended to enhance situation awareness and flight safety, such as cross-checking and verification of communication, preparation, planning, vigilance, speaking up to express concerns, and sharing a mental model of the situation are all means of reducing the likelihood of an error occurring or trapping an error before it has an operational impact. These techniques, along with effective group decision making, and the recognition that they are not immune to the effects of stress, can equip crews to react effectively to, recover from, and mitigate the consequences of, those errors which may threaten the safety of flight (Helmreich & Merritt, 1996).

While there is still yet some distance to travel, CRM has come a long way since its origins in the early 1980's as cockpit resource management training (see

Helmreich, 1993b; Maurino, 1996a). Its principles have been extended from the cockpit to other elements of the aviation system (Hayward, 1995a; Merritt & Helmreich, 1996b), have been employed to achieve significant organisational change (see Hayward, 1995b; 1997), and CRM is now mandated by ICAO for the training of airline flight crews and others (Maurino, 1995). An important discovery is that culture plays a significant role in determining the response of participants to various styles of human factors training. One size does not fit all, and it is important that CRM, and other training, is tailored to fit with the culture - national, organisational, vocational - of the target population.

Enhancing operational safety → "Enhancing op integrity" e.BA.

To conclude, several lessons may be extrapolated from the above to provide for the enhancement of operational safety.

- Recognition that the various cultures within which aviation professionals operate do have an impact on their job performance may go a long way toward mitigating the undesirable effects of some of those cultures, and breaking down barriers between sub-cultures.
- Development of a deeper understanding of the causes and consequences of human error can provide management with the foundation from which to launch effective error management strategies.
- Organisational recognition and acknowledgment of the ubiquity and inevitability of human error is the next step in the development of these strategies.
- Development and introduction of non-punitive policies regarding organisational responses to unintentional human error (*not* violations) is an essential component of error management.
- Development and maintenance of an appropriate organisational culture and a positive safety culture is essential and will be supported by the above.
- Human factors training programs must be operationally relevant, and must be targeted towards practical objectives, such as the avoidance, trapping and mitigation of human error.
- If these programs are targeted at such practical operational objectives, their acceptance and success amongst line personnel will be significantly improved.
- While quality CRM training and other modes of applied human factors training are invaluable aids to the reduction of human error, the best place to start an error management program is at the recruiting point.
- This involves the introduction of an appropriately researched and targeted selection system, which is designed to select-in personnel with desired attributes, and select-out personnel who will not fit within the requisite safety culture of the organisation.

32 Future perspectives

Brent Hayward
Asia Pacific Resource Management, Australia

It would be a foolish manager indeed who believed that their own organisation could emerge unscathed from a rigorous systemic investigation of the kind which has engulfed a variety of maritime, rail, and aviation organisations in recent years (eg., see Bureau of Air Safety Investigation, 1994, 1996; Hidden, 1989; Moshansky, 1992; Sheen, 1987). Thorough systemic investigations will always unearth latent conditions - some of which may have been significant causal factors, and some which patiently await actualisation. However, just as individuals make errors which are more understandable when studied in context, so do organisations, and we must ensure that in broadening the search for contributors to accident causation we do not simply switch the hunt for someone to blame from the flight deck to the boardroom. The systemic investigation of occurrences must be oriented toward making a positive and proactive contribution to the safety health of the organisation, its employees, and the system within which they function. The target of these investigations, and that of any aspiring safety culture, should be to fill as many holes as possible in James Reason's metaphorical layers of 'Swiss cheese' (1990, 1997). However, as he cautions (1997, p. 189), this must be a continuous process: 'As one problem is being addressed, others will spring up in its place. There are no final victories in the safety war.'

In spite of the advances that would appear to have been made in recent years, the 'blood imperative' of organisational safety remains alive and well, and while active failures have traditionally been more summarily dealt with, in most organisations and most systems a major incident or accident is still required before action is taken to effectively deal with all but the most conspicuous of latent conditions. By way of illustration, if we were to go out and conduct a thorough safety audit of those that we regard as 'safe' organisations, we would find that many and perhaps the majority would still be functioning within the bounds of the 'bureaucratic / calculative' stage of safety culture development described by Westrum (1995) and Hudson (1997).[1] In darker moments it is tempting to imagine

---

[1] See chapter 31

287

that the best thing that could happen to many such organisations would be for them to have a serious safety scare through involvement in a significant incident or minor (hopefully casualty-free) accident. The intent would be to shake them from the complacency and conservatism that frequently characterises organisations with 'good' safety records. The harsh reality of life is that it takes just one major accident to turn a very safe organisation into a safety also-ran, and as Reason (1997, p. 192) puts it: 'to put an end to all (previous) worries about the bottom line.'

Turning our thoughts forward, the preferred future to envisage for human factors in accident investigation and prevention is a continuing development *and refinement* of the systemic approach. For some readers this may come as a disappointment, while others will recognise that our concepts of organisational and systemic safety have much further to evolve before we can say with any confidence that they are producing satisfactory results. In spite of recent advances, Maurino (1996b) believes that much needs to be achieved before human factors is paid more than lip service by many investigation agencies, where he believes that the status quo is preferred for reasons of conservatism, convention and convenience (p. xxiii):

> There are reasons for concern as to what the future might hold for human factors in accident investigation, unless air safety investigators as a profession acknowledge that change is imperative. This is an exceedingly important issue because the accident investigation process is a necessary precondition upon which proactive safety builds. If the investigation process does not produce meaningful information, there is no way to feedback and, most important, feed-forward prevention strategies. While likely to be denied by those involved, the evidence in the form of official accident reports aimed at putting losses behind us and reassuring the public, rather than digging out latent failures to address the system's flaws, is a matter of public record.

While it is to be hoped that few experienced air safety professionals would advocate a return to the days of using only the individual, person-centred approach in safety occurrence investigation, it must be acknowledged that there has been some backlash to the ever-increasing focus on the many other factors which can be seen to contribute to organisational accidents. In his excellent new book on this topic, one of the primary architects of the movement to a systemic approach to understanding human error considers if the pendulum may not have swung too far (Reason, 1997, p. 188):

> While it is clear that the present situation represents a major advance over knee-jerk 'human error' attributions, some concerns need to be expressed about the theoretical and the practical utility of this ever-spreading quest for contributing factors. We seem to have reached, or even exceeded, the point of diminishing returns, particularly when it comes to risk management. We need to find some workable middle ground that acknowledges both the psychological and the contextual influences on human performance, as well as the interactions between active failures and the latent conditions that serve, on rare occasions, to breach the system's defences.

Reason is advocating recognition that different approaches to the management of human error and safety do exist, and that there is no reason why they cannot co-exist, even within the same organisation or the same system, so long as their various strengths and weaknesses are recognised. In terms of the focus of this chapter, he has built upon the solid foundation of his previous work to propose a new model to describe the main stages involved in the development and investigation of an organisational accident, as detailed in Figure 1.[2]

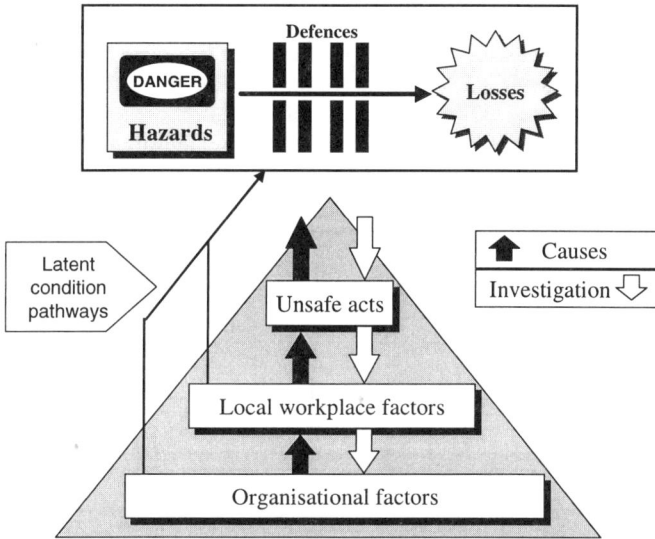

Figure 1   Stages in the development and investigation of an organisational accident (Redrawn from Reason, 1997)

This model seeks to link the various contributing elements into a coherent sequence that runs from the bottom upwards in the causation process, and from the top downwards in the investigation process (p. 14):

> The rectangular block at the top of the figure represents the main elements of an event. The triangular shape below represents the system producing such an event. This has three levels: the person (unsafe acts), the workplace (error-provoking conditions), and the organisation. The black upward arrows indicate the direction of causality, the white downward arrows indicate the investigative steps... Although unsafe acts are implicated in most accidents, they are not a necessary condition. On some occasions, the defences fail simply as a result of latent conditions - as, for example in the *Challenger* and King's Cross Underground disasters. This possibility is indicated... by the latent condition pathways connecting workplace and organisational factors directly to failed defences.

---

[2] I am indebted to Professor Reason for the provision of an advance draft of his new book, and for permission to reproduce this model here.

While the causes of accidents frequently have their roots in factors originating from decisions made at the top levels of an organisation, which are then in turn shaped by the corporate culture of the local workplace, providing the conditions for the production of unsafe acts, the investigative process tends to work in reverse. The systemic accident or incident inquiry begins with the outcome, which is frequently linked to the 'sharp end' actions of individuals or teams (unsafe acts), and then works its way through the various levels of the organisation or system, along the way exposing possible factors which may have contributed to the occurrence, or may have the potential to contribute to future occurrences. Addressing these factors through the investigative process can thus make a very positive contribution to future safety health.

So, where does that leave us with reference to the future of human factors in accident investigation and prevention? Taking stock of the matters discussed above and in previous chapters, we can envisage the following:

- a continuing and logical evolution of the processes for investigating organisational accidents, including refinement of the systemic approach, with a focus on attempting to find some balance between organisational and individual or group responsibility for actions;
- an increased focus on broader elements of the aviation system and their potential contributions (both positive and negative) to safety and efficiency;
- a continuing focus on the development of strategies for the investigation and rectification of latent conditions which have the potential to compromise safety;
- an increased focus in research and practice on learning how accidents are prevented, and further development of applied prevention strategies for operational personnel;
- improved training for air safety investigators, to incorporate awareness and skills training in relation to modern theories of accident causation; principles of human factors, witness interviewing; data analysis, etc;
- improved cooperation and sharing of methodology and resources between national and international safety investigation agencies, societies and regulators;
- last, but perhaps most important, a continuing battle to convince air safety professionals of the potential contribution that applied human factors knowledge can make to the performance of their duties and the safety and efficiency of our industry.

Appendix A

Course Handouts

Bureau of Air Safety Investigation. (1994). *Investigation Report 9301743: Piper, PA31-350 Chieftain, Young, NSW, 11 June 1993*. Canberra: Author.

Bureau of Air Safety Investigation (1996). *Investigation Report 9403038: Boeing 747-312 VH-INH, Sydney (Kingsford-Smith) Airport, NSW, 19 October 1994*. Canberra: Author.

International Civil Aviation Organization. (1989). *Human Factors Digest No 1: Fundamental human factors concepts*. (ICAO Circular 216). Montreal: Author.

International Civil Aviation Organization. (1989). *Human Factors Digest No 2: Flight crew training: CRM and LOFT*. (ICAO Circular 217). Montreal: Author.

International Civil Aviation Organization. (1991). *Human Factors Digest No 3: Training of operational personnel in human factors*. (ICAO Circular 227). Montreal: Author.

International Civil Aviation Organization. (1992). *Human Factors Digest No 5: Operational implications of automation in advanced technology flight decks*. (ICAO Circular 234). Montreal: Author.

International Civil Aviation Organization. (1992). *Human Factors Digest No 6: Ergonomics*. (ICAO Circular 238). Montreal: Author.

International Civil Aviation Organization. (1993). *Human Factors Digest No 7: Investigation of human factors in accidents and incidents*. (ICAO Circular 240). Montreal: Author.

International Civil Aviation Organization. (1993). *Human Factors Digest No 8: Human factors in air traffic control*. (ICAO Circular 241). Montreal: Author.

International Civil Aviation Organization. (1994). *Annex 13 to the Convention on International Civil Aviation: Aircraft accident and incident investigation, Eighth edition, July 1994*. Montreal: Author.

International Civil Aviation Organization. (1994). *Human Factors Digest No 10: Human factors, management and organization*. (ICAO Circular 247). Montreal: Author.

International Civil Aviation Organization. (1995). *Human Factors Digest No 11: Human factors in CNS/ATM systems*. (ICAO Circular 249). Montreal: Author.

International Civil Aviation Organization. (1995). *Human Factors Digest No 12: Human factors in aircraft maintenance and inspection*. (ICAO Circular 253). Montreal: Author.

Appendix B

Course Curriculum

Session A	General Overview
09.00 - 10.30	Introduction and overview of human factors and aviation safety, human performance capabilities and limitations, and the role of the human factors investigator in air safety investigation.

Session B	Human Performance and Systems Safety
11.00 - 12.30	Consideration of human performance capabilities and limitations in the context of an integrated systems approach to aviation safety. Introduction to the Reason Model of systems safety. Case Study 1: The Monarch Investigation

Session C	Applied Systems Safety Investigation
13.30 - 15.00	Further examination of the systemic factors influencing human performance, and how these factors are applied in the context of air safety investigation and accident prevention. Application of the Reason Model of systemic safety to accident investigation. Case Study 2: Accident at Tenerife: DanAir Flight 1008

Session D	Summary and Conclusion
15.30 - 17.00	This session will be used to draw together and summarise the activities of the day to provide an integrated understanding of the role of the human factors specialist in air safety investigation and accident prevention.

Appendix C

Organisational Accident Case Study

This appendix contains an abridged version of a BASI accident investigation report which proved to be highly significant in terms of its effects upon the Australian aviation system - the Monarch Airlines investigation (Bureau of Air Safety Investigation, 1994). The edited report has been published previously by ICAO (ICAO, 1995).

The significance of this investigation to the Australian aviation industry is perhaps best summarised in the following extract from "Plane Safe", the report of the Australian Parliamentary inquiry into the safety of the commuter and general aviation sectors (HORSCOTSI, 1995):

- The catalyst or the chain of events that resulted in the committee inquiry and the establishment of a separate aviation safety authority was the report from the Bureau of Air Safety Investigation (BASI) into the Monarch Airlines crash at Young in June 1993 - Investigation Report 9301743, Piper PA 31-350 Chieftain, Young, NSW, 11 June 1993.
- In his news release of 20 July 1994 following publication of the final BASI report on Monarch Airlines the Minister for Transport 'announced a broad strategy to improve air safety regulation in Australia.' (p. 15).

As a result of the Monarch investigation and the subsequent fatal crash of a Seaview Airlines AeroCommander 690, major changes were made to Australia's aviation regulatory and safety regime. Had the BASI Monarch report concentrated only on the traditional 'sharp end' factors, its significance, and more importantly its contribution to air safety, would have been minimal. If BASI had not investigated the Monarch crash as an organisational accident, to use Reason's (1990) terminology, then BASI itself would have been part of the problem.

The former Australian Civil Aviation Authority was abolished in June 1995 and replaced by two new agencies - the Civil Aviation Safety Authority (CASA), the safety regulator, and Airservices Australia, the provider of Air Traffic Services (ATS) and Rescue Fire Fighting Services.

BASI has been significantly strengthened. Re-allocation of funds within the Department of Transport has enabled the recruitment of additional investigators to meet the substantially increased demands on BASI arising from such diverse factors as the additional complexity of systemic investigations, a greater pro-active accident prevention role for the Bureau, and the unavoidable increasing involvement of BASI investigators in legal matters. The latter was typified by the long-running coronial inquest into the Monarch accident, which effectively removed the chief investigator from the BASI system for approximately six months, in addition to the substantial demands it placed upon all other specialist members of the accident investigation team. It will be of particular interest to the reader that during the coronial inquest into this accident there was extensive cross examination by legal counsel of all members of the investigation team, including the aviation psychologist who provided the specialist expertise on human performance to the investigation team.

Organisational accident - an Australian case study

Reprinted from *ICAO Journal Vol. 50,* No. 7: September, 1995

The circumstances of this tragic accident, which claimed the lives of all five passengers and two pilots on a regional airline service were consistent with controlled flight into terrain. Descent below the minimum circling altitude was the culminating factor in a combination of local contributing factors and organisational failures. The local contributing factors included poor weather conditions, equipment deficiencies, inadequate procedures, inaccurate visual perception, and possible skill fatigue. Organisational and management failures related to this accident were also identified within both the airline, and the regulatory authority.[1]

Investigation facts

History of the flight

At about 1500 hours local time on 11 June 1993 a flight plan was activated indicating that a Piper PA31-350 was to conduct a standard regular public (RPT) transport flight from Sydney, in the state of New South Wales, Australia , to the regional town of Cootamundra via the town of Young. The plan indicated that the flight would depart at 1700 crewed by two pilots and would be conducted in accordance with Instrument Flight Rules procedures. The aircraft was not equipped with an area navigation system and was to navigate by use of ground based radio navigation aids. The flight departed Sydney at 1738 carrying five passengers with a fuel endurance of about 253 minutes. Given the time of year, the flight was to be conducted entirely at night. The pilot-in-command occupied the left cockpit seat.

The aircraft climbed to 8,000 feet tracking initially toward Katoomba. At 1801 hours, now below the Sydney terminal area control steps, the pilot advised Flight Service (FIS) that he was now tracking direct to Young and would report at Riley, on the Katoomba - Young track, although the aircraft would initially track south of that track.

At 1814 the pilot reported at Riley, estimating arrival at Young at 1835. By 1820 the pilot had reported on descent into Young, with in-flight conditions of cloud and heavy rain. Recorded radar data later showed that the aircraft passed 13.5 NM south-east of Riley. When about 18 NM north-east of Rugby, the aircraft initially turned right to track about 280 before turning left to track direct to Young. The only radio navigation aid available at Young was the NDB. When queried by FIS at 1836 regarding his arrival at Young, the pilot amended the estimated arrival time to 1838. At 1842 the pilot reported at Young conducting an NDB approach. He also indicated that he would call again when in the visual circuit prior to landing. Shortly after 1845 witnesses at Young aerodrome saw the lights of an aircraft, which they believed to be the PA31, pass low overhead after approaching from the east. Some minutes later the same aircraft was seen to pass over the aerodrome from the opposite direction and appear to climb away towards the east. On

[1] This article is an abridged version of the official accident report published by the Australian Bureau of Air Safety Investigation in July 1994.

both occasions the runway and aerodrome lights were not illuminated, although the aerodrome was equipped with lighting which is activated by keying a transmitter on a published VHF frequency. It was the responsibility of the pilot to activate the lighting prior to arrival at the aerodrome.

At 1850 FIS advised the pilot of the PA31 that a Cessna 310 was estimating arrival at Young at 1900. This aircraft subsequently reported holding clear of cloud at about 8 NM north of Young. The pilot of the PA31 reported at 1903 that he was on another overshoot at Young, about to commence another approach, and would report again at 1915. At about this time witnesses reported seeing the runway lights illuminate. The Cessna 310 proceeded to Young and landed at about 1912. At 1916 the PA31 reported in the circuit area.

A pilot witness said that he observed the PA31 pass over the northern end of the aerodrome from a westerly direction before turning right and taking up a heading consistent with a right downwind leg for runway 01. The aircraft was then seen to turn right and pass to the south of the aerodrome before entering what appeared to be a right downwind leg for runway 19. When abeam the aerodrome the aircraft turned right again and overflew the aerodrome to enter a second downwind leg for 01. Another witness thought that the aircraft was significantly lower than the previous aircraft (Cessna 310). Shortly after the PA31 turned on to an apparent base leg the navigation lights were lost to sight. Almost immediately a fireball was observed.

Local emergency services were activated but had some difficulty gaining access to the accident site which was located some 2.2 km to the south-east of the aerodrome. An ambulance reached the wreckage at 1952 and resuscitated the only survivor, a teenage girl. She was transported to a Sydney hospital where she died at 0510 the next morning.

Weather conditions

The aerodrome forecast for the arrival time of the PA31 were: wind 320 T at 10 kt, 5 octas of cumulus at 2,000 ft above aerodrome elevation, visibility 10 km or greater, with slight rain showers. Barometric pressure ranged from 1003-1002 hPa. Conditions of 5 octas stratus at 900 ft with visibility reduced to 5,000 m were forecast for temporary periods of 60 minutes, between 1800 and midnight.

The Bureau of Meteorology estimated that the actual weather conditions at Young aerodrome at 1920 were: surface wind 310 at 11 kt gusting to 19 kt, 4 octas stratus at 800 ft, 6 octas stratocumulus at 1,200 ft, and 6 octas cumulus at 1,500 ft. Visibility was 10 km, reduced to 5000 m in light rain. Pilot witness's accounts of the weather were generally consistent with the assessment provided by the Bureau. Crew

The pilot-in-command was aged 42 years and had logged a total of 1822 hours of which 121 was in the last 90 days, 187 at night and 377 on type. He had not flown during the last 24 hours but had flown 47 hours on the actual aircraft in the last 90 days. He held a command multi-engine instrument rating, a Commercial licence and a Class One medical certificate. He is reported to have had a normal sleep period prior to commencing duty and at the time of the accident his duty time was 3 hours.

In the previous 90 days he had conducted three night landings and 15 daylight landings at Young. During this period he had conducted three NDB approaches and one ILS approach. Only the ILS approach was flown in the accident aircraft. He had flown with the second pilot on only one other occasion.

Although the crew included a second pilot, the airline's normal operating procedures called for only a single pilot. No training was provided by the airline to cater for two-pilot operations. A section of the company operations manual concerning take off and landing by co-pilots stated:

...Low Capacity RPT operations does not have any provisions for co-pilot operations since all flights under RPT are single pilot operations.

The inclusion of a second pilot on this flight was required to satisfy a requirement for a second pilot in the event of autopilot unserviceability, which was the case on this flight. An internal company memorandum was the only company document that referred to co-pilots and stated:

....the second pilot is there to fulfil the functions of the autopilot, and the PIC is in command of the aircraft at all times.

The second pilot was aged 24 and had logged a total of 954 hours of which 30 was in the last 90 days, 65 at night and 43 on type. He had flown 2.6 hours in the last 24 hours and 17 on the actual aircraft in the last 90 days. He held an ATPL (Second Class) licence, a command multi-engine instrument rating and a Class One medical certificate.

Aircraft

The aircraft was manufactured in the United States in 1981 and had flown just over 3950 hours since new. Current certificates of registration and airworthiness issued by the Australian Civil Aviation Authority (CAA) were held by the airline. A maintenance release was issued on 1 June 1993 valid to 1 June 1994 or 4,036 hours, whichever came first. Investigation results showed that at the time of the accident the aircraft was loaded within the weight and balance limitations specified in the flight manual. An examination of aircraft components after the accident determined that the landing gear was extended and that the engines were delivering power to the propellers at the time of impact. No abnormalities were detected with the aircraft structure, flight controls, engine or fuel systems.

Removal of autopilot components

On 29 March 1993 the autopilot was reported as unserviceable. Two days later, whilst being checked at a servicing facility, it was determined that removal of the autopilot computer/amplifier disabled the 26VAC power supply to the HSI and RMI heading cards on the pilots instrument panel. They were the only two synchronous magnetic heading indicators immediately available to the pilot. Without those, the pilot was required to use a directional gyro indicator on the co-pilots panel. On 13 April, the servicing facility informed the local office of the CAA about the effect of autopilot component removal on HSI/RMI operation.

On 16 April the General Manager of the airline asked the CAA for permission to operate the aircraft with an unserviceable autopilot for 30 days whilst parts were sought. This request was approved by the CAA on the same day by the issue of a Permissible Unserviceability Schedule (PUS). That document imposed a number of conditions to be met for continued operations without a serviceable autopilot, including the carriage of a second pilot. The PUS was valid for a defined period, or until the required components were available for refitment to the aircraft, whichever occurred first. It was not the intention of the PUS to authorise flight with the computer amplifier removed. In addition, the aircraft Minimum Equipment List (MEL) specifically required at least one serviceable gyro heading indicator to be fitted to the pilot's panel for flight.

On 30 April the aircraft was flown interstate to another servicing facility where the autopilot controller and computer/amplifier were removed for repair. The aircraft then returned to normal RPT service without those autopilot components. At the same time a static pressure line that connects to the autopilot system was blanked-off but was not leak tested. This blank remained in place until the accident.

The servicing facility was unable to commence rectification due to lack of wiring diagrams so on 14 May the airline GM requested return of the components and these were refitted without rectification by persons unknown. The airline GM then requested an extension of the permissible unserviceability for another 30 days. This was approved by the CAA, valid to 16 June. On 1 June the components were again removed and sent to the interstate facility for repair. The aircraft then resumed RPT operations with those components missing.

Aerodrome and NDB approach

The aircraft impacted trees on hilly terrain 275 ft above aerodrome elevation (1,530 ft above sea level) some 2,200 m from the ARP. The Young aerodrome consists of one sealed runway orientated 01/19 at an elevation of 1,255 ft above sea level. Prior to striking terrain, the PA31 was conducting an NDB instrument approach in accordance with a standard procedure published by the CAA. The NDB procedure for Young provided an obstacle clearance of at least 400 ft within the circling area (3 NM radius of the aerodrome reference point, ARP) at the published circling minima of 2,400 ft above sea level (1,145 ft above the aerodrome). The approach procedure was not aligned with a runway, requiring a circling approach to be carried out after becoming visual at or above the MDA.

With the exception of the aerodrome elevation, the instrument approach chart did not indicate the height of obstacles or terrain within the circling area. The associated landing chart, which showed runway layout details, showed a red obstruction light at 1,504 elevation and an unlit spot height of 1,431 ft, both at about 1,900 m from the ARP to the north-east and south-west respectively. This chart did not extend to the full 3 NM radius of the circling area.

The terrain struck by the aircraft was not marked by obstacle lighting. CAA officers suggested that this was probably because it was shielded by other terrain. This was reflected in a minimum circling altitude of 2,400 ft to provide a minimum of 400 ft obstacle clearance within the circling area.

Pilots conducting an NDB approach are required to maintain the circling minima of 2,400 ft until aligned with the runway, unless they can maintain visual reference during the subsequent circling approach at a lower altitude. Included in the requirements of visual reference is the need to maintain sight of lights associated with the approach end of the runway, together with continuous sight of the ground or water, which at night would be impractical without extensive ground lighting. The circuit area at Young was located over sparsely lit terrain.

Active failures

The significant active failure in the accident was that the flight crew did not maintain adequate obstacle clearance whilst conducting a visual circling approach at night.

On becoming clear of cloud at the completion of what was probably his third NDB approach, the pilot had to decide if weather conditions in the circuit area were good enough to permit an approach to land whilst remaining visual. It is clear that he descended below the circling altitude of 2,400 ft in order to maintain visual reference due to the low cloud. To remain clear of the cloud base probably required a descent to about 2,000 ft, some 750 ft above the aerodrome elevation. Having descended below 2,400 ft the 400 ft minimum obstacle clearance provided at the circling altitude was no longer guaranteed. Once below the minimum circling altitude the pilot was required to maintain a minimum obstacle clearance of 300 ft along the flight path. Given the weather conditions of the night, and most importantly the absence of ground lighting, it is unlikely that the flight crew would have been able to maintain adequate visual reference. In addition, the flight crew had no readily available method of determining minimum obstacle clearance along the flight path. This was due to a lack of detailed terrain information published on the NDB approach and landing charts; together with an absence of company procedures for operations at Young.

Examination of the wreckage indicated that the aircraft was in generally level flight at the time of impact with no evidence of sudden loss of height. It is unlikely that the pilot made a deliberate decision to descend to a minimum obstacle clearance based on 300 ft above the aerodrome elevation. Such a decision would have made a collision with terrain almost inevitable, but would not have been necessary since the cloud base would have required descent to only about 750 ft above the aerodrome. It is more likely that the pilot descended only sufficiently to remain clear of cloud and subsequent descent was unintended.

Such an unintended descent may have occurred whilst the pilot attended to some malfunction during the visual circuit to land. This hypothesis could be partly supported by the fact that after overflying the aerodrome and positioning for runway 01, he completed another circuit.

Local factors

Local factors are task, situational or environmental factors which affect task performance and can trigger the occurrence of errors or violations. The local factors identified in this investigation are considered to have had a direct influence on the performance of the flight crew during the conduct of the flight. As well as adverse weather conditions and inadequate terrain guidance information, other local factors which could have induced errors and/or mistakes included; aircraft equipment deficiencies, inadequate flight crew knowledge and skills for the task, visual illusions, high cockpit workload and skill fatigue.

It is certain that the pilot was subjected to additional workload due to the unserviceability of both heading indicators on the left instrument panel, particularly during the NDB letdowns and subsequent circling approach in the prevailing conditions. To determine aircraft heading, the pilot would have had to disrupt his normal instrument scanning pattern to include the directional gyro indicator on the right instrument panel. It is considered that such a scanning procedure would have significantly increased pilot workload. As a result, it is possible that the performance of the pilot was degraded due to skill fatigue. This may have adversely affected his situational awareness, as well as his routine monitoring of the flight instruments. It is not considered that his workload would have been alleviated by the carriage of a second pilot as no formal company procedures had been implemented for two pilot operations. The possible reduction in the pilot's performance due to skill fatigue may account for his apparent lapse in not initially activating the runway lighting. The visual cues available to the flight crew were inadequate as a sole reference to judge terrain clearance during the circling approach. The investigation indicated that the pilot was aware of his lateral position in relation to the runway, but was not aware of his true vertical position. Visual cues which were available could have been misinterpreted as a result of:

- the position of the aircraft in the circuit;
- the pilot's seating position where the pilot was used to seeing the runway at a given position on the aircraft frame in a normal left circuit and transferred that habit inappropriately when flying a right circuit; and
- bifocal trap effect where in the absence of objects to focus on at longer distance, the eyes focus on closer objects such as a windscreen.

Airline organisational deficiencies

The management of the airline had undergone significant changes in the month before the accident. On 17 May the Chief Pilot resigned from his position but remained as Operations Manager. A new Chief Pilot was appointed and approved by the CAA on the same day, and also assumed the responsibilities of the Check and Training captain who had left the company in early May. The next day, 18 May, a consultant GM replaced the previous GM and took over day to day management of the airline.

Investigations showed that the airline was consistently slow to pay accounts for the provision of fuel at company airports, and for accommodation costs incurred by pilots. The airline had not paid any debts to the CAA since late 1991 and was the subject of complaints from a number of creditors. One of these creditors sent letters to government bodies, including the CAA and the Australian Securities Commission (ASC) with concerns about the financial capability of the airline to operate a satisfactory RPT service. However on 19 April 1993, after consideration of those matters within its jurisdiction, the ASC replied that it was not appropriate for any further action to be taken.

The GM who assumed responsibility on 18 May was aware that autopilot components had been removed from the aircraft, and had in fact directed the final removal of these components for repair on 1 June. However, he was unaware of the effects of this action even though the previous GM had been informed of these effects by the servicing facility on 1 April.

In accordance with the requirements of Civil Aviation Orders (CAOs), the airline had an operations manual to provide guidance for flight crew in the conduct of RPT services. The stated objectives of this manual included the requirement for company procedures to '...ensure maximum safety and efficiency of its flight operations.' This manual included a section that contained briefing information on destination airports. Information concerning Young was limited to procedures for engine failure after take-off, and a recommendation to land on runway 01 in light wind conditions. No guidance was provided for terrain avoidance during an approach to land, nor was information provided on the height and extent of obstacles at Young. There was no regulatory requirement for this specific information to be included, even though the CAA had approved the manual.

Also required by CAOs was the provision of a maintenance control system for the airline. The airline maintenance staff consisted of a small core of aircraft maintenance engineers, of whom at least one was required to be licensed to certify maintenance work. There was a history of a high turnover of maintenance staff, especially certifying engineers. The scheduling of maintenance work was carried out by the Maintenance Controller who had no formal aircraft maintenance qualifications and was in fact the pilot of the accident aircraft.

Civil Aviation Regulations required that airlines engaged in RPT services ensure that command pilots were certified as competent for a particular route. In particular, that competency must include a knowledge of terrain and navigation facilities at route aerodromes. No evidence could be found indicating that the captain had been route checked into Young or Cootamundra. His last route check was conducted in daylight hours on a different route on 12-13 March 1993.

The combination of these numerous organisational deficiencies within the airline were found to create an environment within which latent failures would develop and go uncorrected. These latent failures included:

- management priorities which placed the continuation of revenue operations ahead of safety considerations;
- inadequate resources allocated to safety, resulting from the financial situation of the airline;
- organisational factors, relating to management and structural deficiencies in the operation of the airline;
- poor planning and operational procedures, largely driven by financial considerations.
- ineffective communication, particularly regarding safety matters;
- poor control of the safety of flight operations;
- poor maintenance management and control; and
- poor training of flight crew.

Regulatory organisational deficiencies

The CAA was the regulatory authority responsible for the safety regulation of both flying operations and airworthiness matters. Despite the fact that the airline was a CAA debtor, there was no provision in the Civil Aviation Act to cancel an Air Operators Certificate on grounds relating to the financial circumstances of the operator.

As a RPT operator, the airline should have been subjected to en-route operations inspections on 0.5% of revenue hours, as required by CAA documentation. Given the amount of flying conducted by the airline, this should have resulted in a minimum of approximately 14 hours of surveillance in the previous twelve months. In fact, no surveillance of en-route operations was conducted by the assigned Flying Operations Inspector (FOI) during that period.

The investigation found that a factor which affected the CAA's ability to conduct required surveillance was the provision of inadequate resources. This in turn was affected to some degree by a conflict between the mission statement of the Authority and that of the division responsible for operations and airworthiness standards. The mission statement of the Authority placed a clear primacy on the safety of air travel while that of the Standards Division appeared to emphasise the viability of operators within the industry as its major concern.

Although both flying operations and airworthiness inspectors were based at the same airport as the airline, they were responsible to different office managers who in turn reported to different regional managers. The lowest formal level of management in the CAA at which a single individual became responsible for the entire performance of a regional airline was the General Manager of the division based in the national capital.

As a result, flying operations and airworthiness matters were often conducted independently. Although there had been minimal flying operations surveillance of the airline, airworthiness inspectors had been concerned about the supervision of maintenance since February and had been corresponding with the airline's GM. The matter of the unserviceable autopilot was handled as an airworthiness matter since 16 April. Later, the assigned FOI said at no stage was he aware that the aircraft was being operated with the HSI and RMI inoperative. If he had known he would have stopped the operation.

The emphasis on operator viability had been demonstrated on 19 April when a joint operations/airworthiness ramp check was conducted at Sydney to verify that the operator was complying with the terms of the autopilot permissible unserviceability document. This check discovered numerous documentation deficiencies and also the fact that the second pilot on that day was not instrument rated. The attending airworthiness inspector believed he should be instrument rated, but the flying operations inspector commented that in the absence of a CAA-approved copy of the company's Minimum Equipment List (which should have been on the aircraft), the responsibility for dispatch of the aircraft was that of the Chief Pilot. The aircraft subsequently departed on an RPT service with the deficiencies unchanged. It was later determined that the second pilot should have been instrument rated.

Although this incident resulted in concerns about the suitability of the Chief Pilot, no immediate direct action was taken. Nearly a month later, on 17 May, a prepared letter withdrawing the Chief Pilot's approval was not sent as he resigned from that position on the same day.

Although none of these issues concerning the CAA directly affected the conduct of the accident flight, the investigation team believed that such organisational deficiencies contributed to the creation of an environment within which commercial viability appeared to have primacy over the safety of the travelling public.

Postscript

On July 1 1995, a set of new institutional arrangements governing the conduct of aviation in Australia came into effect. In its Advisory Report of May 1995 to the Federal Parliament dealing with the Civil Aviation Legislation Amendment Bill 1995, and the Air Services Bill 1995, the House of Representatives Standing Committee on Transport, Communications and Infrastructure cited the Bureau of Air Safety Investigation's report on this accident as the catalyst for the train of events leading to these new arrangements.

References

Bureau of Air Safety Investigation. (1994). *Investigation Report 9301743: Piper, PA31-350 Chieftain, Young, NSW, 11 June 1993.* Canberra: Author.

Bureau of Air Safety Investigation (1996). *Investigation Report 9403038: Boeing 747-312 VH-INH, Sydney (Kingsford-Smith) Airport, NSW, 19 October 1994.* Canberra: Author.

Chute, R.D., Wiener, E.L., Dunbar, M.G., & Hoang, V.R. (1996). Cockpit/cabin crew performance: Recent research. In *Proceedings of the 48th International Air Safety Seminar, Seattle WA, November 7-9, 1995.* Arlington, VA: Flight Safety Foundation.

Cox, S.J., & Tait, N.R.S. (1991). *Safety, reliability and risk management: An integrated approach.* London: Butterworth-Heinemann.

Degani, A., & Wiener, E.L. (1994). Philosophy, policies, procedures, and practices: The four "P"s of flight-deck operations. In A.N. Johnston, N.J. McDonald, & R.G. Fuller (Eds.), *Aviation psychology in practice.* Aldershot, UK: Avebury Technical.

Edwards, E. (1972). Man and machine: Systems for safety. *Proceedings of the BALPA Technical Symposium.* London: BALPA.

Einhorn, H.J., & Hogarth, R.M. (1986). Judging probable cause. *Psychological Bulletin, 99*(1), 3-19.

Fawcett, H.A. (1986). *Report on human factors definition.* Hull, Quebec: Canadian Aviation Safety Board.

Fennell, D. (1988). *Investigation into the King's Cross underground fire.* Department of Transport, London: HMSO.

Fisher, A.B. (1994, January 24). How to make a merger work. *Fortune,* 58-61.

Hamilton, D. (1993). Human factors initiatives in New Zealand ATC. In B.J Hayward & A.R. Lowe (Eds.), *Proceedings of the 1992 Australian Aviation Psychology Symposium.* Melbourne: AAvPA.

Hawkins, F.H. (1987). *Human factors in flight.* Aldershot, UK: Gower Technical Press.

Hayward, B.J. (1995a). Extending crew resource management: An overview. In N. McDonald, N. Johnston, & R. Fuller (Eds.), *Applications of psychology to the aviation system.* Aldershot, UK: Avebury Aviation.

Hayward, B.J. (1995b). Organisational change: The human factor. In N. McDonald, N. Johnston, & R. Fuller (Eds.), *Applications of psychology to the aviation system.* Aldershot, UK: Avebury Aviation.

Hayward, B.J. (1997). Human factors: Training for organisational change. In R.A. Telfer & P.J. Moore (Eds.), *Aviation training: Learners, Instruction and Organization.* Aldershot, UK: Avebury Aviation.

Helmreich, R.L. (1992). Human factors aspects of the Air Ontario crash at Dryden, Ontario. Technical Appendix to V.P. Moshansky, *Commission of inquiry into the Air Ontario crash at Dryden, Ontario: Final Report.* Ottawa: Canadian Ministry of Supply and Services.

Helmreich, R.L. (1993a). *Anatomy of a system accident: The crash of Avianca Flight 052.* Austin, TX: NASA/UT/FAA Aerospace Crew Research Project.

Helmreich, R.L. (1993b). Fifteen years of the CRM wars: A report from the trenches. In B.J. Hayward & A.R. Lowe (Eds.), *Towards 2000: Proceedings of the 1992 Australian Aviation Psychology Symposium.* Melbourne: AAvPA.

Helmreich, R.L., & Foushee, H.C. (1993). Why crew resource management? Empirical and theoretical bases of human factors training in aviation. In E.L. Wiener, B.G.

Kanki, & R.L. Helmreich (Eds.), *Cockpit resource management.* (pp. 3-45). San Diego: Academic Press.

Helmreich, R.L., & Merritt, A.C. (1996). Cultural issues in crew resource management training. In *Proceedings of the ICAO Global Human Factors Seminar, held at Auckland, New Zealand, April 1996.* Montreal: ICAO.

Hidden, A. (1989). *Investigation into the Clapham Junction railway accident.* London: Department of Transport; HMSO.

Hill, M.W. (1993). Human factors training for the investigator - The results of a systems approach to training development. In R. S. Jensen & D. Neumeister (Eds.), *Proceedings of the Seventh International Symposium on Aviation Psychology* (pp. 1031-1034). Columbus, OH: The Ohio State University.

Hofstede, G. (1980). *Culture's consequences: International differences in work-related values.* Beverly Hills, CA: Sage.

Hofstede, G. (1991). *Cultures and organisations: Software of the mind.* London: McGraw-Hill.

HORSCOTSI. (1995). *Plane Safe.* Report from the House of Representatives Standing Committee on Transport, Communications and Infrastructure. Canberra: Australian Government Publishing Service.

Hudson, P.T.W. (1997). Safety culture in the aviation industry: A system in search of perfection. Paper presented at the Singapore Aviation Academy Air Safety Seminar, Singapore, 18-20 June 1997.

International Air Transport Association. (1975). *Proceedings of the 20th IATA Technical Conference: Safety in Flight Operations, Istanbul.* Montreal: Author.

International Civil Aviation Organization. (1993). *Human Factors Digest No 7: Investigation of human factors in accidents and incidents.* (ICAO Circular 240). Montreal: Author.

International Civil Aviation Organization. (1994). *Annex 13 to the Convention on International Civil Aviation: Aircraft accident and incident investigation, Eighth edition, July 1994.* Montreal: Author.

International Civil Aviation Organization. (1995). Organisational accident - An Australian case study. *ICAO Journal, 50*(7), September.

Johnston, A.N. (1991). Organisational factors in human factors accident investigation. *Proceedings of the Sixth International Symposium on Aviation Psychology* (pp. 668-673). Columbus, Ohio: Ohio State University.

Johnston, A.N. (1993). CRM: Cross-cultural perspectives. In E.L. Wiener, B.G. Kanki, & R.L. Helmreich (Eds.), *Cockpit resource management.* San Diego: Academic Press.

Johnston, A.N. (1996). Managing risk in flight operations. In B.J. Hayward & A.R. Lowe (Eds.), *Applied aviation psychology: Achievement, change and challenge.* Aldershot, UK: Avebury Aviation.

Kern, A.T. (1995). *Darker shades of blue: A case study of failed leadership.* Colorado Springs: United States Air Force Academy.

Lauber, J. (1994a). Management, corporate policy and corporate culture. *Proceedings of 22nd IATA Technical Conference: Human factors in aviation.* Montreal: International Air Transport Association.

Lauber, J. (1994b). Safety cultures and the importance of human factors. *CRM Advocate, 94*(4), 1-3.

Lee, R. (1988). *Corporate factors in air crew decision-making.* 41st FSF Air Safety Seminar. Washington: Flight Safety Foundation.

Lee, R. (1994). Corporate factors, risk management and accidents: The air safety investigation perspective. *Proceedings of 22nd IATA Technical Conference: Human factors in aviation.* Montreal: International Air Transport Association.

Lee, R. (1996). Aviation psychology and safety: Implementing solutions. In B.J. Hayward & A.R. Lowe (Eds.), *Applied Aviation Psychology: Achievement, Change and Challenge.* Aldershot, UK: Avebury Aviation.

Lightbody, M., & Wheeler, T. (1985). *Papua New Guinea - a travel survival kit.* Melbourne: Lonely Planet Publications.

Margerison, C., McCann, D., & Davies, R. (1987). Aircrew team management program. In H.W. Orlady & H.C. Foushee (Eds.), *Cockpit resource management training: Proceedings of a NASA/MAC workshop* (NASA CP 2455). Moffett Field, CA: NASA Ames Research Center.

Maurino, D.E. (1994). Cross-cultural perspectives in human factors training: Lessons from the ICAO human factors programme. *The International Journal of Aviation Psychology, 4*(2), 173-181.

Maurino, D.E. (1995). ICAO annex amendment introduces mandatory human factors training for airline flight crews. *ICAO Journal, 50*(7), September 1995.

Maurino, D. (1996a). Eighteen years of the CRM wars: A report from headquarters. In B.J. Hayward & A.R. Lowe (Eds.), *Applied aviation psychology: Achievement, change and challenge* (pp. 99-109). Aldershot, UK: Avebury Aviation.

Maurino, D. (1996b). Foreword. In B.J. Hayward & A.R. Lowe (Eds.), *Applied aviation psychology: Achievement, change and challenge* (pp. xx-xxv). Aldershot, UK: Avebury Aviation.

Maurino, D.E., Reason, J., Johnston, N., & Lee, R.B. (1995). *Beyond aviation human factors.* Aldershot, UK: Avebury Aviation.

McCullough, E. & Hill, M. (1993). Human factors training for the investigator - A systems approach to transportation accident investigations. *Proceedings of the 26th Annual Conference of the Human Factors Association of Canada* (pp. 115-120). Toronto: HFAC.

Merritt, A.C. (1993). The influence of national and organisational culture on human performance. *Invited paper at an Australian Aviation Psychology Association Industry Human Factors Seminar,* Sydney, 25 October 1993.

Merritt, A.C. (1996). *National culture and work attitudes in commercial aviation: A cross-cultural investigation.* Unpublished doctoral dissertation, The University of Texas at Austin.

Merritt, A.C., & Helmreich, R.L. (1996a). Creating and sustaining a safety culture: Some practical strategies. In B.J. Hayward & A.R. Lowe (Eds.), *Applied aviation psychology: Achievement, change and challenge.* Aldershot, UK: Avebury Aviation.

Merritt, A., & Helmreich, R.L. (1996b). CRM in 1995: Where to from here? In B.J. Hayward & A.R. Lowe (Eds.), *Applied aviation psychology: Achievement, change and challenge.* Aldershot, UK: Avebury Aviation.

Moshansky, V.P. (1992).*Commission of inquiry into the Air Ontario crash at Dryden, Ontario: Final Report.* Ottawa: Canadian Ministry of Supply and Services.

National Transportation Safety Board. (1979). *United Airlines DC-8-61, Portland, OR, 12/28/78 (NTSB Report No. AAR-79/07).* Washington, DC: Author.

Nottrodt, J., Hill, M., & McCullough, B. (in press). Investigating for human factors: an integrated approach. *Proceedings of the Ninth International Symposium on Aviation Psychology, April, 1997.* Columbus, OH: Ohio State University.

O'Hare, D., Wiggins, M., Batt, R., & Morrison, D. (1994). Cognitive failure analysis for aircraft accident investigation. *Ergonomics, 37*(11), 1855-1869.

Ooi, T.S. (1991). Cultural influences in flight operations. Paper presented at the *SAS Flight Academy International Training Conference, Stockholm, Sweden.*

Ooi, T.S. (1992). Multicultural pilot research project: Preliminary report. In *Proceedings of the 8th IATA General Flight Crew Training Meeting, Stockholm.* Montreal: International Air Transport Association.

Pariès, J. (1996). Evolution of the aviation safety paradigm: Towards systemic causality and proactive actions. In B.J. Hayward & A.R. Lowe (Eds.), *Applied aviation psychology: Achievement, change and challenge.* Aldershot, UK: Avebury Aviation.

Pidgeon, N.F., & O'Leary, M. (1994). Organizational safety culture: Implications for aviation practice. In A.N. Johnston, N.J. McDonald, & R.G. Fuller, (Eds.), *Aviation psychology in practice.* Aldershot, UK: Avebury Technical.

Rasmussen, J. (1983). Skills rules and knowledge: Signals, signs and symbols, and other distinctions in human performance models. *IEEE Transactions on Systems, Man and Cybernetics, Vol. SMC-13*(3), 257-266.

Rasmussen, J. (1987). The definition of human error and a taxonomy for technical system design. In J. Rasmussen, K. Duncan, & J. Leplat (Eds.), *New technology and human error.* Toronto: Wiley & Sons.

Reason, J. (1990). *Human error.* New York: Cambridge University Press.

Reason, J. (1991a). Identifying the latent causes of aircraft accidents before and after the event. *Proceedings of the 22nd ISASI Annual Air Safety Seminar,* Canberra, Australia. Sterling, VA: ISASI.

Reason, J. (1991b). The contribution of latent failures to the breakdown of complex systems. *BASI Journal, 9.* Canberra: BASI.

Reason, J. (1991c). Too little and too late: A commentary on accident and incident reporting systems. In T. van der Schaaf, D. Lucas, & A. Hale (Eds.), *Near miss reporting as a safety tool* (pp. 9-26). Oxford, UK: Butterworth-Heinemann.

Reason, J. (1994a). Organisations, corporate culture and risk. *Proceedings of 22nd IATA Technical Conference: Human factors in aviation.* Montreal: International Air Transport Association.

Reason, J. (1994b). Incident monitoring: Capturing the human contribution. *Proceedings of the Conference on Incident Monitoring and Risk Management in the Health Care Sector, Melbourne, 29-30 November, 1994.* Canberra: Department of Human Services and Health.

Reason, J. (1995). A systems approach to organizational error. *Ergonomics, 38*(8), 1708-1721.

Reason, J. (1997). Organizational accidents: The management of human and organizational factors in hazardous technologies. Draft manuscript, March 1997. To be published (autumn 1997) as: *Managing the risks of organizational accidents.* Aldershot, UK: Ashgate.

Russell, P.D. (1994). Management strategies for accident prevention. *Air Asia (Special Issue on flight safety strategy), 6,* 31-41. Mauritius.

Semin, G.R., & Rubini, M. (1990). Unfolding the concept of person by verbal abuse. *European Journal of Social Psychology, 20,* 463-474.

Sheen, Mr. Justice (1987). *MV Herald of Free Enterprise. Report of Court No. 8074 Formal Investigation.* London: Department of Transport; HMSO.

Smith, P.B., & Bond, M.H. (1993). *Social psychology across cultures - analysis and perspectives.* New York: Harvester Wheatsheaf.

Transportation Safety Board of Canada. (1996, May). *A guide for the investigation of human factors: An integrated approach.* Quebec: Author.

Westrum, R. (1993). Cultures with requisite imagination. In J. Wise, V.D. Hopkin, & P. Stager (Eds.), *Verification and validation of complex systems: Human factors issues.* Berlin: Springer-Verlag.

Westrum, R. (1995). Organisational dynamics and safety. In N. McDonald, N. Johnston, & R. Fuller (Eds.), *Applications of psychology to the aviation system.* (pp. 75-80). Aldershot, UK: Avebury Aviation.

Wilde, G.J.S., & Stinson, J.F. (1980). *Human factors considerations in locomotive cab design* (CIGGT Project No. 80-9). Kingston, Ontario: Queen's University, Canadian Institute of Guided Ground Transport.

Zotov, D.V. (1996, October). Reporting human factors accidents. *ISASI Forum, 29*(3), 4-20.